THE BACKROOM BOYS

Also by Noam Chomsky

American Power and the New Mandarins
(*Penguin*)

At War with Asia
Problems of Knowledge and Freedom: The Russell Lectures
For Reasons of State
(*Fontana*)

NOAM CHOMSKY

THE BACKROOM BOYS

FONTANA/COLLINS

This edition first published in Great Britain
by Fontana 1973

© Noam Chomsky 1973

Much of 'Endgame: the Tactics of Peace in Vietnam'
originally appeared in *Ramparts*, April 1973

Printed in Great Britain by
Richard Clay (The Chaucer Press) Ltd
Bungay, Suffolk

ISBN 0 00 633614 0 (paperback)
        0 00 216053 6 (hardback)

CONDITIONS OF SALE

This book is sold subject to the condition that it shall
not, by way of trade or otherwise, be lent, re-sold,
hired out or otherwise circulated without the
publisher's prior consent in any form of binding or
cover other than that in which it is published and
without a similar condition including this condition
being imposed on the subsequent purchaser.

Contents

Introduction	7
1 The Backroom Boys	23
2 Endgame: the Tactics of Peace in Vietnam	149
Notes	173
Index	215

Introduction

Although the two essays that follow deal peripherally with Indochina, their focus is the United States and its image as reflected in its South-east Asian wars – a distorted image, fortunately, but one that reveals facets of reality that no serious person will ignore. The first chapter is devoted primarily to the 'Pentagon Papers.' It went to press in the American edition in June 1972 and has not been revised for publication here. The second chapter is an assessment of the situation as it appears shortly after the signing of the Paris Agreements of January 1973.

The Pentagon Papers are of considerable value as a source of insight into the exercise of power by the United States Executive. They bear only indirectly on the Vietnam war, and offer a valuable opportunity to turn attention to Washington. Whatever the outcome in Indochina, the framework of ideology and policy-making, political culture and popular attitude, has not been substantially modified by this catastrophe, and significant changes in the system of institutions and doctrine that gave rise to it are most unlikely. America has wearied of this war, and in the narrow groups that determine foreign policy, many have long concluded that it is pointless, a venture that should be liquidated. But official doctrine nevertheless prevails. It sets the terms of debate, a fact of considerable importance. Possible consequences for Indochina itself are discussed briefly in Chapter 2, but the significance of the matter is much more general.

The savagery of the American attack on the people of Indochina is often condemned, but more fundamental questions are rarely raised in the mainstream of opinion. We may therefore expect new interventions in South-east Asia and beyond. If resistance is again miscalculated, there may be new Vietnams; or if the planners are more successful, new Guatemalas, to be quickly forgotten.

An observer capable of extricating himself from the grips of state propaganda would recognize that the American intervention has been, from the beginning, a campaign directed against much of the rural population of South Vietnam, expanding in stages throughout Indochina. United States troops landing in Normandy in 1944 did not discover, as the Marines did in March 1965, that 'the toughest war for them was the war in the villages behind them' near their bases, and they did not have to 'turn . . . away from the enemy to a grueling and painfully slow effort to pacify the villages' in their rear.[1] Nor did they attempt to imprison the French in 'strategic hamlets' or devise 'experiments with population and resources control methods'[2] or concentrate the population by massive bombardment, crop destruction and levelling of villages. Yet it is striking that even vast and systematic operations of coercion designed to control the population of South Vietnam aroused little protest in the West as long as there were prospects of success, nor do they today in retrospect.

Consider as a case in point the strategic hamlet programme of 1962–3. Bernard Fall described this as 'the most mammoth example of "social engineering" in the non-Communist world.'[3] The purpose was 'systematically to cut [the guerilla force] off from its true base of support – the people' – to provide the peasant with 'physical security' so that 'he could make a free choice between the Viet Cong and the government.'[4] No one, of course, asked 'the people' whether they wanted the security. In fact, as Hilsman reported to the President, 'it is difficult if not impossible to assess how the villagers really feel,'[5] but still we drive them into hamlets, where they will have a 'free choice.' Both Hilsman and the designer of the programme, Sir Robert Thompson, observe that the programme failed in part because police work within the hamlets was inadequate. Hilsman explained to the President that 'you have strategic hamlets going up enclosing Communists inside their boundaries with no provision for winkling out those communists . . . it seemed obvious that putting up defenses around a village would do no good if the defenses enclosed Viet Cong agents . . .'[6] How could there be a 'free choice' between the government and the communists as long as the communists were permitted to exist?

In the first district where the programme was implemented, the Saigon psychological warfare services estimated that of 38,000 inhabitants, 60 per cent were 'communist-intoxicated.' Not surprisingly, they 'had to be convinced at gunpoint' to abandon their homes and to move to 'security,' and most able-bodied men escaped. Observers sympathetic to the programme compared the hamlets to prison camps.[7] Areas outside of the strategic hamlets were declared 'open zones' for 'random bombardment by the newly-arrived artillery and aircraft so as to drive the inhabitants into the safety of the strategic-hamlet belt.' This 'was the principal cause of a huge migration of tribesmen in the summer of 1962, which gave the President [Diem] the personal satisfaction of being voted for by about a quarter of a million feet.'[8] In January 1962 Hilsman personally observed a United States FARMGATE bombing mission which struck a Cambodian village by mistake, then hitting the Vietnamese village that was the designated target. He states that napalm was a 'standard item of issue' and that United States General Harkins, asked about the political consequences of napalm attacks on villages, replied that it 'really puts the fear of God into the Viet Cong . . . and that is what counts.'[9] By October 1962 it was reported that 30 per cent of all air missions in South Vietnam had American pilots at the controls.[10]

According to the Saigon government, 8,700,000 people, about two-thirds of the population, were moved into strategic hamlets within a little over a year, with full United States support. The programme was accurately described by Marine Colonel William Corson as 'forced resettlement, physical oppression, coercion, and political "persuasion" by the club.'[11] There was no doubt in the mind of any observer that the 'enemy' consisted of South Vietnamese, including, after 1959, 'regroupees' who were permitted to return to the South to take part in the ongoing rebellion against the tyranny of the United States-backed regime, which had formally renounced the Geneva agreements by January 1955.[12]

Information about all of this was readily available in the West at the time. The Pentagon Papers historian does not depart from attitudes generally held by 'responsible' commentators in his cool and detached account of the strategic hamlet programme. The basic question, as he sees it, is 'the validity of that body of writings which one may call the theory and doctrine of counter-insurgency. Neither the military nor the political aspects of this doctrine can be upheld (*or* proved false) by an examination of the Strategic Hamlet Program,' which was 'an attempt to translate the newly articulated theory of counter-insurgency into operational reality.' The evidence, he concludes, 'is not sufficient for an indictment; still less is one able to validate the counter-insurgent doctrine with reference to a program that failed.'[13] That there might be another notion of 'validity,' or another form of 'indictment' (irrespective of failure), is a possibility that he does not raise, a fact that is unremarkable, given the premises of political analysis in the major industrial societies.

On such technical matters as the strategic hamlet programme, the United States government is guilty of little deceit. Rather, it relied on the expectation that if successful, such programmes would be criticized only by moralistic fanatics. But to provide a more general justification of the war, substantial deception was necessary. It was also very successful. Shortly after the Pentagon papers appeared, Richard Harwood wrote in the *Washington Post* that a careful reader of the press could have known the facts all along, and he cited cases where the facts had been truthfully reported. He failed to add that the truth had been overwhelmed, in the same pages, by a flood of state propaganda. With rare exceptions, the press and the public accepted the framework of government deceit on virtually every crucial point. Hawks and doves alike speak of the conflict as a war between North Vietnam and South Vietnam, with the United States coming to the defence of the South – perhaps unwisely, the doves maintain, and with means disproportionate to the just ends sought. It was a tragic miscalculation – the implication being that had limited means sufficed, the American intervention would have been legitimate.

Summarizing after the January 1973 Paris Agreements, two liberal critics of the war write: 'The United States went to the aid of the government of South Vietnam with the best intentions, yet the good intentions have been the most costly the Vietnamese have known.'[14] That the original intentions were good requires no proof: it is an axiom of responsible political analysis. The situation is complex: 'there are elements of a Greek tragedy in Vietnam: two rights are in conflict with one another; the value of peace is at loggerheads with the value of democracy.'[15] Or, we read in a strong editorial statement against the war: 'This is not to say that Americans, including the political and military commands and the GI's themselves, did not originally conceive their role quite honestly as that of liberators and allies in the cause of freedom; but such idealistic motives had little chance to prevail against local leaders skilled in the art of manipulating their foreign protectors.'[16] Here we have the image of the American political leadership, noble and virtuous, bewildered and victimized, but not responsible, never responsible for what it has done. The corruption of the intellect and the moral cowardice revealed by such statements, which abound, defy comment. What they plainly reveal is that nothing fundamental changed in the mainstream of public opinion as the piles of corpses grew higher in Indochina. Others were to blame; the American political leadership was merely a victim of factors beyond its control, not an active agent of disruption in world affairs. Therefore it is free to try again elsewhere when circumstances are more propitious.

Introduction 11

The axiom that the United States merely responds to external challenges is deeply entrenched in academic scholarship as well. This is true, in fact, even of the most perceptive and intelligent criticisms of cold war illusions and related ideological pronouncements within the domain of 'responsible scholarship.' I will return to some recent examples in Chapter 1, section V, but it is important to recognize that the assumption dominates academic scholarship, even among the 'realist' critics of United States foreign policy. Consider one of the earliest and best, Norman Graebner.[17] United States foreign policy, he concludes, has been guided by the 'Wilsonian principles of peace and self-determination.' But after surveying some examples, he observes: 'It was ironic that this nation generally ignored the principle of self-determination in Asia and Africa [and, we may add, Greece, Latin America] where it had some chance of success and promoted it behind the Iron and Bamboo curtains where it had no chance of success at all.' Consider the logic. A general principle is proposed: the United States follows the Wilsonian principle of self-determination. But in the specific instances surveyed, where the principles could be applied, they were not applied. Conclusion: it is ironic that the general thesis fails when tested. By similar logic, a physicist might formulate a general hypothesis, test it, discover that it is refuted in each specific instance, and conclude that it is ironic that the facts are the opposite of what the principle predicts – but the principle nevertheless stands. The example reveals the difference between ideological subjects such as academic history and political science on the one hand, and subjects that are expected to meet intellectual standards that are inapplicable to the state religion and its proponents, on the other.

Graebner is an excellent and critical historian. He argues along Kennanesque lines that United States policy was in error. 'Error,' however, is a socially-neutral category. To invoke it is to remain within the bounds of the primary dogma of state ideology; that the United States merely responds to external challenges, and its policy reflects no special material interests of dominant social groups.

It is remarkable how resistant this doctrine is to challenge. Consider, for example, the question of the influence of corporations on foreign policy. A neutral and dispassionate observer, noting that the state executive is largely staffed by representatives of major corporations that are much concerned with the global economy and its organization, might be led to entertain the hypothesis that corporate interests influence foreign policy – indeed, that foreign policy is virtually an expression of such interests. The gross phenomena would surely suggest this as a kind of null hypothesis. How does American scholarship deal with this rather plausible idea?

In a recent summary, Dennis Ray observes that:

> The influence of corporations on the foreign policy process . . . remains clouded in mystery. My search through the respectable literature on international relations and US foreign policy shows that less than 5 per cent of some two hundred books granted even passing attention to the role of corporations in American foreign relations. From this literature, one might gather that American foreign policy is formulated in a social vacuum . . . There is virtually no acknowledgement in standard works within the field of international relations and foreign policy of the existence and influence of corporations.[18]

Note that he is referring only to the 'respectable literature.' There is also the literature of 'advocacy,' including 'radical and often neo-Marxist analyses' which develop the thesis that Ray himself discovers to be correct in his own brief investigation, namely, that corporate interests appear to influence foreign policy quite significantly, exactly as one would expect. It is striking that Ray never raises the question why the 'respectable literature' so systematically avoids any investigation of the obvious hypothesis with regard to the determination of foreign policy, preferring rather to study third-order effects and minor perturbations, ignoring the main theme. Furthermore, his own investigation of the question does not lead him to modify his attitude towards those who develop the conclusions that he discovers to be accurate: they are not respectable scholars, in his view, but are engaged in 'advocacy,' while the scholarly mainstream, which carefully avoids any scrutiny of the major formative influence in foreign policy does not lose its 'respectability' for this curious oversight, and does not seem to him to be engaged in 'advocacy.' Once again, we note the effective controls of the central dogmas of state ideology. All of this is the more interesting when we observe that the society is really free of ugly forms of totalitarian control and coercion that are prevalent elsewhere.[19]

In fact, it has long been a deeply-rooted premise in American political culture that the United States has the right to intervene in the internal affairs of others. Writing in 1947, A. A. Berle, a typical member of the American ruling elite, presented the 'revolutionary' thesis that the world is entering a new stage in which the rights of peoples take precedence over the rights of sovereign governments. The United States must serve as guarantor of the rights of peoples, intervening if necessary to defend these rights, acting with the same solicitude it has always shown to the nations protected from harm by the Monroe Doctrine ('for nearly a century' the United States has maintained its 'dominant objective' of securing world peace). Why are we justified in taking on this exalted role, replacing even the United Nations where it proves ineffective? The reason is simple. Along with Great Britain, the United States is more representative of the people than other powers, and therefore naturally pursues the popular demand for world peace – a refutation of Marxist doctrine, he sagely observes. To illustrate the necessity for intervention in defence of the rights of peoples, Berle cites the case of Greece, where 'Russian-inspired aggression' is implemented by 'subsidized bands of irregulars and local renegades acting under local leaders, but directed from abroad.'[20] Despite the important challenge to American conservative ideology in the past few years, such views largely maintain their hold on American opinion, and Berle's disdain for historical fact is no less typical of contemporary 'leaders of opinion.'

Notice that Berle's analysis, in 1947, conforms entirely to the state ideology as expressed in academic scholarship. American policy reflects no special interests in domestic American society. Rather, American leaders 'embrace the cause of humanity.'[21] Correspondingly, American intervention is not a disruptive element in world affairs. Rather, it is a contribution to stability, decency and the rule of law.

With regard to the Vietnam war, there were (and probably still are) the 'optimists,' who believed that with persistence we could win, and the 'pessimists,' who held that the United States could not, at reasonable cost, guarantee the rule of the regime of its choice in South Vietnam. These were the two positions that appeared in the secret 'Kissinger Papers', released by the *Washington Post*.[22] The pessimists expected 'pacification success in 13·4 years,' while the interpretation of the optimists 'implies that it will take 8·3 years to pacify the 4·15 million contested and VC population of December 1968.' As always, the pessimists differ from the optimists in their estimate of how long it will take to beat the Vietnamese resistance into submission – nothing more.

It is not very surprising that within the National Security Council there is no one to express the view that the United States *should not* (rather than *cannot*) pacify Vietnam or secure the rule of the regime it has instituted. But it is, perhaps, surprising that outside of the government the debate has so commonly remained within the same channels, a fact that I have documented at length elsewhere. There are the Joseph Alsops who believe that victory is within our grasp, and the Arthur Schlesingers who 'pray that Mr Alsop will be all right,' but doubt it. Much the same, apparently, is true in Great Britain. Consider the following editorial analysis of the spring 1972 offensive:

> The anti-communists have argued that the North Vietnamese may well lose in this desperate last gamble, and will henceforward be unable, or unwilling, to repeat it. The critics of American policy have argued that the South Vietnamese look the more likely losers, and that South Vietnam may crumble like a house of cards. Such arguments have some force; according to one's politics one can pick the first or the second.[23]

The assumptions of United States government propaganda are adopted here without qualification. The North is fighting the South – long forgotten is the fact that the war has been waged by the United States and the local forces it assembled against much of the rural population of South Vietnam. According to one's politics, one may be a hawk or a dove, an Alsop or a Schlesinger, an optimist or a pessimist in the sense of the National Security Council. But 'one's politics' cannot reflect a commitment to the principle that the United States has no right to play any role in the internal affairs of Indochina.

It is curious, and of some importance, that within a substantial component of Anglo-American opinion, opposition to forceful intervention by the United States is regarded as a 'radical' or 'extremist' view. One has to cross the English Channel to find it generally characterized, more accurately, as a moderate position, established in international law and 'solemn treaty obligations,' hence domestic United States law as well. Such is the power of endlessly repeated lies linked with overwhelming force in a political culture that so easily adopts the long-standing premises of imperialist doctrine and patterns of thought.

One mark of a culture in the firm grip of ideological controls is that what must be believed to justify state policy will be believed, regardless of the facts. The American war in Indochina offers many remarkable examples, from the start, when the United States undertook to restore Western rule. The internal record, to which we return, reveals that United States government analysts recognized that Western intervention must destroy the most powerful nationalist movement in Indochina. But a victory of the forces of revolutionary nationalism in Indochina was regarded as inconsistent with American global objectives, and therefore it was necessary to define the Viet Minh as agents of foreign aggression, while the French were defending the independence of Indochina. The necessary premise was soon embodied in state ideology, and rarely questioned thenceforth in internal documents or official propaganda.

In passing, I might note that it is quite misleading to describe the Pentagon Papers as a record of lies, as many commentators have. There is a striking similarity of internal to external rhetoric and expressed beliefs. What had to be believed for the justification of American policy was, apparently, efficiently internalized. 'Lying' is not quite the right term for this kind of behaviour.

The United States undertook at once to subvert the Geneva Accords of 1954, quite explicitly, as we shall see. But it was necessary to believe that this government committed to the rule of law was concerned only to restore the *status quo* as established at Geneva. The required premise became official doctrine, reiterated endlessly by political commentators.

To justify American escalation under Kennedy, it was necessary to believe that an American victory was of cosmic importance. The appropriate premise was duly adopted. As the 'legendary' General Lansdale expressed it:

> If Free Vietnam is won by the Communists, the remainder of South-east Asia will be easy pickings for our enemy, because the toughest local force on our side will be gone. A communist victory also would be a major blow to US prestige and influence, not only in Asia but throughout the world . . .[24]

Official pronouncements elevated Vietnam to a 'test case'; the outcome of the struggle there would virtually determine the course of world history. When, Blair Seaborn, Canadian member of the International Control Commission, conveyed United States warnings to Hanoi in July 1964, he 'cautioned that US stakes in resisting a North Vietnamese victory were high, since the United States saw the conflict in South-east Asia as part of a general confrontation with guerrilla subversion in other parts of the world.'[25]

Later the alleged aggressive expansionism of Communist China was offered as a reason for the United States escalation. Fantasy piled on fantasy, in accordance with the exigencies of policy.

There is ample evidence that the success of the NLF can be traced to the appeal of its constructive programmes to the peasantry.[26] But to concede this would discredit the American enterprise (though it is permissible to concede the point in retrospect; only fanatics are concerned with ancient history). Accordingly, government spokesmen and the press, generally, speak only of the 'control' of the peasants by the Viet Cong. The same inability to perceive facts that are inconsistent with the requirements of official propaganda is a common feature of intelligence analyses,[27] which one might have expected to be immune to such distortion. To cite one case, peasant discontent was recognized as a factor in the deterioration of Diem's position in 1960, but in a revealing manner. According to intelligence, 'most of the Vietnamese peasants are politically apathetic,' but they do have grievances against the government, specifically, 'lack of effective protection from Viet Cong demands.'[28] Defense Department analyses took this 'lack of security' to be 'the single significant peasant grievance, or the overwhelming predominant one, or the basis of the others,' so the Pentagon historian reports; but CIA and State, more perceptive, recognized that the oppressiveness of the Diem regime was another factor. At issue, then was the question whether the inability of the government to protect the peasants from the Viet Cong was one among many grievances, or the basis of all grievances. That the peasants might have some positive reason for supporting the NLF was a possibility too remote for consideration, though there are hints. E.g., SNIE 63.1–60 reports that the Viet Cong 'have exploited the tendency of the largely passive population to accommodate to their presence and thereby avoid reprisals,' though 'In some areas of operations . . . they have obtained the active cooperation of the local population,' for reasons that go unreported, at least in the available record.

The effectiveness of NLF programmes was, to be sure, tacitly conceded. In Vietnam, as in Laos, the United States has sought to mimic some of the achievements of the revolutionary nationalists in an effort to gain support for its accomplices. This homeopathic character[29] of United States programmes for treating the Viet Cong infection has some intriguing consequences. Thus a recent survey shows that the Saigon land reform has progressed in areas where 'the Viet Minh and the Viet Cong broke the landlords' hold years ago,' so that the programme 'appears to some merely to confirm a distribution of land already made by the Communists.' Where the Communists had not paved the way, 'landlords have intimidated their tenants and made deals with local officials' and the reforms are at a standstill. The land reform differs from that of the Communists in that it excludes farm labourers, the poorest peasants.[30] Though it owes such success as it has achieved to the Viet Minh and NLF, the programme is hailed as a major accomplishment of the United States and the GVN. One writer comments that one feature of the land reform of the Saigon regime 'considered highly progressive and revolutionary' is that it gives peasants 'formal entitlement to the land they have been tilling in recent years'[31] – that is, the land given to them in the NLF land redistribution.

By 1964 it was evident that even with extensive United States involvement the American-instituted regime would be unable to control the southern insurgency.[32] Therefore, the United States took over the war directly, invaded South Vietnam, ultimately devastating the peasant society. In so doing, it was again defending Free Vietnam from 'agression from the North.' At the same time, the United States began the sustained bombing of North Vietnam in an effort to compel the DRV to use its alleged 'directive powers' to call off the insurgency. When the DRV dispatched regular armed forces to the South, this reaction was incorporated into the structure of state propaganda, quite effectively, as a proof of North Vietnamese aggression. The press and the public generally conformed.

In the spring of 1972, the 'enemy' – now the NFL/PRG and the DRV after seven years of full-scale American war – was once again on the verge of victory. The Administration thus shifted to a broader, international confrontation in which it hoped to prevail. The sinking of a Russian ship in the first air strike on Haiphong, the attack on two Russian ships several weeks later,[33] and the mining of Haiphong harbour signalled that the leaders of the Free World were prepared to risk general war to achieve their objectives. Meanwhile, as in 1965, the United States intensified its attack on Indochina within the context of a heightened confrontation, and state propaganda recorded another triumph as American and British moralists brooded over the relative blame that attached to the Americans and the North Vietnamese for the incredible carnage. The violence of the Saigon army against the people of South Vietnam was mysteriously absent from these calculations, and as to the NLF/PRG, the American reader was generally spared any knowledge of its existence. Exploring Nazi archives, one might find angry denunciations of the Anglo-American invaders in 1944, who compounded their aggression with brutal attacks on civilians in the peaceful French countryside.[34] Why then be surprised when American officials indignantly denounce North Vietnamese aggression – in regions laid waste by American violence years before, in regions where a Marine Colonel described one of the milder American exercises as not war, but genocide?[35]

The analogy, to be sure, should not be pressed too far. The Anglo-American invaders were foreign forces. What is more, they were most assuredly intent on conquering France, whereas the alleged North Vietnamese objective of conquering South Vietnam or even part of its territory is, again, asserted not on the basis of any evidence that has been produced but rather because of the necessary role of this hypothesis in the system of state propaganda. North Vietnamese tactics appeared consistent with those of earlier years:[36] to draw the forces of the United States and the army it created away from populated areas, so that the indigenous guerrillas would have an opportunity to rebuild the structure that was severely damaged by the terror tactics of the post-Tet 'pacification' programmes, with their innumerable atrocities, of which My Lai is the best-known example.[37] More revealing was the massacre at nearby My Khe, with scores of civilians dead, revealed by the Peers Panel investigation of My Lai. General Peers falsely stated to newsmen that no evidence had been presented of another massacre. Proceedings against the officer in charge of the operation were dismissed on the grounds that there had been no massacre, merely a normal operation in which a village was destroyed and its population forcibly relocated.[38] His exoneration for this routine operation tells more about the war in Vietnam than a dozen books. The accidental discovery of the My Khe massacre also bears a message. Consider the likely density of atrocities, given the manner in which this event was discovered. Still more significant were the tactics of General Ewell in the Mekong Delta, where thousands were murdered in routine operations in NLF-controlled areas.[39]

The fact is that after the Tet offensive of January–February 1968, the United States Command, which had already torn much of the country to shreds in its effort to eradicate the NLF, undertook campaigns of unprecedented savagery. We shall probably never know the scale of this frenzied attack. Coupled with the massive terrorism of the Phoenix programme and other US–GVN operations, this war of annihilation reportedly restored 'security' to the countryside, seriously weakening the NLF.

It is in this context that we must consider the contributions of the subtle moralists who condemn both sides. Consider this rather typical example:

> The North's attack was not merely immoral; it has demonstrated that Hanoi has not persuaded the people of the South to throw off the yoke of Washington's 'puppets' in Saigon to embrace their 'liberators'. The North Vietnamese armies are winning hegemony over the South by right of conquest, not popular demand (the refugees are fleeing South, not North).[40]

The tacit presupposition is clear: the 'moral approach' for the DRV would have been to stand back while the United States imposed the rule of its collaborators by the means just described,[41] crushing the remnants of the Southern resistance whose victory was blocked by United States force in 1965. As for the miserable refugees, once again driven from their homes, I would not presume to assess their preferences and desires, having no more information than those who speak so confidently of their deepest wishes. The fact that they were fleeing South rather than remaining in their homes or fleeing North to be wiped out by the most vicious aerial assault in history seems less than a compelling proof that they preferred the Saigon regime to communist rule, as a moment's reflection might have suggested.

Throughout, the underlying assumption, variously expressed, is that United States intervention is uncontroversial if only it can succeed without too great a cost. Thus it is immoral for Vietnamese to resist American aggression or to come to the aid of resistance forces that cannot withstand its savagery. It should be clear that to insist upon the malicious character of this pervasive assumption is to imply nothing about the tactics used by any group of Vietnamese.

Nixon and Kissinger have pursued a variant of the strategy implicit in the long-term United States commitment to the imposition of Western-oriented regimes, a variant foreshadowed in the policy debates of 1967–8. Like their predecessors, they were free to murder and destroy without fear of reprisal. Since much of the 'responsible' criticism is easily neutralized, for reasons already discussed, the domestic restraints have been limited. Well before the expanded air war of 1972, it had been demonstrated that the level of United States violence tends to increase as domestic restraints diminish. In the limiting case, where the restraints are null, the destruction will be total. Consider the Plain of Jars in Northern Laos. The press was unaware or silent. United States military activities were the focus of no peace movement activity. The Plain of Jars is now a deserted wasteland, probably uninhabitable for decades to come.[42] There is little reason to doubt that the same factors will continue to operate, whatever their effectiveness, with respect to intervention in Southeast Asia and elsewhere in years to come.

Some believe that the Nixon–Kissinger diplomacy spells an end to the global interventionism of the post-war period, but this seems a most dubious interpretation. The new diplomacy is an effort to institutionalize the cold war system with more rational controls. The cold war was never simply a zero-sum game, a conflict between the superpowers in which the gain of one is the loss of the other. Rather, it has functioned as a marvellously effective device for mobilizing support, in each superpower, for ventures that carry a significant cost, economic and moral. The citizen must agree to bear the burdens of imperial wars and of government-induced production of waste, a critical device of economic management.[43] He has been whipped into line by the fear that we will be overwhelmed by an external enemy if we let down our guard.

The case of Vietnam, once again, is instructive. It would have been difficult to convince Americans that Ho Chi Minh posed a threat to their welfare or survival. The USSR or Dean Rusk's billion Chinese are another matter. Government doctrine therefore identified Ho as an agent of a Kremlin-directed conspiracy or Chinese militant expansionism. The pattern has been as persistent in international affairs as the fakery with regard to bomber and missile gaps.

A conservative alliance of great powers, each free to control its own domains, with arrangements (e.g. the recent SALT agreements) for a controlled expansion of the system of military production, offers definite advantages to the great powers. Its international consequences are not obscure:

> The day of the maverick states – North Vietnam, and North Korea, Albania and Cuba, Egypt and Israel – appears to be ending; no longer can aggressive adventures which threaten

the greater peace rely on the automatic ideological and material support of the communist giants. Those small nations which have been willing to play a role in international affairs similar to that of aircraft hijackers are finding that they no longer have *carte blanche* to threaten the safety of the majority in pursuit of their own fanatical minority goals.[44]

Here we see a clear expression of the ideology of imperialism: it is North Vietnam that is aggressive and fanatic, not the country that deployed half a million ground troops to destroy the NLF and dropped seven million tons of bombs on Indochina. More important, it is a fair assessment of the intent of the Nixon–Kissinger diplomacy by an informed observer who is sympathetic to its goals. What it will imply, in practice, is that the fanatics who seek independence and social change are to be crushed by their respective imperial masters, with no fear of great power conflict.

Rational control of the cold-war system by high-level diplomacy may reduce the danger of nuclear war, which can be calmly faced only by the criminally insane.[45] It should also reduce the freedom of bargaining of weaker states that might hope to play one great power against the other in pursuit of their 'fanatical minority goals.' But there are also potential difficulties. It may not be quite so simple a matter to invoke the external enemy in times of need. This problem is more severe in a more democratic society, where public opinion is a more potent force and a potential brake on policy. A possible solution is to transform the United States into a more disciplined and controlled society. The Nixon Administration has taken steps in this direction, with its flagrant defiance of Congressional directives, the authoritarian reconstruction of the Supreme Court, and the attack on the media for occasional departures from official doctrine.

It is useful to bear in mind, however, that the commitment to a tightly-managed, centrally-controlled society finds its place in liberal (and so-called 'socialist') ideology as well. Consider, for example, some of the views of Robert McNamara on social organization. 'Vital decision-making,' he holds, 'particularly in policy matters, must remain at the top.' Apparently, this is a divine imperative:

God – the Communist commentators to the contrary – is clearly democratic. He distributes brain power universally, but He quite justifiably expects us to do something efficient and constructive with that priceless gift. That is what management is all about. Its medium is human capacity, and its most fundamental task is to deal with change. It is the gate through which social, political, economic, technological change, indeed change in every dimension, is rationally spread through society.

> ... the real threat to democracy comes not from overmanagement, but from undermanagement. To undermanage reality is not to keep it free. It is simply to let some force other than reason shape reality ... if it is not reason that rules man, then man falls short of his potential.

And reason is to be identified as centralization of decision-making at the top, in the hands of management. Popular involvement in decision-making is a threat to liberty, a violation of reason, a surrender to 'unbridled emotion,' 'greed,' 'aggressiveness,' and so forth. Management is 'a mechanism whereby free men can most efficiently exercise their reason, initiative, creativity and personal responsibility.' We must therefore strengthen the institutions in which management can function successfully in its 'adventurous and immensely satisfying task ...'[46]

This is, in fact, the authentic voice of the technical intelligentsia, whether in the service of private capital, or state power under state capitalism of the American variety, or associated with statist forces of the left. The Dutch Marxist Anton Pannekoek remarked, shortly before the Second World War, that:

> The aim of the Communist Party – which it called world-revolution – is to bring to power, by means of the fighting force of the workers, a layer of leaders who then establish planned production by means of State-Power; in its essence it coincides with the aims of social democracy. The social ideals growing up in the minds of the intellectual class now that it feels its increasing importance in the process of production: a well-ordered organization of production for use under the direction of technical and scientific experts – are hardly different.[47]

The technical intelligentsia find their natural place in a state management, testing the validity of counter insurgent doctrine and transforming it into operational reality, organizing society for purportedly liberal and humane ends. The style and rhetoric of the Pentagon Papers history is authentically theirs. As for the events recorded, it would be a serious error to dismiss recent history in the hope that it will prove to be some mad aberration, of little consequence for the international order.

ONE

The Backroom Boys

I. INTRODUCTION

If the next edition of the Pentagon Papers is to contain an epigraph, I would suggest a remark by a war correspondent who is unusual, if not unique, in her concern for the Vietnamese and her detailed reporting on the meaning of the war to them. A year of exposure to the Nixon–Kissinger war, the one that is winding down, left her with 'a deep, angry suspicion and scorn' for the White House, the Pentagon, the army, the diplomats, the experts in Vietnam, 'for among them are some stunning lunatics and liars who have done their own country much damage, and nearly killed this one.'[1]

The Pentagon Papers have a cool and antiseptic quality that readers may find revolting if they are at all aware of the reality that seems so remote from the minds of the planners in Washington. At least, that was my personal reaction. Perhaps that is why, after closing volume IV, I found myself thumbing through a study of the real Vietnam by the British photographer-writer Philip Jones Griffiths.[2] His technique is simple and effective. On one page there is a photograph of a serious looking American pilot with a skull on his helmet, and facing it, a victim of napalm, with a brief text:

> Some of its finer selling points were explained to me by a pilot in 1966: 'We sure are pleased with those backroom boys at Dow. The original product wasn't so hot – if the gooks were quick they could scrape it off. So the boys started adding polystyrene – now it sticks like shit to a blanket. But then if the gooks jumped under water it stopped burning, so they started adding Willie Peter [WP – white phosphorus] so's to make it burn better. It'll even burn under water now. And just one drop is enough, it'll keep on burning right down to the bone so they die anyway from phosphorus poisoning.'

The Pentagon Papers do not deal with murder and destruction.

They are not – nor do they purport to be – a history of the war or of the American involvement in Indochina. But they do provide much insight into the thinking and machinations of the backroom boys who bear the primary responsibility for a catastrophe of which they seem unaware. The study deals, not with the war, but with the perception of the war in Washington, a rather different matter. The account is sometimes inaccurate and misleading, reflecting what the policy makers persuaded themselves to believe. The relative attention given to various phases of the conflict also reflects the perception of Washington, rather than the significance of the events themselves.

There is, for example, much agonizing over the air war in North Vietnam. In contrast, the bombing of the South, far greater in scale, is barely mentioned. '*It takes time to make hard decisions,*' John McNaughton wrote. 'It took us almost a year to take the decision to bomb North Vietnam.'[3] The decision is studied in painstaking detail. There is scarcely a word about the decision to bomb South Vietnam, at greater than triple the intensity by 1966 (IV, 49). A few remarks prior to February 1965 indicate some interest in 'explicit use of US air in South Viet-Nam' (III, 618 – inexplicit use of helicopters and tactical air support for combat operations is reported from 1960 and was extensive by early 1962).[4] These remarks are so insignificant that the Pentagon historians – properly, given a narrow interpretation of their task – do not enter them into their record of planning in Washington.

In February 1965, 'for the first time, US jet aircraft were authorized to support the RVNAF in ground operations in the South without restriction' (III, 391), and the roof fell in on the rural population of South Vietnam. From the third week of February, 'jet bombers commenced attacks against Southern targets on a daily basis.'[5] This was the fundamental policy decision of early 1965. As Bernard Fall pointed out not long after, 'what changed the character of the Vietnam war was *not* the decision to bomb North Vietnam; *not* the decision to use American ground troops in South Vietnam; but the decision to wage unlimited aerial warfare inside the country at the price of literally pounding the place to bits.'[6] But of this decision, we learn next to nothing. And only a few scattered sentences indicate the effects of the bombing.

The contrast is all the more remarkable given the fact that South Vietnam, beginning in early 1965, was subjected not only to massive aerial attack but also to artillery bombardment which may well have been even more destructive. There is an extensive RAND Corporation study, still secret, that provides detailed evidence on United States air and artillery tactics and their effects on peasant attitudes and 'Viet Cong morale,' based on interviews with prisoners, defectors, and refugees. It may well be an extension of the study introduced by Robert McNamara in congressional testimony in January 1966.[7] This report is concerned 'especially to highlight some VC vulnerabilities which appear to provide opportunities for exploitation,' for example, the vulnerability to bombardment by B-52s, 'the most devastating and frightening weapons used so far against the VC'; 'VC soldiers and civilians said that they felt there is no protection against these attacks.' The report states: 'The air and artillery attacks – the latter being far more frequent than the former – while disrupting VC activities and intensifying the cleavage between the population and the VC, often appear to cause [deleted] damage and casualties to the villagers [deleted].' The [deleted] damages and casualties lead the villagers 'to move where they will be safe from such attacks . . . regardless of their attitude to the GVN.' This is very helpful. 'The effects of the departure of large numbers of villagers for GVN areas are beginning to be felt,' with a consequent reduction in manpower available to the Viet Cong and the threat of 'a major deterioration of their economic base.' The report quotes a Viet Cong cadre: 'Each person that moves out [of a Viet Cong area] will cause one VC to die of hunger. Viet Cong units find that they are 'unable to buy food in abandoned villages.' Thus the popular sea in which the guerrillas swim 'is receding.' Things are looking up for our side.[8]

The public record provides ample evidence that by late 1965 the United States command appreciated the logic of this analysis. In December 1965, General Westmoreland, in a briefing for war correspondents, explained that previously the peasant had three options: he could 'follow his natural instinct' and remain in his home, or move to a government-controlled area, or join the Viet Cong. But now, with the escalated war, 'if he stays put there are additional dangers.' 'The VC can't patch up wounds,' and they 'no longer have secure areas,' because of B-52 bombings and other tactics. Asked whether this gives the villager 'only the chance of becoming a refugee,' Westmoreland replied, 'I expect a tremendous increase in the number of refugees,'[9] an expectation that was rapidly fulfilled.

The contrast in the Pentagon Papers between the attention to

26 *The Backroom Boys*

the decision to bomb the North and the decision to conduct extensive aerial and artillery bombardment of the South is striking. The reason for this seems clear enough. The bombing of North Vietnam was highly visible, very costly to the United States, and quite dangerous, with a constant and perceived threat of general war. The far more vicious bombing of the South, on the other hand, was merely destroying the rural society of South Vietnam, and thus did not merit the attention of the backroom boys.

The Pentagon Papers are a study of decision making, nothing more. They do not deal with the results of decisions, except in terms of military success and cost – cost, that is, to the planners and the interests they represent. There are no memoranda on bombs that tear the flesh with tiny arrows, designed to cause maximum pain and impossible to extract without grave injury. There are no scenes of cratered fields and poisoned rice paddy,[10] no smell of burning flesh. We find no description of an old woman searching the rubble of her napalmed 'hooch,' or of a child, chained to a hospital bed, insane since the age of two when his mother was killed by a helicopter gunship as she held him in her arms. Nor is there a word of comment on the wreckage of the village society of Vietnam, or on life in the densely packed urban slums to which villagers have fled because 'they don't like our artillery and air strikes,'[11] or because they are starving, or because they have been moved by force. Such sentimentality is far from the minds of the men whose thoughts are recorded in the Pentagon study.

The sense of remoteness from reality conveyed by the documentary record is heightened by the accompanying analysis. Two of the authors have commented on

> the well carpeted stillness and isolation of those government offices where some of the Pentagon Papers were first written. The efficient staccato of the typewriter, the antiseptic whiteness of nicely margined memoranda, the affable, authoritative and always urbane men who wrote them – all of it is a spiritual as well as geographic world apart from piles of decomposing bodies in a ditch outside Hue[12] or a village bombed in Laos, the burn ward of a children's hospital in Saigon, or even a cemetery or veteran's hospital here.[13]

The essence of the Pentagon Papers is conveyed in a summary and analysis of the situation after the Tet offensive of 1968 (II),

414–15). The analyst ponders the question whether the United States can

> overcome the apparent fact that the Viet Cong have 'captured' the Vietnamese nationalist movement while the GVN has become the refuge of Vietnamese who were allied with the French in the battle against the independence of their nation? Attempts to answer this question are complicated, of course, by the difficult issue of Viet Cong allegiance to and control by Communist China.

He goes on to muse over 'the question of the adequacy of counterinsurgent theory and doctrine' and the problem of 'its transformation into operational reality,' a 'difficult, frustrating business,' where 'there exists no "control" by which laboratory comparisons of alternative courses can be made,' but a problem that must be studied 'in order better to guide future policy.'

The United States, in short, is supporting the former agents of French colonialism against the nationalist movement captured – by implication, illegitimately – by the Viet Cong, like the Viet Minh before it. Twenty years earlier, a State Department policy statement noted that the Communists under Ho Chi Minh had 'capture[d] control of the nationalist movement,' thus impeding the 'long-term objective' of the United States, 'to eliminate so far as possible Communist influence in Indochina.'[14] The biographies of Thieu, Ky, and Khiem indicate the continuity of policy; all served with the French forces.[15] This poses no moral dilemma, but rather a technical one. As Dean Acheson once explained, 'Question whether Ho as much nationalist as Commie is irrelevant.' He is an 'outright Commie,' and that is all that matters (besides, 'All Stalinists in colonial areas are nationalists'; *DOD*, bk 8, p. 196). At worst, this fact poses one of those dilemmas of counterinsurgency, and as the theorists are quick to point out, 'All the dilemmas are practical and as neutral in an ethical sense as the laws of physics.'[16] If the children in a burn ward in the Quang Ngai hospital disagree, well, they probably don't understand the laws of physics either. By defining the problems as technical, one appears hardheaded and realistic, any moral considerations are displaced, and the public is effectively excluded, since clearly technical problems are to be left to experts.

Furthermore, the technician who is concerned with transforming counterinsurgent theory into operational reality in the absence of laboratory control need not concern himself with the origin of the idea that the Viet Cong may be Chinese agents. This 'issue,' a hypothesis originating in someone else's department, merely sets the terms of the technical problem, which the counterinsurgent theorist is therefore free to address, understanding nothing. Facts are no more relevant to him than they were to Dean Acheson when he urged aid and recognition for the Bao Dai government in May 1949 to safeguard Vietnam from 'aggressive designs Commie Chi,' *DOD*, bk 8, pp. 190–1.

In fact, the function of the hypothesis is transparent: by assuming it, one can squarely face the problem of repressing the nationalist movement of Vietnam, untroubled by sentimental moral qualms, since the enemy is really China (or perhaps the Kremlin, which is directing a 'coordinated offensive' against South-east Asia),[17] not Vietnam. This kind of thinking, if that is the right word, goes a long way towards explaining the barbarism of the Vietnam war, in which the world's most advanced technology is pitted against the nationalist movement 'captured' by the Viet Cong. If the backroom boys at Dow were forced to walk through the burn ward of a children's hospital, they might think twice about what they are doing in their laboratories. It is conceivable that even the modern Metternich might be shaken by a face-to-face confrontation with refugees from the Plain of Jars, if one of his jaunts happened to bring him to the place where the fun and games are 'transformed into operational reality.' The same is true more generally of the planners in Washington and academia, insulated from the facts, posing as technical experts and problem solvers.[18]

The analyst noted above is, finally, perceptive in recognizing that the technical problem must be studied 'in order better to guide future policy' in Indochina and elsewhere, in pursuit of a stable world order in which the rights of the privileged will be guaranteed. Vietnam was seen as a great experiment, challenging and almost exhilarating, a laboratory of counterinsurgency and a test of the feasibility of 'wars of national liberation' – by definition, inspired by 'international communism' when they take place within the 'free world.' Under the Kennedy administration, 'there was an emphasis on counterguerrilla and counterrevolutionary training.'[19] Kissinger's doctrine of 'limited war,' extricated from its rationalization in terms of great-power conflict, is a natural theme of United States political–military global policy, given the relations between the industrialized countries and the developing world. Advanced technology makes a dual contribution. On the one hand, it provides the antipersonnel weapons, electronic battlefield, automated fire-control systems, and the like, all designed for wars against the weak. It also provides an intellectual framework to protect the decision maker from any realization of what he is in fact doing and to deflect the attention of the public – an important matter, since most people are not gangsters by nature and tend to be unhappy about murder and destruction. It is difficult to plot aggression 'under the klieg lights of a democracy.'[20] How much more convenient it is merely to face technical problems, as neutral in an ethical sense as those of physics.

The technical pose also allows the Pentagon historians to slip into unquestioning acceptance of the assumptions that guide the thinking of the policy planners themselves. Following Secretary McNamara's guidelines, the Pentagon historians do not undertake to inquire seriously into the American role in world affairs and its long-term motive and objectives, nor do they try to place the material that they investigate within the general context of post-war history. Thus the analysts describe the variants of the 'domino theory' that appear throughout the record. The director of the study, Leslie Gelb, points out that 'this theory, whether more or less completely articulated, appears in the relevant NSC papers of the Indochina war period, and underlies all major US policy decisions taken relevant to the area.'[21] But the Pentagon historians do not analyse the implicit content of the domino theory – the fact, as Gabriel Kolko expresses it, that 'translated into concrete terms, the domino theory was a counter-revolutionary doctrine which defined modern history as a movement of Third World and dependent nations – those with economic and strategic value to the U.S. or its capitalist associates – away from colonialism or capitalism and toward national revolution and forms of socialism.'[22] Nor do they take note of the important fact that the same domino theory was formulated for other areas as well, in rather similar terms, as when Secretary of State Marshall told a group of key congressional leaders in February 1947 that 'if Greece should dissolve into civil war,' Turkey might then fall, and 'Soviet domination might thus extend over the entire Middle East and Asia.'[23]

Furthermore, the interpretation given by the analysts generally reveals an unspoken but prevailing commitment to the faith that the position of the United States was defensive and responsive, that it was not an active disruptive agent in world affairs. At times this general stance leads to a serious misrepresentation of the documentary record. To mention one crucial case (see pp. 111–13), the documentary record reveals plainly that the United States intended to undermine the Geneva Agreements from the start, but the Pentagon historians do not accurately report the content of the basic document and speak only of the United States 'response' to the prevailing situation, giving a generally inaccurate account of events in Vietnam and Laos at the time. Similarly, the Pentagon history underplays or entirely fails to mention clandestine American activities in Indochina. It does not take note, for example, of the fact that in late 1963 and early 1964 there was a marked expansion of American and American-sponsored military actions in all of the countries of Indochina, or of the coincidence of American-sponsored subversion in Laos and in Cambodia in the late 1950s. United States initiatives elsewhere in South-east Asia, particularly in Thailand, also go unreported, though it is only by considering this broader context that one can hope to gain any real insight into evolving American plans for South-east Asia.

Nevertheless, these limitations of the Pentagon Papers as history, like the exclusive preocupation with the question of cost to the imperial power, provide a faithful and often revealing reflection of the limitations within which the designers of policy themselves operate, at least at the secondary level that is richly illustrated by the documentary record presented here. It is hardly surprising that policy planners raise no searching questions about the people whose lives and fate they manipulate, about the validity of their own beliefs or their own vision of a properly organized society, or about their right to act upon these beliefs to impose social and economic arrangements on others. Correspondingly, the planners tend not to see themselves as imperialist aggressors, a hostile and disruptive force in some foreign land; rather, they defend civilized values and the status quo. They seek peace and order. They are victims, not agents, and merely respond to the acts of their great-power rivals or of the obstinate, recalcitrant, and perverse elements in foreign lands who do not bend to the will of the superpower, reject its vision of their future, and even forcefully resist its intrusions, thereby becoming violent aggressors in their own homes. The technician who merely studies the day-by-day moves of the imperial planners can also easily avoid the painful questions that arise at once for anyone who extricates himself from the framework of official ideology.

The issues raised by the Pentagon Papers fall into several categories. There are, in the first place, questions relating to the public release of the material and the government response: the matter of executive privilege, the scope of the First Amendment, the rights and duties of a citizen (section II below). The contents of the study also bear directly on problems of law and conscience and legitimate social action (section III). It is also important to explore the broader lasting value of this collection of documents and analyses as a contribution to the historical record (section IV) and to the understanding of the objectives of American global strategy (section V), as well as for the insight it provides into the mentality of the planners and the functioning of government (section VI). All of these matters merit extensive study. I would like to comment on each of them, in the sequence indicated.

II. ON THE PUBLIC RELEASE OF THE PENTAGON PAPERS

Senator Sam Ervin, who has been conducting an inquiry into the separation of powers, observed recently:

> Throughout history, rulers have imposed secrecy on their actions in order to enslave the citizenry in bonds of ignorance. By contrast, a government whose actions are completely visible to all of its citizens best protects the freedoms embodied in the Constitution.[24]

Ervin is referring specifically to the doctrine of executive privilege, invoked with increasing frequency as a device for withholding information from Congress and the public so that 'those who govern are not accountable for their actions.' On this matter, Senator Ervin takes his stand within a distinguished tradition. Thomas Jefferson warned that if citizens 'become inattentive to the public affairs,' then the government 'shall all become wolves'[25] – a perceptive remark, and an accurate prediction. The story revealed by the Pentagon Papers is just what we should expect of a system of centralized power insulated from public scrutiny and democratic control, and unmindful – perhaps even ignorant – of the human consequences of its acts.

For a generation, there has been a contrived inattention to public affairs in the domain of foreign policy. Government secrecy has been a contributing factor, far outweighed in importance by the intense indoctrination that had rendered the public inert until very recently, when the Vietnamese resistance awakened some degree of scepticism and open-mindedness with regard to the behaviour of the state executive and its official claims. With the partial collapse of the ideological consensus of the post-war years, it is much easier to undertake some serious inquiry into the United States role in world affairs. The release and publication of the Pentagon Papers are in part a result of this more healthy intellectual climate, and should contribute to it, one may hope.

Naturally, the government response is to try to shore up the dikes. The Nixon–Kissinger administration has gone even beyond its predecessors in invoking the 'inherent executive power,' in particular the proclaimed right to withhold information from Congress and the public. This is consistent with the Nixon ideology of radical authoritarianism (often mislabelled 'conservatism') and Kissinger's belief in the need for tight central management in foreign policy.[26]

A related matter is the flagrant disregard for law on the part of the Nixon administration, perhaps even beyond that of its predecessors. As a revealing if minor illustration, consider the use of Thai mercenaries in Laos, recently the subject of some acid commentary in Congress. An executive session of the Senate was called to consider the CIA war in Laos, particularly the fact 'that the United States is currently paying for foreign troops, for mercenaries, if you will, despite legislation which, by letter as well as intent, was designed to prohibit any such practice.'[27] Despite repeated efforts on the part of Senator Fulbright, information was withheld until reporters determined that thousands of Thai troops, recruited and funded by the CIA, were fighting in Laos under Thai officers in a new phase of the decade-long war conducted under CIA direction 'without the authorization of the Congress; and largely without the knowledge – therefore obviously without the consent – of either the Congress or the American people.'[28] With these acts, the administration moves another step towards realizing the proposal of George Ball in 1965: 'Securing the Mekong Valley will be critical in any long-run solution, whether by the partition of Laos with Thai–U.S. forces occupying the western half or by some cover arrangement' (IV, 618; Ball has been widely praised for his appreciation, in this memorandum, of the difficulties of fighting an unpopular war against a large part of the population of South Vietnam).

In Senate hearings Alexis Johnson, speaking for the administration, was asked whether he considered Thais in Laos to be local forces, as required by law. 'I do consider them local forces,' he replied. Asked further whether he believed that under the terms of the legislation it would be permissible to 'recruit Cambodians and Malaysians, Australians or anybody you felt, by calling them local forces,' Mr Johnson explained that he did indeed; they would then become 'Lao forces or local forces,' as required by the legislation restricting funds to local Lao forces.[29]

In the face of such blatant violation of law, Senator Symington raised the question, 'If we pass a law and the law can be honored in the breach, what real reason is there to be a Senator of the United States?'[30] And Senator Fulbright noted, 'I and some of my colleagues have almost been reduced to the situation where it makes no difference what is put into law, the administration will not abide by it,' adding that perhaps some day 'this country will return to its senses and we will then have an opportunity to resurrect the basic principles of law on which this country was founded.'[31]

The example is, to be sure, a minor one in the context of general executive lawlessness in Indochina, but it serves to indicate why the administration must continue to 'enslave the citizenry [and Congress as well] in bonds of ignorance.' It is no surprise, then, that there was an effort at prior restraint, the first in American history, followed by an indictment alleging a conspiracy involving Daniel Ellsberg, Anthony Russo, and others, with further indictments pending. The point was captured succinctly in a Mauldin cartoon showing a worried Nixon whispering to LBJ, 'If I let them print the truth about you, I'd be their next victim.' What the administration fears is a breakdown in the system of secrecy that has so facilitated the planning and execution of policies that cannot be defended before the public.

In an important study of the First Amendment, Thomas Emerson points out that 'limitations of expression are by nature an attempt to prevent the possibility of certain events occurring rather than a punishment of the undesired conduct after it has taken place.'[32] In the present instance, this observation applies with a slight modification. The punishment is intended to prevent efforts to inform the public about events still to occur. Reviewing earlier efforts to restrict First Amendment rights, Emerson concludes, I think correctly, that in each case the alleged need for restriction upon freedom of expression was seriously exaggerated, administration of the limitations created an 'obnoxious' enforcement apparatus, and, most significantly, 'in practice the restrictions were employed to achieve objectives quite different from the theoretical purposes of the laws,' with social losses that proved significant. The response to the publication of the Pentagon Papers is a case in point.

The central issue in this case is that, legalisms aside, there is an element of absurdity in any investigation or prosecution of those who released the Pentagon Papers to the American public. Any indictment of those involved in making this information available represents nothing more than an effort on the part of the government to punish the exposure of its crimes. We may ask whether it is the law itself that is absurd, in that it permits such proceedings, or whether the law is again being contravened.

It can be plausibly argued that the First Amendment provides a proper framework for exposing the absurdity of the proceedings. The government alleges that release of this material to the American public violates various statutes, for example, the sections of the Espionage Act which prohibit the transmission of documents 'relating to the national defense' or of 'information relating to the national defense which information the possessor has reason to believe could be used to the injury of the United States or to the advantage of any foreign nation.'[33] Congress has, however, passed no law prohibiting the release of documents or information relating, not to the national defence, but to a history of aggression (the executive, of course, will always characterize aggression as 'national defense'); or prohibiting the release of information which the possessor has reason to believe will be used to the advantage of the United States – that is, the people of the United States and the Congress. If it was not the intent of the Espionage Act to protect the executive from embarrassing disclosures, or to permit it to conceal its actions from the public and from Congress, there is no reason to suppose that release of the Pentagon Papers, in an effort to inform the American people about the acts – perhaps criminal acts – of successive administrations, is in violation of the Espionage Act.

It might be argued further that under the First Amendment, no congressional statute can inhibit transmission of information to the press. The courts, however, have never adopted a strict interpretation of the First Amendment. They have held, rather, that the press cannot, for example, publish 'the sailing dates of transports or the number and location of troops,'[34] appealing to the First Amendment for protection against prosecution. Several cases that might fall under this proscription are mentioned in the Pentagon Papers. The White House called off a planned attack on the Tchepone barracks in southern Laos in December 1964 (it was 'deleted as a secondary mission') 'because a Hanson Baldwin article had named it as a likely target' (III, 255). Later, strikes against North Vietnamese petroleum facilities at Haiphong were temporarily cancelled when the Dow Jones news wire reported the plans, 'an extremely serious leak, because of the high risk of U.S. losses if NVN defenses were fully prepared' (IV, 106). In another incident, the president seems to have announced the Tonkin Gulf 'retaliatory strike' before American planes were intercepted by North Vietnamese radar. The reason, according to Anthony Austin's important study, is that although 'if the President spoke too soon he would be tipping off Hanoi,' nevertheless 'if he delayed much longer he would lose his audience on the whole Eastern seaboard' (the hour being past 11 pm Washington time).[35]

In recent years, the courts have held that First Amendment rights must be balanced against other interests. Emerson suggests that this 'balancing' test has been construed so broadly that the First Amendment may be reduced 'to a limp and lifeless formality . . . threatened with disintegration.'[36] However one regards the balancing doctrine, it applies in the present case only if the government represents some legitimate public interest in its efforts to prosecute those who released the Pentagon study to the American public. If so, then one might ask whether this interest, whatever it may be, outweighs the First Amendment. But the question does not even arise if the government represents no legitimate public interest. In this instance, the public interest lies squarely in the strict and literal interpretation of the First Amendment, which affords the citizen some protection against the state, in that inquiry may reveal secret plans that might be criminal, or might simply be condemned by an informed public. Such considerations are particularly important in a political system with no opposition party in the domain of foreign affairs and no system of parliamentary questioning. Deprived of the information revealed by a press that is substantially free, the citizen has no defence against the conniving of the state executive. It is therefore essential for the press to play an adversary role, as the First Amendment permits. To the extent that the press is inhibited by ideological constraints, intimidation, or simply the concentration of wealth and power, fundamental rights are infringed. The government can make no legitimate claim to abridge these rights in the interest of 'enslaving the citizenry in bonds of ignorance.' The First Amendment alone suffices to block the government's current efforts to intimidate the press and restrain its further investigations by prosecuting and otherwise harassing individuals who expose its ugly secrets.

In the case of the Pentagon Papers, the issue is particularly clear because the government is seeking to punish the release of historical information. But the same would be true in the more interesting case of plans for the future. For example, on February 26, 1966, the president stated: 'We do not have on my desk at the moment any unfilled requests from General Westmoreland.'[37] In fact, there was at this time a request to double the troop commitment, and the president had on his desk a memorandum from the secretary of defence stating that with deployments of the kind recommended (to about 400,000 by the end of 1966 and perhaps more than 600,000 in the following year), Americans killed in action could be expected to reach 1,000 per month (IV, 309, 623–4). The president and his advisers did not consider it appropriate that the American people should be aware of what was in store for them. To cite another case, when Secretary Rusk spoke on television on January 3, 1965, 'ruling out . . . a major expansion of the war' (III, 138, 263), the basis for the escalation that soon followed had already been solidly laid, as he knew. He also knew the possible consequences, whatever his personal estimate of the probabilities may have been. A National Security Council working group had predicted that the commitment 'to maintain a non-Communist South Vietnam' would 'involve high risks of a major conflict in Asia,' which would 'almost inevitably involve a Korean-scale ground action and possibly even the use of nuclear weapons at some point.'[38] Earlier, Secretary Rusk himself had emphasized to General Khanh that the United States 'would never again get involved in a land war in Asia limited to conventional forces,' and that 'if escalation brought about major Chinese attack, it would also involve use of nuclear arms' (II, 322; May 1964).

To those in power, it seems obvious that the population must be cajoled and manipulated, frightened and kept in ignorance, so that ruling elites can operate without hindrance in 'the national interest,' as they choose to define it. The citizen should be informed of only 'the things he needs to know to be a good citizen and discharge his functions,' as Maxwell Taylor explained in commenting on the peoples' 'right to know,' after the release of the Pentagon Papers.[39] If policies are to be modified, then 'a conditioning of the U.S. public' is necessary, and where this cannot be done expeditiously, the executive may find itself trapped by its own earlier misrepresentations.[40]

But officials of the government have no legal authority to act in accordance with their contempt for the public and to lie with impunity.[41] And under a reasonable interpretation of the First Amendment, they have no authority to prosecute the exposure of their deceit and their acts.

The Pentagon Papers provide documentary evidence of a conspiracy to use force in international affairs in violation of law. One may debate the sufficiency of the evidence, but hardly its existence. The Justice Department, which initiates criminal investigation and prosecution, is at the service of the conspirators. Naturally, instead of investigating a possible conspiracy to involve the United States in an expanding war of aggression in Indochina, with continual and recognized risks of nuclear war (see above, p. 36),[42] it will rather try to protect the inheritors of these policies from scrutiny and will prosecute those who bring the facts to the public, which must know these facts if it is to act to restrain the executive. In short, it will seek to demonstrate that Proudhon was quite right when he wrote that laws are 'spiderwebs for the powerful and the rich, chains that no steel can break for the small and weak, fishing nets in the hands of the government.'[43]

The Bill of Rights represents an effort of great historical significance to protect the citizen from state power. The true content of these formal rights is determined by the willingness of the public to defend them. One essential element in the protection of the citizen is his access to information about the acts and plans of the state executive. It will require energy and determination to overcome the natural tendency of the state executive to conceal its doings. This, it seems to me, is the fundamental issue raised by the release of the Pentagon Papers and subsequent events relating to that release.

III. CRIMES AGAINST PEACE

The contents of the Pentagon Papers, not merely the circumstances of their release, bear directly on problems of law and conscience and legitimate social action. The Pentagon study is not concerned with the character of United States military and police activities in Indochina, and therefore provides little information about war crimes in the narrow sense: forced evacuation, destruction of the land, massacres, and so on. But it does provide important documentation with respect to a second category of possible crimes, namely, the 'planning, preparation, initiation or waging of a war of aggression or a war in violation of international treaties, agreements or assurances,' or a conspiracy to this end, in the wording of Nuremberg.[44]

It is important to be clear about the issues that are at stake in an inquiry into the legality of the American war in Indochina. It is not in dispute among rational people with some concern for the facts, that the United States command is responsible for major crimes in the layman's sense of this term. What we may reasonably ask is whether the acts that are documented beyond dispute are also crimes in the lawyer's sense, recognizing that when we raise this question, it is not the war that is on trial but the law. We are asking – if we are serious – whether the law is a sufficiently precise and delicate instrument so that it can label a monstrous crime as a violation of law. Similarly, in considering the legality of the intervention itself (apart from the means employed), a person who is serious about the matter is not examining the propriety of the act, but rather the adequacy of the law. Suppose we were to determine that international law does not condemn the United States intervention as criminal in the technical sense. Then a rational person will regard the law, so understood, with all the respect accorded to the divine right of kings.[45] In fact, it seems to me that the law is not so deficient as to be unable to rule this intervention illegal, but it is, again, important to be clear about what is at stake when the issue is raised.

The fundamental treaty obligation of the United States is to the United Nations Charter, to which other treaties, such as SEATO, are explicitly subordinate. The United Nations Charter, which as a valid treaty is part of the supreme law of the land, specifies a series of 'peaceful means' (negotiations, etc.) that must be employed in the event of a dispute that might endanger peace (article 33). It is the sole responsibility of the United Nations Security Council to 'determine the existence of any threat to the peace, breach of the peace, or act of aggression' and to determine what measures shall be taken (article 39). Member states are required to 'settle their international disputes by peaceful means' and to 'refrain in their international relations from the threat or use of force against the territorial integrity or political independence of any state, or in any other manner inconsistent with the Purposes of the United Nations'; and even the United Nations is not authorized 'to intervene in matters which are essentially within the domestic jurisdiction of any state' (article 2), in particular, domestic insurgency and civil war. There is only one exception: 'Nothing in the present Charter shall impair the inherent right of individual or collective self-defense if an armed attack occurs against a Member of the United Nations, until the Security Council has taken the measures necessary to maintain international peace and security' (article 51). The distinction between 'aggression by means of armed attack' and threats 'other than by armed attack' (including 'subversive activities directed from without') is written into the SEATO treaty, which permits only consultation in the latter case, while reaffirming the right of collective self-defence in the case of 'armed attack.' Article 51 is consistent with the remainder of the charter on the assumption that 'armed attack' is construed narrowly, for example, as an attack that is 'instant, overwhelming, and leaving no choice of means, and no moment for deliberation,' in a classic formulation.[46]

The law is reasonably clear and straightforward. The open questions have to do with historical interpretation. The questions concern the 'state of South Vietnam,' a state established and maintained in existence by United States force; a state which claims, in its 1967 Constitution, that 'Viet-Nam is a territorially indivisible, unified and independent republic,' thus extending from the borders of China to the Camau Peninsula (article 1; this is, furthermore, the only provision of the Constitution not subject to amendment or deletion),[47] as the Geneva Agreements of 1954 also stipulate. The question is: Was this state subjected to a sudden and overwhelming attack, leaving no opportunity for the Security Council to determine the existence of a threat to peace, so that the United States was entitled to intervene in collective self-defence under article 51 of the United Nations Charter?

We hardly need the Pentagon study to refute this claim. This study merely provides further and still more conclusive evidence that the alleged 'aggression from the North,' far from constituting an armed attack, was claimed by the United States executive to be a matter of 'support and direction' for the domestic insurgency at a time when the United States was directly engaged in combat operations in South Vietnam[48] and was providing 'our leadership, and our officer direction, and equipment as we can furnish them.'[49] It also adds supporting evidence to the conclusion that direct North Vietnamese military involvement followed upon the regular bombardment of all Vietnam and the invasion of South Vietnam by an American expeditionary force in early 1965,[50] a consequence that was always anticipated by American planners. It further reveals that each step of American escalation was undertaken to sustain a regime incapable of withstanding a rebellion that was overwhelmingly indigenous, and that American policy was to avoid 'premature negotiations' which would enable the 'enemy,' holding all the cards, to achieve his objectives through peaceful means.

The United States executive is granted no authority to determine that the North Vietnamese involvement it believed to exist constituted armed attack, or to respond to the Southern insurgency by deployment of United States military force from the early 1960s. It had no authority to implant a terroristic dictatorship in South Vietnam in 1954 (or even a benevolent democracy), or to carry out covert activities or direct military action elsewhere in Indochina.

The war planners were never in doubt about these issues. They understood that article 51 of the United Nations Charter is the only possible basis for a defence of the legality of United States intervention and that appeal to it would require 'a major public relations effort' (III, 229). The public-relations effort had several facets. One component was outright misrepresentation with regard to 'North Vietnamese aggression,' as in testimony by Secretary Rusk before the Senate Foreign Relations Committee. State Department legal experts developed the theory that the return of Southern regroupees to their homes from 1959 (to take part in the ongoing struggle against the terror of the American-imposed regime that had refused to abide by the Geneva Accords) constituted an 'armed attack' against 'South Vietnam.' Still more subtle minds devised the concept of 'internal aggression,' used earlier by Dean Acheson with respect to the Viet Minh. It was even claimed that political activity contrary to United States goals constituted aggression. To disguise the absurdity of these formulations, it was alleged that the 'internal aggressors' were agents of a foreign Communist power. Lack of evidence was never a problem.

More significantly, before the ink was dry on the Geneva

Agreements of 1954, the National Security Council set forth an explicit programme to undermine the agreements and undertake the use of force in violation of law. In later years, the planners developed an explicit (and patently illegal) policy of exercising force prior to the recourse to peaceful means, to compensate for the political weakness of the American position in Indochina.

We will return to all of these matters in section VI, with explicit documentation.

It should be noted that the defence of the American intervention has given rise to some curious constructions by the more inventive geopoliticians. At one stage of the twenty-five-year war it was necessary to defeat the Vietnamese Communists to prevent Kremlin rule over Indochina, at another, to save the Vietnamese people from the alien influence of China, and at still another, to prevent the militant Chinese ideology from gaining ascendance over the more moderate Kremlin version within the Communist world. Tomorrow, we shall very likely hear that the United States must continue to pound Indochina to dust to further the common United States–Chinese interest in preventing Soviet hegemony over South and South-east Asia. It is noteworthy that as the premises replace one another in rapid succession, nevertheless the conclusion deduced from them remains constant: Kill Cong.

It must also be emphasized that the direct involvement of DRV ground forces in South Vietnam was a response to American escalation of the ground and air war in the South and the bombing of the North, and that Russian and Chinese involvement in Indochina was a response to American escalation from 1964. But once the 'intervention' had taken place, government propagandists were quick to exploit it as a justification for still further American escalation to save the people of South Vietnam from aggression.

It is possible to devise a defence for United States intervention that is less disreputable intellectually than the appeal to article 51 of the United Nations Charter, and probably this defence will be heard more frequently now that the Pentagon Papers have further undermined the argument based on the inherent right of collective self-defence against armed attack[51] It might be argued that the charter does not explicitly prohibit a government from calling on its allies to suppress an indigenous rebellion. Under this interpretation, it is legitimate to use force to destroy an indigenous movement within the territory of another state on request of the incumbent government. It is necessary, under this interpretation, to argue that such use of force is consistent with article 2(7) of the charter, which forbids even the United Nations to intervene in matters of the domestic jurisdiction of any state, and that it is consistent with the purposes of the United Nations (see article 2(4)), which include the commitment to peaceful means for settlement of disputes, respect for self-determination of peoples, and so on. The defence must further reject the position taken by the General Assembly that 'no State has the right to intervene, directly or indirectly, for any reason whatever, in the internal or external affairs of any other State,' or to 'interfere in civil strife in another State.'[52] But at least it does not fly in the face of historical facts, and it can appeal to some ambiguity in the charter as well as to a tradition granting rights to incumbent governments.

The primary virtue of this defence is that it avoids hypocrisy. The interpretation of law that underlies it is explicitly counter-revolutionary and expresses the fact that regardless of the law great powers will do as they wish to achieve the objectives of their ruling elites ('the national interest'), restrained only by cost or competing force. The Bangkok Conference of Asian Jurists (1965) concluded that 'on the former colonial territories, the Rule of Law is viewed more as a malevolent instrument of tyrannical rule than as a force of emancipation or of protection of human rights.'[53] As a general conclusion, this is accurate enough.

'The right to aid incumbent governments,' whether claimed by the United States in South Vietnam or the Soviet Union in Hungary, is merely a flimsy disguise for imperial ambition. The same is true of the concept of 'limited sovereignty' developed by the United States in the Caribbean, and later, in almost the same terms, by the Soviet Union in Eastern Europe. In both cases, the essence of the doctrine is that 'a regional organization may designate a particular sociopolitical ideology as alien to the region,' and its advocacy by indigenous groups a form of aggression.[54] In accordance with this doctrine, Guatemalans, Vietnamese, Hungarians, and Czechs become aggressors in their own country if they are inspired by an ideology held to be alien and intolerable by the great power dominating that sphere of influence.

Under a reasonable interpretation of the United Nations Charter, intervention under these conditions is not permissible, but this fact in no way inhibits great-power practice. The conclusion is similar to that of section II above. There is a reasonable interpretation of the existing body of laws under which the law is not absurd and the behaviour of the state executive is improper, even criminal. But state power will construct, and seek to implement, a different interpretation under which it suffers virtually no restraints. The law, so conceived, has no legitimacy. Which interpretation prevails, in the international sphere at least, is determined not by legal or historical argument – much as we may deplore the fact – but by the distribution of power.

It is in this connection that the Pentagon Papers raise some uncomfortable questions concerning legitimate social action. Confirming other evidence, they indicate that fear of domestic disruption was an effective constraint on policy. The analyst recognizes that one of the more serious problems for the administration was 'the massive anti-war demonstration organized in Washington on October 21 [1967],' with the 'massive march on the Pentagon': 'the sight of thousands of peaceful demonstrators being confronted by troops in battle gear cannot have been reassuring to the country as a whole nor to the President in particular' (IV, 217, 197). McNaughton was concerned that escalation of the land war beyond South Vietnam might lead to massive civil disobedience, particularly in view of opposition to the war among young people, the underprivileged, the intelligentsia, and women (IV, 482, 478). In considering additional troop deployments to Vietnam after the Tet offensive, the Joint Chiefs had to make sure that 'sufficient forces would still be available for civil disorder control' (IV, 541). A memorandum in the Defense Department a few weeks later was concerned that increased force levels would lead to 'increased defiance of the draft and growing unrest in the cities,' running the risk of 'provoking a domestic crisis of unprecedented proportions' (IV, 564).

Considerations of cost are the sole factors inhibiting policy makers, so these volumes indicate. I have found no exception to this conclusion. Among the effective costs are those just noted. It was and still remains within the power of American citizens to raise these costs and thus to restrain the criminal violence of the state.

IV. THE PENTAGON STUDY AND THE HISTORICAL RECORD[55]

Though in no sense a history of American involvement in Indochina, the Pentagon study adds important details to the historical record. As a general assessment, it seems fair to say that it corroborates reasonable inferences drawn in the most critical literature on the war. The Pentagon historians do at times try to distinguish the evidence they present from the conclusions in the critical literature, but unsuccessfully; they misrepresent the views of the critics of the war whom they discuss, and severely distort the historical record as well.

Not surprisingly, the Pentagon historians, in case after case, reiterate United States government claims as if they were established fact. Often they go far beyond government propaganda in attempting to justify United States policy and to uphold the view that North Vietnam was the disruptive and aggressive force in Indochina, sometimes even misrepresenting the documentation on which their account is based. Their reasoning, when they go beyond the documentary record, also reveals the extreme progovernment bias that one would naturally expect in a study of this sort. To cite one case, consider the interpretation of the post-Geneva period by Leslie Gelb, the director of the Pentagon study. In his view, the United States and the GVN, though not 'fully cooperative,' nevertheless 'considered themselves constrained by the Accords' and did not 'deliberately . . . breach the peace.' 'In contrast, the DRV proceeded to mobilize its total societal resources scarcely without pause from the day the peace was signed, as though to substantiate the declaration' of Pham Van Dong that 'we shall achieve unity' (I, 250). Thus by mobilizing its total societal resources for social and economic reconstruction, the DRV clearly demonstrated its intent to upset the accords, in contrast to the peace-loving United States and GVN, who were merely maintaining the status quo as established at Geneva as they rejected the central elections provision of the accords and launched a murderous repression of the Viet Minh and other opposition elements, in violation of article 14(c) of the accords. The DRV could have demonstrated its sincerity only by succumbing to the famine that appeared imminent in 1954 (cf. *At War with Asia*, p. 282, and *For Reasons of State*, Chapter 5), refraining from economic development, and permitting the

United States to succeed in its efforts to undermine it. The logic of the historian is rather like that of Dean Acheson when he declared in 1950 that recognition of Ho Chi Minh by China and the Soviet Union 'should remove any illusion as to the nationalist character of Ho Chi Minh's aims and reveals Ho in his true colors as the mortal enemy of native independence in Vietnam' (I, 51). To Acheson, apparently, Ho could prove his nationalist credentials only by capitulating to the French, who, as Acheson saw it, were defending liberty and national independence in Vietnam against Viet Minh aggression (see pp. 124–5 below).

On similar ideological premises, Gelb states that 'no direct links have been established between Hanoi and perpetrators of rural violence' in the 1956–1959 period (I, 243). By 'perpetrators of rural violence' Gelb means the resistance forces in South Vietnam who undertook measures of self-defence (contrary to the policy of the Vietnamese Communists) in response to the reign of terror instituted by President Diem and his associates, who organized massive expeditions to peaceful Communist-controlled areas, killing innumerable peasants and destroying villages by artillery bombardment, killing, torturing, and imprisoning tens of thousands of dissidents.[56] In this regard, Gelb merely states that 'at least through 1957, Diem and his government enjoyed marked success with fairly sophisticated pacification programs in the countryside' (I, 254), though he affirms that Diem instituted various 'oppressive measures' (I, 253, 255). But he concludes that the Diem regime 'compared favorably with other Asian governments of the same period in its respect for the person and property of citizens' (I, 253; in particular, for the property of the 2 per cent of landowners who owned 45 per cent of the land by 1960; I, 254). Diem and his associates are not described as 'perpetrators of rural violence.' There is, incidentally, little difficulty in establishing 'direct links' between Washington and the organizers of the 'sophisticated pacification programs,' a fact not discussed in this connection.

When the Pentagon study appeared there was loud protest that it was biased, misleading, a chorus of doves. In a sense, this is correct. The Pentagon historians do, in general, seem to believe that the United States involvement in Vietnam may well have been a costly error. At the same time they tend to accept uncritically the framework of official ideology and rarely question government assertions. As the term has been used in American political discourse, they are doves, by and large, and they have naturally been subjected to much criticism on that account by the statist ideologues who are scandalized when the mass media or scholarship or public opinion shows the slightest signs of intellectual independence or scepticism with regard to official dogma.

The general bias of the analysts must be appreciated by anyone who hopes to make serious use of this material. Disinterested scholarship on contemporary affairs is something of an illusion, though it is not unusual for a commitment to the prevailing ideology to be mistaken for 'neutrality.' Such naiveté is not infrequently apparent in these analyses, though no more so than in most professional work. Nevertheless, no reader will fail to learn a great deal about the United States involvement in Vietnam, and the attitudes and goals that underlie it, from a careful study of the analyses and the documentation on which they are based.

The most striking feature of the historical record, as presented in the Pentagon study, is its remarkable continuity. Perhaps the most significant example has to do with the political premises of the four administrations covered in the record (and we may now add a fifth). Never has there been the slightest deviation from the principle that a noncommunist regime must be imposed, regardless of popular sentiment. True, the scope of the principle was narrowed when it was finally conceded, by about 1960, that North Vietnam was 'lost.' Apart from that, the principle was maintained without equivocation, the record indicates. Given this principle, the strength of the Vietnamese resistance, the military power available to the United States, and the lack of effective constraints, one can deduce, with almost mathematical precision, the strategy of annihilation that was gradually undertaken.

In May 1949, Acheson informed United States officials in Saigon and Paris that 'no effort should be spared' to assure the success of the Bao Dai government (which, he added, would be recognized by the United States when circumstances permitted) since there appeared to be 'no other alternative to estab[lishment] Commie pattern Vietnam.' He further urged that the Bao Dai government should be 'truly representative even to extent including outstanding non-Commie leaders now supporting Ho.'[57] Of course, Acheson was aware that Ho Chi Minh had 'captured control of the nationalist movement.'[58] But to Acheson, Ho's popularity was of no greater moment than his nationalist credentials.

In May 1967, McNaughton and McNamara presented a memorandum that the analyst takes to imply a significant reorientation of policy, away from the early emphasis on military victory and towards a more limited and conciliatory stance. McNaughton suggested that the United States emphasize 'that the sole US objective in Vietnam has been and is to permit the people of South Vietnam to determine their own future.' Accordingly, the Saigon government should be encouraged 'to reach an accommodation with the non-Communist South Vietnamese who are under the VC banner; to accept them as members of an opposition political party, and, if necessary, to accept their individual participation in the national government.'[59] Precisely Acheson's proposal of eighteen years earlier (restricted now to South Vietnam).

The final words of the Pentagon Papers analysis describe a new policy, undertaken after the Tet offensive of 1968 had shattered the old: 'American forces would remain in South Vietnam to prevent defeat of the Government by Communist forces and to provide a shield behind which that Government could rally, become effective, and win the support of its people' (IV, 604). Again, the same assumption: the United States must provide the military force to enable a noncommunist regime, despite its political weakness, corruption, and injustice, somehow to manage to stabilize itself. Nowhere is there the slightest deviation from this fundamental commitment.[60] The same policy remains in force today, despite tactical modifications.[61]

Small wonder, then, that many Vietnamese saw the Americans as the inheritors of French colonialism. The analyst cites studies of peasant attitudes demonstrating 'that for many, the struggle which began in 1945 against colonialism continued uninterrupted throughout Diem's regime: in 1954, the foes of nationalists were transformed from France and Bao Dai, to Diem and the US . . . but the issues at stake never changed' (I, 295; see also I, 252). Correspondingly, the Pentagon considered its problem was to 'deter the Viet Cong (formerly called Viet Minh)' (May 1959; *DOD*, bk 10, p. 1186; also II, 409).[62] Diem himself, on occasion, seems to have taken a rather similar position. Speaking to the departing French troops on April 28, 1956, he pledged that 'your forces, who have fought to defend honor and freedom, will find in us worthy successors.'[63] In January 1964 General Minh warned of the 'colonial flavor to the whole pacification effort.' The French he said, in their worst and clumsiest days never went into villages or districts as the Americans were about to do. (Note the date.) In response to Lodge's argument that most of the teams were Vietnamese, General Minh pointed out that 'they are considered the same as Vietnamese who worked for the Japanese.' The United States reaction was to reject Minh's proposals as 'an unacceptable rearward step' and to extend the adviser system even below 'sector and battalion level' (II, 307–8). A year and a half later, it was quite appropriate for William Bundy to wonder whether people in the countryside, who already may be tempted to regard the Americans as the successors to the French, might not 'flock to the VC banner' after the full-scale United States invasion then being planned (IV, 611).

The Thieu regime today has a power base remarkably like Diem's, perhaps even narrower.[64] By now, substantial segments of the urban intelligentsia – 'the people who count,' as Lodge put it (II, 738) – regard American intervention as blatant imperialism. Of course, one may argue that the popular mood counts for less than in former years, now that the United States has succeeded, at least partially, in 'grinding the enemy down by sheer weight and mass' (Robert Komer; IV, 420).

V. VIETNAM AND UNITED STATES GLOBAL STRATEGY

With regard to long-term United States objectives, the Pentagon Papers again add useful documentation, generally corroborating, I believe, analyses based on the public record that have been presented elsewhere.[65] In the early period, the documentary record presents a fairly explicit account of more or less rational pursuit of perceived self-interest. The primary argument was straightforward. The United States has strategic and economic interests in South-east Asia that must be secured. Holding Indochina is essential to securing these interests. Therefore we must hold Indochina. A critical consideration is Japan, which will eventually accommodate to the 'Soviet bloc' if South-east Asia is lost. In effect, then, the United States would have lost the Pacific phase of World War II, which was fought, in part, to prevent Japan from constructing a closed 'co-prosperity sphere' in Asia from which the United States would be excluded. The theoretical framework for these considerations was the domino theory, which was formulated clearly before the Korean War, as was the decision to support French colonialism. The goal: a new 'co-prosperity sphere' congenial to United States interests and incorporating Japan.

It is fashionable today to deride the domino theory, but in fact it contains an important kernel of plausibility, perhaps truth. National independence and revolutionary social change, if successful, may very well be contagious. The problem is what Walt Rostow and others sometimes call the 'ideological threat,' specifically, 'the possibility that the Chinese Communists can prove to Asians by progress in China that Communist methods are better and faster than democratic methods.'[66] The State Department feared that 'a fundamental source of danger we face in the Far East derives from Communist China's rate of economic growth which will probably continue to outstrip that of free Asian countries, with the possible exception of Japan,' a matter of real as well as psychological impact elsewhere (*DOD*, bk 10, p. 1198; June 1959). The Joint Chiefs repeated the same wording two weeks later (p. 1213), adding further that 'the dramatic economic improvements realized by Communist China over the past ten years impress the nations of the region greatly and offer a serious challenge to the Free World' (p. 1226). State therefore urged that the United States do what it can to retard the economic progress of the Communist Asian states (p. 1208),[67] a decision that is remarkable in its cruelty.

A few years later, in the midst of the autumn 1964 planning to escalate the war, Michael Forrestal argued that we must be concerned with Chinese 'ideological expansion,' its need 'to achieve ideological successes abroad,' and the danger than any such ideological success will stimulate the need for further successes. Therefore 'our objective should be to "contain" China for the longest possible period' (III, 592; November 4, 1964); or, as the analyst puts it a bit more accurately, paraphrasing Forrestal, 'the US object should be to "contain" Chinese political and ideological influence' (III, 218). William Sullivan picked up the same theme, viewing 'Chinese political and ideological aggressiveness ... as a threat to the ability of these peoples to determine their own futures, and hence to develop along ways compatible with US interests' (III, 218; analyst's paraphrase).

Note the typical assumption that self-determination is equivalent to United States interest, an assumption that is more than usually insipid in the light of what the Pentagon Papers reveal about the actual American response to Vietnamese efforts at self-determination. The same assumption, in effect, appeared much earlier in the important State Department policy statement of September 1948, mentioned earlier, which took note of 'our inability to suggest any practicable solution of the Indochina problem.' This inability arose from the incompatibility of our long-term objectives with certain unpleasant facts. One long-term objective is to eliminate Communist influence so far as possible and to prevent Chinese influence, and 'the unpleasant fact [is] that Communist Ho Chi Minh is the strongest and perhaps the ablest figure in Indochina and that any suggested solution which excludes him is an expedient of uncertain outcome.' What is particularly interesting is the reason why we must 'prevent undue Chinese penetration and subsequent influence in Indochina.' The reason is 'so that the peoples of Indochina will not be hampered in their natural developments by the pressure of an alien people and alien interests.'

This laudable concern for the 'natural developments' of the people of Indochina, free from alien interests, is coupled with the statement of another long-term objective of United States policy: 'to see installed a self-governing nationalist state which will be friendly to the US and which ... will be patterned upon our conception of a democratic state,' and will be associated 'with the western powers, particularly with France with whose customs, language and laws [the peoples of Indochina] are familiar, to the end that those peoples will prefer freely to cooperate with the western powers culturally, economically and politically' and will 'work productively and thus contribute to a better balanced world economy,' while enjoying a rising standard of income (*DOD*, bk 8, pp. 148, 144). The United States and France, in short, do not constitute 'alien people and alien interests' so far as the peoples of Indochina are concerned, and association with them does not hamper 'natural developments.'

The National Security Council working group of November 1964, in discussing the domino theory, pointed out the danger that mainland South-east Asia might fall to Communist domination if South Vietnam does, noting that 'if either Thailand or Malaysia were lost, or went badly sour in any way, then the rot would be in real danger of spreading all over mainland South-east Asia' (III, 627). The Joint Chiefs added that they were 'convinced Thailand would indeed go.' The NSC working group was further concerned with the 'effects on Japan, where the set is clearly in the direction of closer ties with Communist China, with a clear threat of early recognition'; and with the possibility that 'if the rest of South-east Asia did in fact succumb over time,' the effects might be 'multiplied many times over' and might, 'over time, tend to unravel the whole Pacific defense structure.' The Joint Chiefs added that the loss of South Vietnam alone would have these effects, that the United States would not be able to prevent the rot from spreading, very likely, except through 'general war,' and that the time-frame for the unravelling of the whole Pacific defence structure would be brief.

Shortly after, William Bundy and John McNaughton noted that the 'most likely result' of the least aggressive option they were considering (option A) 'would be a Vietnamese-negotiated deal, under which an eventually unified Communist Vietnam would reassert its traditional hostility to Communist China and limit its own ambitions to Laos and Cambodia.' They added: 'In such a case . . . whether the rot spread to Thailand would be hard to judge.' It would, however, be likely that the Thai 'would accommodate somehow to Communist China even without any marked military move by Communist China,' because they would 'conclude we simply could not be counted on' (III, 661).

Option A was unacceptable: the United States was unwilling to accept its 'most likely result,' a Vietnamese-negotiated deal leading to a unified Vietnam, Communist-led and hostile to China, its ambitions limited to Laos and Cambodia. Therefore the planners quickly moved to heightened aggression. They are vague as to just how the rot will spread to Thailand or why they fear a Thai 'accommodation' to China. This imprecision cannot be an oversight; these are, after all, the crucial issues, the issues that led the planners to recommend successive stages of aggression in Indochina, at immense risk and cost. But even internal documents, detailed analysis of options and possible consequences, refer to these central issues in loose and almost mystical terms. Occasionally, as in the document just cited, the planners make it clear that military conquest is not the mechanism by which the rot will spread. Surely they did not believe that Ho Chi Minh was going to conquer Thailand or Malaya or set sail for Jakarta or Tokyo. One must assume they were sufficiently in touch with reality to comprehend that Vietnamese support for guerrilla movements could hardly be very significant in Thailand or Malaya (and would be of no significance beyond). Such movements could succeed only if they had powerful roots and were capable of rallying the local population. If nothing else, repeated failures to incite resistance in North Vietnam would have sufficed to establish this fact. And it is difficult to believe that the planners, not ignorant men, feared Chinese aggression in Southeast Asia. As we see from the cited document, they regarded even a unified Vietnam that would be hostile to China as a danger to their plans, and anticipated that the mysterious Thai 'accommodation' would take place even without any overt military moves by China.

In fact, the American political leadership desperately sought some indication that China had aggressive intentions. A case in point was their interpretation of Lin Piao's statement of September 1965, which emphasized that national liberation movements must be self-reliant and cannot count on China for meaningful support. To McNamara, Rusk, and others, this was a new *Mein Kampf*.[68] The response of the Kennedy intellectuals to Mao's talk about the East Wind prevailing over the West Wind,[69] or to Khrushchev's statements of support for wars of national liberation, was of the same order. It would be misleading to say that such statements inspired fear or concern in Washington; rather, ideologists eagerly seized upon them in an effort to justify programmes that they wished to undertake or had already set in motion. As we shall see directly, United States intelligence agencies made determined (though unavailing efforts to unearth evidence that would prove the Viet Minh to be agents of 'international communism,' after having decided, with certain qualms, to support the reconquest of Indochina by France.

There is only one rational explanation for these and many similar incidents, and for the imprecision of the planners with regard to the spreading of the rot and the accommodation that they so feared. The 'rot' is the Communist 'ideological threat,' which must be combatted by direct intervention against local Communist rebellion, whether or not armed attack is involved (see p. 112 below). The Thai elite, they fear, will 'conclude we simply could not be counted on' to help them prevent internal social change in Thailand or to suppress a domestic insurgency. The only 'threat' posed by a unified Vietnam, hostile to China and limiting its ambitions to Laos and Cambodia, is the threat of social and economic progress within a framework unacceptable to American imperial interests. This is the rot that may spread to Thailand, inspiring a Communist led nationalist movement there. But no skilful ideologist would want to see the implications spelled out too clearly, to himself or others. Consequently the central factors noted are left a mystery, apart from occasional comments such as those just cited.

Recall that in this period there was much talk of competition between the Chinese and the Indian models of development (see note 66). In this context, fear of Chinese 'ideological expansion' gave substance to the domino theory, quite apart from any fantasies about Chinese troops roaming at will through northern Thailand or Kremlin directed aggression by the Viet Minh (see note 210 and pp. 56–7, 124–5 below).

It is important to be clear about what is at stake in discussion of the domino theory and related matters. The reality of perceived dangers is, of course, irrelevant to determining the motivation of policy makers. The fact that threats were perceived and taken seriously suffices to establish motive. The question of the reality of the threats is nevertheless of interest, for a different reason. If, in fact, foolishness or ignorance led to the perception of imaginary dangers, as is often alleged (see notes 86, 97, 98), then policy could be 'improved' (for whose benefit is another question) by replacing the policy makers by others who are more intelligent and better informed. The issues are sometimes not kept separate, with much resulting confusion.

In South-east Asia, the threat was heightened by a look at the allies of the United States. When Lyndon Johnson returned from Vietnam in May 1961, he spoke of the problem of reassuring our friends: in addition to Diem, these were Chiang, Sarit, and Ayub (II, 56). Such friends as these – the only ones mentioned – surely were endangered by the 'ideological threat' that Rostow and others perceived. The threat would be enhanced if Vietnam were to be united under communist leadership and successful in mobilization of the population for social and economic development, as might well have occurred had United States force not been introduced.

The comparison of development in South and North Vietnam was not particularly encouraging to the United States in this regard. An intelligence estimate of May 1959 concluded that 'development will lag behind that in the North, and the GVN will continue to rely heavily upon US support to close the gap between its own resources and its requirements' (*DOD*, bk 10, p. 1191). In the North, the standard of living is low and 'life is grim and regimented,' but 'the national effort is concentrated on building for the future.' The South has a higher standard of living (and 'there is far more freedom and gaiety' – for whom is not specified, nor is there discussion of the distribution of wealth), but 'basic economic growth has been slower than that of the north.' The alleged higher standard of living in the South was not unrelated to the more than $1 billion of American nonmilitary aid, the bulk of which financed import of commodities (*DOD*, bk 10, pp. 1191–3). In a similar context a few years later, an NSC working group took note of the discouragement in South Korea 'at the failure to make as much progress politically and economically as North Korea' (III, 627).

Perhaps the threat has now diminished, with the vast destruction in South Vietnam and elsewhere and the hatred and social disruption caused by the American war. It may be that Vietnam can be lost to the Vietnamese without the dire consequence of social and economic progress of a sort that might be meaningful to the Asian poor. Perhaps the 'second line of defense' of which American planners spoke can be held, at least for a time.

If our friends were toppled by popular movements, perhaps ultimately leading Japan to realign, influencing India, affecting even the oil-rich Middle East and then Europe, as the domino theory postulated, there would be a serious impact on the global system dominated by the United States and United States-based international corporations. Although some of the formulations of the domino theory were indeed fantastic, the underlying concept was not. Correspondingly, it comes as no surprise to discover that it is rarely challenged in this record. The analyst regards support for the French against Ho Chi Minh as 'the path of prudence rather than the path of risk'; it 'seemed the wiser choice,' given the likelihood that all of South-east Asia might have fallen under Ho's leadership (obviously not by military conquest, say, in Indonesia). This he regards as 'only slightly less of a bad dream than what has happened to Vietnam since' (I, 52). The domino principle, he notes 'was at the root of U.S. policy' since Chiang's defeat. It was also at the root of French policy, though the dominoes they were concerned with were in North Africa (I, 54). The domino theory was firmly reiterated by McGeorge Bundy in mid-1957 (IV, 159; cf. p. 126 below), and by many others.

In the years between, there is debate only over timing and probability. A CIA analysis of June 1964 has frequently been described as a challenge to the validity of the domino theory.[70] However, this analysis (III, 178) merely states that the surrounding nations probably would not '*quickly* succumb to communism as a result of the fall of Laos and South Vietnam' (my emphasis) and the spread of communism would not be 'inexorable' and might be reversed, though the loss of South Vietnam and Laos 'would be profoundly damaging to the US position in the Far East,' and might encourage the 'militant policies' of Hanoi and Peking.

The documentation for the pre-Kennedy period gives substantial support to this interpretation of United States motives. By April 1945 the United States had publicly supported the reconstitution of French authority, somewhat evasively, while a 'more liberal' pattern, specifically 'liberalization of restrictive French economic policies,' was recommended 'for the protection of American interests' (*DOD*, bk 8, pp. 6–10). The American interest in Indochina ('almost exclusively a French economic preserve, and a political morass') was considerably less than in Indonesia, where 'extensive American and British investments . . . afforded common ground for intervention' (I, 29). It was urged that France move to grant autonomy to its colonies (or the people 'may embrace ideologies contrary to our own or develop a Pan-Asiatic movement against all Western powers') and that open-door policies be pursued (*DOD* bk 8, p. 23). By December 1946, it was noted that 'French appear to realize no longer possible maintain closed door here and non-French interests will have chance to participate in unquestioned rich economic possibilities' (p. 87). Although the resources of Indochina itself are repeatedly mentioned (e.g., p. 183), it was of course the whole region (on the hypothesis of the domino theory) that was the primary consideration: 'if COMMIES gain control IC, THAI and the rest SEA will be imperilled' (p. 220; June 1949).

A National Security Council report of December 1949 went into the situation in some detail (NSC 48 1; *DOD*, bk 8, pp. 226–7). The problem is that now and for the foreseeable future, the Soviet Union threatens to dominate Asia, an area of significant political, economic, and military power. The 'Stalinist bloc' might achieve global dominance if Japan, 'the principal component of a Far Eastern war-making complex,' were added to it. 'Whether [Japan's] potential is developed and the way in which it is used will strongly influence the future patterns of politics in Asia.' 'In the power potential of Asia, Japan plays the most important part' by reason of its economic potential and strategic position. 'The industrial plant of Japan would be the richest strategic prize in the Far East for the USSR.' Communist pressure on Japan will mount, because of proximity, the indigenous Japanese Communist movement which might be able to exploit cultural factors and economic hardship, and 'the potential of Communist China as a source of raw materials vital to Japan and a market for its goods.' Japan requires Asian food, raw materials, and markets; the United States should encourage 'a considerable increase in Southern Asiatic food and raw material exports' to avoid 'preponderant dependence on Chinese sources.' Analogous considerations hold for India. Furthermore, these markets and sources of raw materials should be developed for United States purposes. 'Some kind of regional association . . . among the non-Cummunist countries of Asia might become an important means of developing a favorable atmosphere for such trade among themselves and with other parts of the world.'

As John Dower among others has emphasized, 'the United States has never intended to carry the burden of anti-Communist and anti-Chinese consolidation alone. It has always seen the end goal as a quasi-dependent Asian regionalism.'[71] The Pentagon Papers enrich the available documentation on this matter in a rather interesting way.

Continuing with NSC 48/1, it is recommended that under certain restrictions, trade with Communist China should be permitted, for the health of the Japanese and American economies. The industrial plant of Japan and such strategic materials as Indonesian oil must be denied to the Soviet Union and kept in the Western orbit. The particular problem in South-east Asia is that it 'is the target of a coordinated offensive directed by the Kremlin' (this is 'now clear'), and has no responsible leaders, outside of Thailand[72] and the Philippines. If South-east Asia 'is swept by communism we shall have suffered a major political rout the repercussions of which will be felt throughout the rest of the world, especially in the Middle East and in a then critically exposed Australia.'

The general lines of this analysis persist through the Truman and Eisenhower administrations. NSC 64 (I, 361–2) conclude that Thailand and Burma would 'fall under Communist domination' and the rest of South-east Asia would be 'in grave hazard' if Indochina were 'controlled by a Communist-dominated government.' The Joint Chiefs urged 'long-term measures to provide for Japan and the other offshore islands a secure source of food and other strategic materials from non-Communist held areas in the Far East' (I, 366; April 1950; they also recommended military aid and covert operations). A State Department policy committee interpreted NSC 64 as asserting that 'the loss of Indochina to Communist forces would undoubtedly lead to the loss of Southeast Asia' (*DOD*, bk 8, p. 351; October 1950). NSC 48/5 saw the Soviet Union as attempting to bring the mainland of East Asia and eventually Japan under Soviet control (pp. 425–6; May 1951). Given Asian population, military capacity, critical resources, and Japanese industrial capacity, it is essential to block this programme. An NSC staff study of February 1952 warned:

> The fall of Southeast Asia would underline the apparent economic advantages to Japan of association with the communist-dominated Asian sphere. Exclusion of Japan from trade with Southeast Asia would seriously affect the Japanese economy, and increase Japan's dependence on United States aid. In the long run the loss of Southeast Asia, especially Malaya and Indonesia, could result in such economic and political pressures in Japan as to make it extremely difficult to prevent Japan's eventual accommodation to the Soviet Bloc [I, 375]

It went on to speak of the importance of South-east Asian raw materials (for example, Indonesian oil, and the significance of Malaya, the largest dollar earner of the United Kingdom, to Britain's economic recovery) and United States strategic interests, developing the domino theory in detail.

NSC 124/2 in June 1952 identified China as the main enemy and gave a clear formulation of the domino theory, emphasizing again the problem of raw materials and the threat of Japanese accommodation to communism (I, 83–4, 384–5). The same themes persist, with added and even clearer emphasis, under the Eisenhower administration. It was emphasized that Japan is the keystone of United States policy and that the loss of South-east Asia (a likely consequence of the loss of Indochina, or even Tonkin) would drive Japan to accommodation with the Communist bloc permitting Red China (now the main culprit, though some analyses still refer to 'the Soviet Communist campaign in Southeast Asia'; cf. *DOD*, bk 9, p. 214; January 1954) to construct a military bloc more formidable than that of Japan before World War II. The world-wide effects would be disastrous. Therefore Indochina must be saved and its countries encouraged to integrate themselves into the 'free world' system and to stimulate the flow of raw-material resources to the free world, Japan being the critical factor (see I, 436, 438, 450, 452). In June 1956, John F. Kennedy gave a clear formulation of the basic thesis:

> Vietnam represents the cornerstone of the Free World in Southeast Asia, the keystone to the arch, the finger in the dike. Burma, Thailand, India, Japan, the Philippines and, obviously, Laos and Cambodia are among those whose security would be threatened if the red tide of Communism overflowed into Vietnam. . . . Moreover, the independence of Free Vietnam is crucial to the free world in fields other than the military. Her economy is essential to the economy of all of Southeast Asia; and her political liberty is an inspiration to those seeking to obtain or maintain their liberty in all parts of Asia – and indeed the world. The fundamental tenets of this nation's foreign policy, in short, depend in considerable measure upon a strong and free Vietnamese nation.[73]

Intelligence estimates repeated, with various nuances, the general assumptions of the domino theory (see *DOD*, bk 10, p. 999, September 1955, for a qualified statement). Memoranda of the NSC and of the Joint Chiefs of Staff also elaborate the same assumptions consistently, adding conventional recommendations that the investment climate for United States capital be improved (p. 1206) and that South-east Asian countries be integrated into the free-world economic system (pp. 1206, 1228, 1234, 1288).

It is sometimes argued that at best, 'citation of these views [which can now be documented extensively from internal documents as well as the public record] proves no more than conviction, and a mistaken conviction at that,' and therefore the 'radical argument' that Japanese relations with South-east Asia were a dominant consideration in American planning can be discounted.[74] The argument is an obvious nonsequitur, a particularly clear example of the fallacy noted earlier (p. 53 above). Documentation of the *conviction* suffices to establish motive; its *accuracy* is clearly irrelevant to the determination of motive. Robert W. Tucker compounds his logical fallacy with a factual error when he states that 'the radical argument of Japanese dependence on Southeast Asia is difficult to take seriously.' This is not a 'radical argument' but rather the expressed conviction of United States policy makers. By arguing merely the irrelevant question of the accuracy of the conviction, Tucker in effect concedes the actual 'radical argument' while appearing to reject it.

To make matters still worse, when he turns to the question whether the conviction was held, he hedges, claiming only that 'at least after 1964' one cannot attribute Vietnam policy to this conviction. Again irrelevant, since what has actually been argued is that this was the operative factor through the 1950s, of diminishing importance in later years as deepening American involvement became self-motivating and increasingly irrational on imperialist grounds, leading finally to serious disenchantment on the part of rational imperialists and a 'split in the ruling class.' From every point of view, then, Tucker's discussion of this point is entirely inept, yet it is the only attempt I know of to respond to what Tucker calls 'the radical argument.'[75]

In the 1960s, there is an increasing component of irrationalism and posturing, with much talk of psychological tests of will, humiliation, the American image, and so on. The insistence that the other fellow blink first is not without its ironic aspects. Thus the analysis regards 1961 as 'a peculiarly difficult year' for the United States because of 'the generally aggressive and confident posture of the Russians . . . and the generally defensive position of the Americans' (II, 21). It was therefore difficult to make concessions or to give ground to the Soviets, a matter which indirectly affected Vietnam. Anything, anywhere, that 'was, or could be interpreted to be a weak US response, only strengthened the pressure to hold on in Vietnam.' Chester Cooper believes, however, that 'Kennedy's foreign policy stance was given an added fillip in late 1962 following his dramatic success' in the Cuban missile crisis. Vietnam then provided an opportunity to prove to Peking and Moscow that their policy of 'wars of liberation' was dangerous and unpromising, and also 'provided both a challenge and an opportunity to test the new doctrines' of counterinsurgency.[76] Thus whether the United States stance with respect to its great-power rival is defensive or not, the determination to win in Indochina is fortified.

It is, I believe, reasonable to attribute the increasing irrationality of United States Indochina policy in the 1960s at least in part to the influx of technical intelligentsia into Washington and the expansion of the state role in the system of militarized state capitalism that has been evolving in the United States since World War II. The primary allegiance of the technical intelligentsia is to the state and its power, rather than to the specific interests of private capital, insofar as these interests can be distinguished. Furthermore, the claim of the technical intelligentsia to a share in power rests on their alleged expertise. For this reason, it is difficult for them to concede error or to shape state policy in terms of a pragmatic calculation of interests, once a commitment has been made to a particular policy. By admitting error, they concede that their claim to power was fraudulent. These problems are not faced in the same measure by someone whose authority is based on his role in controlling private empires or on an aristocratic heritage. If his policies founder and his judgments prove erroneous, his right to power is not correspondingly diminished and he is therefore somewhat more free to terminate an enterprise that is wasteful, failing, or indecisive.

By early 1964, concern over the effects of the 'loss' of South Vietnam reached a peak of what can perhaps properly be called 'hysteria.' In the analyst's phrase, referring to the February deliberations, 'Stopping Hanoi from aiding the Viet Cong virtually became equated with protecting US interests against the threat of insurgency throughout the world' (III, 153). Ralph Stavins hardly exaggerates when he describes the 'clouds on the horizon' as seen from Washington in the early 1960s: 'Hanoi would overthrow Diem with a few guerilla bands, and the United States as a direct consequence, would be forced to retire from the arena of world politics.'[77] Such fears were incorporated into the important NSAM 288 of March 1964, which presented what the analyst calls 'a classic statement of the domino theory' (III, 3). Throughout the world, it held, 'the South Vietnam conflict is regarded as a test case of US capacity to help a nation to meet the Communist "war of liberation." Thus, purely in terms of foreign policy, the stakes are high. . . .' The memorandum stated in clear terms that 'we seek an independent non-Communist South Vietnam' free to accept outside – meaning American – assistance, including 'police and military help to root out and control insurgent elements.' And it stated that unless we can achieve this objective, 'almost all of Southeast Asia will probably fall under Communist dominance' or 'accommodate to Communism,' with an increased threat to India, Australia, and Japan and indeed throughout the world, given that the conflict is a 'test case' (III, 50–1; II, 459–61). Although these views were modulated later on (cf. III, 220, 658), the essential idea of South Vietnam as a 'test case' remained, and the commitment to a noncommunist South Vietnam was never modified.

Despite the hyperbole, the rational core of policy making remained in the early 1960s, and in fact can even be detected in the exaggerated doctrine of Vietnam as a 'test case.' In one sense, Vietnam was indeed to serve as a test case. Developing countries were to be taught a harsh lesson. They must observe the rules of the international system as determined by the powerful – who, like many a stern disciplinarian, saw themselves as benign, even noble in intention. Developing countries must not undertake 'national liberation' on the Chinese model, extricating themselves from the international system dominated by Western and Japanese state capitalism, with mass mobilization, a focus on internal needs, and exploitation of material and human resources for internal development. If they are so foolhardy as to disobey the international rules, they will be subjected to subversion, blockade, or even outright destruction by the global judge and executioner.

The problem of Japan continued to be a serious though much less central issue. In November 1964 an important NSC working group, considering the problem of escalation, discussed 'the effect on Japanese attitudes through any development that appears to make Communist China and its allies a dominant force in Asia that must be lived with.' They already perceived a danger that Japan would move towards closer ties with Communist China, and 'the growing feeling that Communist China must somehow be lived with might well be accentuated' if the United States were not to prevail in Indochina (III, 623, 627; William Bundy's draft). It is important, in short, that Japan not accommodate to China or drift towards a readiness to live with China. Again in June 1965, William Bundy warned of the importance of considering Japanese views in choosing policy, for fear that Japan may turn to 'accommodation and really extensive relationships with Communist China' (IV, 614). We know from other sources that in the 1950s Japan was pressured to break trade relations with China, and that access to South-east Asia was explicitly offered as an inducement.[78] Japan's need for markets was also an important consideration for President Kennedy.[79] It must, of course, be kept in mind that Japan in those years was not generally perceived as an immediate rival; in fact, until 1965 Japan always had an unfavourable trade balance with the United States.[80] Japan was perceived as a potential threat if it drifted from the United States global system and began to 'live with' China.

Failure to appreciate the historical circumstances and the range of options actually available to policy makers sometimes leads to superficial commentary on this matter. For example, Charles Kindleberger argues that Japan is a 'difficult counterexample' to the theory that American economic foreign policy is motivated by self-interest,[81] specifically to the theory that 'foreign aid to less developed countries is to keep these countries dependent' and that United States policies 'are designed to use the dollar as a main instrument of control over the capitalist world.' Putting aside the question whether the theory is defensible, consider the logic of Kindleberger's argument: why does he regard Japan as a 'difficult counterexample?' His reason is that Japan has been assisted by the United States in various ways but is not 'a puppet of the United States.' By the same logic, we can prove that Soviet aid to China and Rumania was not granted out of self-interest. In fact, Kindleberger's argument holds only on the further assumption that the United States is omnipotent: on this assumption, if American aid is intended to induce some nation to remain within the American-dominated system, then that nation must be a puppet; and if the nation is not a puppet, it follows that American assistance cannot have been intended as a device to maintain control or influence.

In the real world, United States policy makers faced a rather different problem. They had a variety of means at hand to influence postwar Japanese development towards integration into the 'free world' system. A possible alternative, which they successfully overcame, was that 'the workshop of the Pacific' might undergo revolutionary social change or 'accommodate' to the closed systems developing in East Asia (cf. NSC 48/1, discussed above). The option of guaranteeing that Japan would be 'a puppet' was not available; whether it would have been chosen had it been feasible is another question.[82]

The results are a mixed blessing to American capital – bad for textiles and a bonanza for oil interests, to mention two examples – but surely preferable to the perceived alternatives. In any event, once Kindleberger's untenable implicit hypothesis is removed, the 'difficult counterexample' becomes quite manageable. Reasonable discussion of the matter is impeded by a kind of paranoia that is developing about 'Japan, Inc.' For example, Zbigniew Brzezinski, in an article which is critical of such exaggeration, nevertheless predicts that Japan will seek to 'exclude' computers from its liberalization policy on foreign investment, failing to mention that a wholly owned subsidiary of IBM, IBM Japan, has an estimated 40 per cent share of the Japanese computer market (apart from other arrangements between American and Japanese companies in the computer fields).[83] In fact, Japanese liberalization is proceeding, and if the outcome of the competition between American and Japanese capital may be in doubt, it should not be forgotten that quite apart from questions of scale, the United States holds many cards – for example, control of most of Japan's sources of petroleum.[84] Prior to the full-scale United States invasion of South Vietnam, with its vast and unanticipated costs, it was quite reasonable to suppose that Japan would remain for some time a reasonably well-behaved junior partner in the American dominated system.

Perhaps a word might be added with regard to the commonly heard argument that the costs of the Vietnam war prove that the United States has no imperial motives (as the costs of the Boer War prove that the British Empire was a figment of the radical imagination). The costs, of course, are profits for selected segments of the American economy, in large measure. It is senseless to describe government expenditures for petroleum, jet planes, cluster bombs, or computers for the automated air war simply as 'costs of intervention.' There are, to be sure, costs of empire that benefit no one: 50,000 American corpses or the deterioration in the strength of the United States economy relative to its industrial rivals. The costs of empire to the imperial society as a whole may be considerable. These costs, however, are social costs, whereas, say, the profits from overseas investment guaranteed by military success are again highly concentrated in certain special segments of the society. The costs of empire are in general distributed over the society as a whole, while its profits revert to a few within. In this respect, the empire serves as a device for internal consolidation of power and privilege,[85] and it is quite irrelevant to observe that its social costs are often great or that as costs rise, differences may also arise among those who are in positions of power and influence. While serving as a device for internal consolidation of privilege, the empire also provides markets, guaranteed sources of inexpensive raw materials, a cheap labour market, opportunities for export of pollution (no small matter for Japan, for example), and investment opportunities. On the assumptions of the domino theory, even in its more rational versions, the stakes in Vietnam in this regard were considerable.

The same fallacy is one of several that undermine the familiar argument that our economic stake in the third world is too slight a fraction of the gross national product to play any significant role in motivating Third World interventions.[86] The private interests that stand to gain from foreign intervention are undeterred by its social costs and will exert their often substantial influence to engage state power in support of their aims, irrespective of the percentage of GNP at stake. Quite apart from this, it is in general impossible to uncouple economic interests in the Third World from those in industrial societies, as the case of Vietnam clearly illustrates, with the long-standing concern of the policy makers over the fate of the farther dominoes such as Japan, and in the early stages, the relationship to the critical problem of reconstructing Western European capitalism (cf. the matter of Malayan dollar-earning capacity, noted above, p. 57; or the matter of French unwillingness to accept West Germany as an unrestricted participant in a Western alliance prior to successful reconstruction of the French imperial system).

Still, it might very well be true that had the costs been anticipated, the Vietnam venture would not have been undertaken. But in the real world, policy makers do not operate with a knowledge of ultimate costs and cannot begin all over again if plans go awry. At each point, they consider the costs and benefits of future acts. On these grounds, the Vietnam involvement might very well have seemed reasonable within the framework of imperialist motives, though by the 1960s, with the influx to Washington of ideologists and crisis managers, it can be argued that other and more irrational considerations came to predominate.

Furthermore, even now that the bill is in, the effect might be judged a moderate success for those segments of American society that have a major interest in preserving an 'integrated global system' in which American capital can operate with reasonable freedom. Consider the assessment of the editor of the *Far Eastern Economic Review*, generally committed to economic liberalism. He speaks of 'the ring of success stories in East and Southeast Asia,' with the Japanese economy serving as 'the main factor in pulling the region together and providing the shadowy outlines of a future co-prosperity sphere . . . and neatly complement[ing]' the economics of the rest of the region. 'The US presence in Vietnam,' in his view, 'has won time for Southeast Asia, allowing neighbouring countries to build up their economies and their sense of identity to a degree of stability which has equipped them to counter subversion, to provide a more attractive alternative to the peasant than the promises of the terrorist who steals down from the hills or from the jungles at night' – or on different ideological premises, allowing these countries to become more securely absorbed within the neocolonial global system. Whatever premises one adopts, the fact is that 'American businessmen . . . are convinced of the potential of Asia and the Pacific Basin as the world's third largest and fastest-growing market area,' and are moving rapidly into the region, a process that is continuing 'since the initiation of "Vietnamisation."' American investments now total nearly 70 per cent of all foreign investments in the region.[87]

The imperial drive that is clearly expressed in many documents may have been blunted by the unexpected resilience and obstinacy of the Vietnamese resistance. Nevertheless, it has partially achieved its aims, though in retrospect it might be argued that other means would perhaps have been more efficacious.

To be sure, the imperial drive is often masked in defensive terms: it is not that we are seeking to dominate an integrated world system incorporating Western Europe and Japan, but rather that we must deny strategic areas to the Kremlin (or 'Peiping'), thus protecting ourselves and others from their 'aggression.' The masters of the Russian empire affect a similar pose, no doubt with equal sincerity and with as much justification. The practice has respectable historical antecedents, and the term 'security' is a conventional euphemism. The planners merely seek to guarantee the security of the nation, not the interests of dominant social classes.

There is, in fact, a sense in which the 'defensive' rhetoric is appropriate. It is natural for the managers of the world's most advanced industrial superpower, organized more or less along capitalist lines, to seek free and open competition throughout the world in fair confidence that the interests they represent will tend to predominate. Thus they seek only to deny various areas to closed systems, national or imperial. The United States, like Britain in the period of its world dominance, tends towards the 'imperialism of free trade,' while maintaining the practice of state intervention for the benefit of special interests and demanding special rights (as in the Philippines) where they can be obtained.[88]

Many commentators deny that United States policy was determined or even influenced by long-term imperial objectives, and argue that the Pentagon Papers reveal no imperial drive. A case can be made for this view, specifically in the 1960s. Leslie Gelb makes the interesting point that 'no systematic or serious examination of Vietnam's importance to the United States was ever undertaken within the government.'[89] He attributes the persistence of the Vietnam ventures, in the face of this oversight, to multiple factors: the stranglehold of cold-war assumptions, bureaucratic judgments, anticommunism as a force in American politics and other domestic pressures, and so on.[90] He points out that although the view that 'Vietnam had intrinsic strategic military and economic importance' was argued, it never prevailed; properly, of course, since Vietnam has no such *intrinsic* importance. Rather its importance derives from the assumptions of the domino theory, in his formulation the theory 'by which the fall of Indochina would lead to the deterioration of American security around the globe.' 'It was ritualistic anti-communism and exaggerated power politics that got us into Vietnam,' he maintains, noting that these 'articles of faith' were never seriously debated (*New York Review*). Nor, we may add, is there any record of a debate or analysis of just how American 'security' would be harmed by a victory of the Communist-led nationalist movement of Indochina, or just what components of 'American security' would be harmed by the triumph of a nationalist movement which, it was expected, would be hostile to China and would limit its ambitions to Laos and Cambodia (see p. 51 above).

Hannah Arendt has discussed a variety of rather different irrational factors that impelled policy makers in Vietnam.[91] 'The ultimate aim,' she concludes, 'was neither power nor profit [nor] particular tangible interests,' but rather 'image making,' 'something new in the huge arsenal of human follies.' 'American policy pursued no real aims, good or bad, that could limit and control sheer fantasy,' in particular no imperial strategy. Ignorance, blind anticommunism, arrogance, and self-deception lie behind American policy. She is certainly correct in noting these elements in the Pentagon history. Thus in the face of all historical evidence, the American authorities persisted in the assumption, a point of rigid doctrine, that China was an agent of Moscow, the Viet Cong an agency of North Vietnam, which was in turn the puppet of Moscow or 'Peiping' or both, depending on the mood of the planners and propagandists, who surely had more than enough information at hand to refute these assumptions, or at the very least to shake their confidence in them. A kind of institutionalized stupidity seems a possible explanation.

There is ample material in the Pentagon Papers to support

such interpretations, from the time when Dean Acheson, in a cable to Saigon, spoke of the need to aid the French and the Associated States of Indochina 'to defend the territorial integrity of IC and prevent the incorporation of the ASSOC[iated] States within the COMMIE-dominated bloc of slave states' (I, 70; October 1950), and on to the present. One of the most remarkable revelations of the Pentagon study is that the analysts were able to discover only one staff paper, in a record of more than two decades, 'which treats communist reactions primarily in terms of the separate national interests of Hanoi, Moscow, and Peiping, rather than primarily in terms of an overall communist strategy for which Hanoi is acting as an agent' (II, 107; an intelligence estimate of November 1961). Even in the 'intelligence community,' where they are paid to get the facts straight and not to rant about helping the French defend the territorial integrity of Indochina from its people and the Commie-dominated bloc of slave states, it was apparently next to impossible to perceive, or at least express the simple truth, that North Vietnam, like the Soviet Union, China, the United States, and the NLF, has its own interests, which are often decisive.

It is amusing to trace the efforts to establish that Ho Chi Minh was merely a Russian (or Chinese) puppet – as obviously must be the case. The State Department, in July 1948, could find 'no evidence of direct link between Ho and Moscow' (but naturally 'assumes it exists').[92] State Department intelligence, in the fall, found evidence of 'Kremlin-directed conspiracy . . . in virtually all countries except Vietnam.' Indochina appeared 'an anomaly.' How can this be explained? To intelligence, the most likely explanation is that 'no rigid directives have been issued by Moscow' or that 'a special dispensation for the Vietnam government has been arranged in Moscow' (I, 5, 34). In September 1948, the State Department noted: 'There continues to be no known communication between the USSR and Vietnam, although evidence is accumulating that a radio liaison may have been established through the Tass agency in Shanghai' (*DOD*, bk 8, p. 148, grasping at straws). American officials in Saigon added: 'No evidence has yet turned up that Ho Chi Minh is receiving directives either from Moscow, China, or the Soviet Legation in Bangkok.' 'It may be assumed,' they conclude from this, 'that Moscow feels that Ho and his lieutenants have had sufficient training and experience and are sufficiently loyal to be trusted to determine their day-to-day policy without supervision' (p. 151).

By February 1949, they were relieved to discover that 'Moscow publications of fairly recent date are frequently seized by the French,' indicating that 'satisfactory communications exist,' though the channel remains a mystery (p. 168); also, 'there has been surprising[ly] little direct cooperation between local Chinese Communists and the Viet Minh.'

'We are unable to determine whether Peiping or Moscow has ultimate responsibility for Viet Minh policy,' an intelligence estimate of June 1953 relates (I, 396), but it must be one or the other – that is an axiom. In the context of a discussion of Chinese Communist strategy, Intelligence concludes that the Communists are pursuing their present strategy in Indochina because it 'diverts badly needed French and US resources from Europe at relatively small cost to the Communists' and 'provides opportunities to advance international Communist interests while preserving the fiction of 'autonomous' national liberation movements, and it provides an instrument, the Viet Minh, with which Communist China and the USSR can indirectly exert military and psychological pressures on the peoples and governments of Laos, Cambodia, and Thailand' (I, 399). Might there be another reason why the Viet Minh fight on?

It is tempting to use such evidence to support the claim that ignorance, mythology, and institutionalized stupidity led United States policy-makers into a series of disastrous errors. If only they had realized that Stalin was lukewarm or negative towards Mao and the Greek guerrillas, that there was no 'pattern of Communist conquest... manifest' in Guatemala in 1954[93] that the Vietnamese were conducting their own struggle for national liberation. If only William Bundy had had a course in Vietnamese history at Yale. But ignorance and paranoia obscured the facts.

This theory, however, leaves too many questions unanswered. To mention only the simplest: Why were policy makers always subject to the same form of ignorance and irrationality? Why was there such a systematic error in the delusional systems constructed by post-war ideologists? Mere ignorance or foolishness would lead to random error, not to a regular and systematic distortion: unwavering adherence[94] to the principle that whatever the facts may be, the cause of international conflict is the behaviour of the Communist powers and all revolutionary movements within the United States system are sponsored by the Soviet Union, China, or both.[95] Why was the latter assumption so far beyond challenge that no examination of Vietnam's importance was ever undertaken (Gelb)? Ignorance and stupidity can surely lead to error, but hardly to such systematic error or such certainty in error. And there is a second and even more obvious question: Why is the United States anti-communist?

With respect to the first question, whether it is Acheson, Rostow, Stevenson, Kissinger, or whoever, one generally finds the same distortion as in the sorry record of the 'intelligence community.' From one or another such source we hear that Stalin supported Mao and incited the Greek guerrillas and Ho Chi Minh, China attacked India, the Viet Cong are agents of international Communist aggression, and so on. These are, indeed, articles of faith. The crisis managers do not argue these claims; they merely intone them. All are at best highly dubious and probably false, so the available record indicates, but questions of fact are beside the point in theological disputation.

What is not beside the point is that these articles of faith are highly functional. The fact is that anticommunism provides a convenient mythology to justify colonial wars, and to gain the popular support that is often hard to rally, given the grisly nature and substantial costs of such endeavours. But to explain the United States attack on Vietnam on grounds of anticommunist delusions would be as superficial as explaining the Russian invasion of Czechoslovakia or Hungary merely on grounds of fear of West Germany or Wall Street. No doubt at some level the Soviet leadership believes what it says and is bewildered at the bitter reaction to its selfless and benevolent behaviour. Perhaps Russian public opinion indeed 'is proud of its country's armed power in Prague and speaks of Czechoslovak weakness, ingratitude, irresponsibility, etc.'[96] Similarly, Washington claims to be defending democracy and warding off 'internal aggression' or subversion by agents of international communism when it helps to destroy a mass popular movement in Greece, supports an invasion of Guatemala, invades the Dominican Republic, and devastates the peasant societies of Indochina. Its defenders, and many critics as well, are at most willing to concede error if the costs mount too high, and cannot conceive that any 'responsible' or 'qualified' observer might have a rather different view. Some still insist that for the most part the United States pursues its foreign policy 'for reformist, even utopian goals,' and that this policy can be faulted only for being 'callow, sentimental, savagely stupid . . . too little the work of an intellectually serious leadership.'[97] It is remarkable how difficult it is, even for those who see themselves as critics, to interpret United States behaviour by the standards of evaluation and analysis that would, properly, be applied to any other great power.

The fact that policy makers may be caught up in the fantasies they spin to disguise imperial intervention, and may sometimes even find themselves trapped by them, should not prevent us from asking what function these ideological constructions fulfil – why *this* particular system of mystification is consistently expounded in place of some alternative. Similarly, one should not be misled by the fact that the delusional system presents a faint reflection of reality. It must, after all, carry some conviction. But this should not prevent us from proceeding to disentangle motive from myth.

The efforts of the 'intelligence community' to establish the thesis that the Viet Minh were agents of international communism reveal quite clearly the function of the 'international Communist conspiracy' in post-war American foreign policy. There is no doubt that the Soviet Union, within the limits of its power, established its harsh and oppressive imperial rule. But it was not this fact that determined American policy in South-east Asia. Contrary to the fantasies of Walt Rostow (see note 192) and others, the United States did not first discover that the Viet Minh were agents of a Kremlin-directed conspiracy and then proceeded to help France beat back Russian aggression against South-east Asia. Rather, the United States merely applied in Indochina the general policy of establishing Western-oriented regimes that would cooperate ('freely') with the West and Japan, 'culturally, economically, and politically,' and 'contribute to a better balanced world economy' – the 'world economy' in question being, of course, that of the 'free world' (cf. p. 50 above). In its essentials, the policy was not fundamentally different from, say, American policy in Italy in 1943, or in Greece and Korea shortly after.[98] To implement this policy in Vietnam, it was necessary to destroy the forces that had 'captured the nationalist movement,' since these forces had a different model of social and economic development in mind. But this would have appeared too cynical, if stated frankly. Therefore it was necessary to recast the issue in 'defensive' terms, and to establish that these nationalist forces were really the agents of aggression by an international conspiracy, aimed ultimately at destroying the freedom of the United States itself. The 'intelligence community' thus was assigned the task of demonstrating the thesis that was required as the ideological underpinning of the American intervention. It is interesting, but not very surprising given the background, that the failure of intelligence to establish the needed link in no way impeded the ideologists, who simply continued to insist that the required thesis was correct, accepting and proclaiming it as an article of faith. The same pattern has appeared elsewhere, with predictable regularity.

Turning to the second question: Why is the United States anti-communist? A conventional answer is that the United States opposes communism because of its aggressive, expansionist character. Thus it is argued that we do not seek to overthrow communism where it represents the status quo, as in Eastern Europe; and that when President Kennedy, in an often-quoted remark, said that we would always prefer a Trujillo to a Castro,[99] he meant that 'the power requirements of the struggle with the Soviet Union took precedence over the commitment to a "decent democratic regime".' As to China:

> The containment of China has not been pursued simply because China has a communist government, but because of China's outlook generally and her policy in Asia particularly. It is China's insistence upon changing the Asian status quo, and the methods she has used, that explain American hostility.[100]

Such proposals cannot withstand analysis. It is true, but irrelevant, that the United States will not risk nuclear destruction to roll back communism; again, one should not overlook the objective limits on American power. Tucker's interpretation of Kennedy's remarks seem to presuppose that American hostility towards Castro was a consequence of his turn towards the Soviet Union, which is of course untrue. Perhaps one can argue that American hostility was not a determining factor in this move, but that it preceded it is beyond argument.[101] With respect to China, Tucker's argument is weaker still. What methods did China use in changing the status quo beyond its borders? In what respect were these methods 'objectionable' in comparison with American methods in the Far East? In what sense was the forceful reimposition of French colonialism, in opposition to a Communist-led Vietnamese nationalist movement, an attempt to preserve the status quo after World War II? Why the effort to demonstrate that the Vietnamese revolutionaries – or the backers of Arbenz or Bosch – were Russian or Chinese agents, despite the evidence at hand, leading ultimately to the religious faith that this must be so? The answers to these questions entirely undermine Tucker's effort to 'explain American hostility.'

Tucker is in fact mistaken about what counts as an explanation of policy. He is nearer the mark when he points out that Castro 'would refuse to do our bidding' and 'would stand as a challenge to our otherwise undisputed hegemony in this hemisphere,' but he does not pursue these observations to the degree of specificity that any serious discussion of policy must achieve. In what respects would Cuba refuse to do our bidding and challenge our hegemony? This question Tucker does not answer, or even pose. He says merely that 'America's interventionist and counter-revolutionary policy . . . may be accounted for in terms of a reasonably well-grounded fear that the American example might become irrelevant to much of the world,' along with the 'will to exercise dominion over others.' Tucker is in error when he states that 'a radical critique cannot *consistently* accept this explanation.'[102] It would, however, be quite accurate to say that no serious critique can accept such proposals *as an explanation of policy*. Rather, any serious critique will pursue the matter further, asking what elements of 'the American example' a foreign society must adopt to allay these fears. Was it fear that Guatemala would choose soccer rather than baseball as its national sport that precipitated the 1954 intervention? Was the Bay of Pigs invasion rooted in the fear that Cuban intellectuals would prefer Continental phenomenology to American-style analytic philosophy? Is it our concern that the model of American political democracy might prove 'irrelevant' that explains why the United States executive so prefers Brazil to Chile under Allende? Again, a serious look at real historical examples reveals at once the emptiness of Tucker's proposals. He believes himself to be offering a more cogent alternative to a 'radical critique,' whereas in fact he is offering no alternative at all, but merely abstracting away from the particular specific questions that must be faced by any serious effort, radical or not, to explain the American policy of counter-revolutionary intervention.

Tucker's failure to come to grips with the real problems follows a familiar pattern. It is commonly argued that American interventionism is not attributable to the normal workings of state capitalism, but to some deeper motive, such as the 'drive for power.' The reasoning is shoddy, and it is important to see why. The failure of the argument does not lie in the identification of the 'power drive' as the cause of imperialist intervention; this premise is sufficiently vague so that we can grant it to be true without fear of refutation. Rather, the argument fails because it does not recognize that a generalization is not refuted by rephrasing it in terms that are logically equivalent, or even by tracing it to deeper theses from which it derives. Thus suppose one were to argue that the normal behaviour of a businessman is not governed by the pursuit of profit (or, say, growth, assuming this to be an empirically distinguishable thesis), but rather by a 'deeper' drive for power. Again, we may accept the claim that the normal behaviour of the businessman is explained by a drive for power, which manifests itself in a capitalist society in the pursuit of profit. This claim merely restates, and does not contradict, the hypothesis that the behaviour of a businessman in a capitalist society is governed by the pursuit of profit.

Much the same is true of the vague musings about a 'generalized drive for power' which often appear in discussions of American foreign policy. It may well be true that any autocratic system of rule will support and intensify the 'drive for power' and give it free rein. In a capitalist society, the operative form of autocratic rule is the private control of the means of production and resources, of commerce and finance, and further, the significant influence on state policy of those who rule the private economy, and who indeed largely staff the government. Elements of the private autocracy who have a specific concern with foreign affairs will naturally tend to use their power and influence to direct state policy for the benefit of the interests they represent. Where they succeed, we have imperialist intervention, quite commonly.

It might be argued that a healthy democracy would impede imperial planners, for two reasons: in the first place, considerations of self-interest would serve as a brake on imperial ventures with their often substantial social cost; and secondly, a functioning democracy might foster other values beyond domination and power – solidarity, sympathy, co-operative impulses, a concern for creative and useful work, and so on. The prevailing ideology tends to downgrade and scoff at such motives, often appealing to the alleged discoveries of the 'behavioral sciences,' but this farce need not detain us here (see *For Reasons of State*, Chapter 5). The important point is that the resort to a 'power drive' as the explanation of imperial intervention is not false, but irrelevant, once its true character is laid bare. It is fair, I think, to suggest that this 'alternative explanation' merely serves as a form of mystification; it serves to obscure the actual workings of power.

The question remains: Why is American ideology and policy anti-communist? Or a further question: Why has the United States been antifascist (though selectively)? Why was fascist Japan evil in 1940, while fascist Greece and Portugal (preserving the status quo with American arms in Africa) are quite tolerable today? And why is the United States generally anticolonialist, as in Indonesia shortly after World War II, when the conservative nationalist leadership appeared at first to favour foreign investment, but (reluctantly) not in Indochina, where the alternative to a barely disguised French colonialism was an indigenous Communist resistance?

It is not too difficult to discern a criterion that serves rather well to determine which elements in foreign lands receive support and which are labelled enemies. It is surely not the humanitarian impulse (see pp. 76–7 below); nor is it the prospects for development that determine the official United States response: China or Cuba might well have profited from capital grants for development – more so, at least, than from blockade, invasion, and harassment. Nor is it the fear of our great-power rivals that leads us to intervene halfway around the world, as is plainly shown by the determined effort to prove that Russia and China were responsible for the 'internal aggression' in Vietnam, in the face of the evidence that they were not, and analogous efforts in the Caribbean and elsewhere. Nor do democratic or authoritarian rule, blood-thirstiness, aggressiveness, or a threat to United States security (in the proper sense of the term) provide a plausible criterion. Brazil and South Africa are as vicious as they come. The horrendous Indonesian massacre of 1965 was greeted with calm. China has been the least aggressive of the great powers. The Viet Minh and the Pathet Lao are hardly a threat to United States security. Fascist Japan was no doubt an aggressive power. in some ways, not unlike the United States today[103] – but the United States was prepared to seek a *modus vivendi* in 1939 provided that its rights and interests on the mainland were guaranteed. And fascist Greece is quite all right today; it plays its NATO role, provides bases for American naval forces,[104] and as an added attraction there is – as Secretary of Commerce Maurice Stans put it so lyrically not long ago – 'the welcome that is given here to American companies and the sense of security the Government of Greece is imparting to them.'[105]

Friends and enemies can be identified, to a rather good first approximation, in terms of their role in maintaining an integrated global economy in which American capital can operate with relative freedom. The so-called 'Communist' powers are particularly evil because their 'do-it-yourself' model of development tends to extricate them from this system. For this reason, even European colonialism, which was bad enough, is preferable to indigenous communism. For the same reason, Washington will prefer a Trujillo to a Castro.

The study group of the Woodrow Wilson Foundation and the National Planning Association was perceptive, and more honest than many contemporary ideologists, when it described the primary threat of communism as the economic transformation of the Communist powers 'in ways which reduce their willingness and ability to complement the industrial economies of the West,'[106] their refusal to play the game of comparative advantage and to rely primarily on foreign investment for development. If the 'developing nations' choose to use their resources for their own purposes, or to carry out internal social change in ways which will reduce their contribution to the industrial economies of the state capitalist world, these powers must be prepared to employ sufficient force to prevent such unreasonable behaviour, which will no doubt be described as aggression by agents of international communism. The Soviet Union reacts no differently when Czechoslovakia seeks a degree of independence or social change.

At a much different level of domination, British auto workers must not be permitted to demand too great economic benefits or a share in management in the Ford plant, and must remain subject to the threats that can be wielded quite effectively by an international corporation.[107] In East Asia, which many regard as a most promising region for the 'internationalization of production' as well as for supplying raw materials (see *For Reasons of State*, Chapter 2), the problems will be particularly acute. Surely such considerations lie at the very core of American foreign policy. Though they are far from the sole operative factors in United States policy, and are often overwhelmed by the impact of ideological commitments which themselves grow out of such concerns, it is surely the beginning of wisdom to recognize their crucial role.

It is often maintained that United States policy is motivated by a commitment to political democracy. To test the force of this concern, we can consider how United States policy typically evolves when political democracy is destroyed, while American economic intervention is freed from constraints – and we can compare such policy with the typical United States reaction when an economy is closed to American economic penetration, whether or not political democracy is more or less maintained. Latin America provides an ample set of test cases. Considering American policy towards Brazil and Chile, Guatemala for the past two decades, the Dominican Republic in 1965, and so on, there can be little doubt as to the outcome of such an investigation. Gordon Connel-Smith puts the matter in terms that seem quite adequate:

> ... United States concern for representative democracy in Latin America is a facet of her anti-communist policy. There has been no serious question of her intervening in the case of the many right-wing military coups, from which, of course, this policy generally has benefited. It is only when her own concept of democracy, closely identified with private, capitalistic enterprise, is threatened by communism that she has felt impelled to demand collective action to defend it.[108]

Those who are called upon to implement and defend United States policy are often quite frank about the matter. The director of USAID for Brazil, to take one recent and very important case, explains clearly that protection of a favourable investment climate for private business interests is a primary United States objective. To be sure, he mentions other objectives as well: our 'humanitarian interests' and our 'security objectives.' As to our humanitarian interests, they seem a bit selective, and correlate remarkably well with 'the protection and expansion, if possible, of our economic interests, trade and investment, in the hemisphere.'[109] Thus our humanitarian interests in Brazil, as measured by the aid programme, showed a marked upsurge after the April 1964 'revolution' which, among other achievements, overcame the 'administrative obstacles to remittance of income developed under the Goulart regime' (pp. 185–7, 215). Another achievement that correlated with the vast flow of aid was the rise of private investment from 50 per cent to 75 per cent of total investment.[110]

Or perhaps our humanitarian interests, as measured by the aid flow, were stirred by the incidence of state violence and torture in Brazil under the new regime, or by the significant decline in the share of GNP of the bottom 80 per cent of the population,[111] and the reported decline in wages for most workers that accompanied the significant rise in production under 'a dictatorship, established to protect the privileges of a small property-owning class and to assure the growing control of the nation's economy by imperialistic interests.'[112] As for the security objectives, the fear that Brazil under Goulart posed a security threat to the United States seems a bit far-fetched; and as far as Brazil itself is concerned, the military perceive no external threat to the country,[113] so that the extensive American military aid is clearly either for 'internal security' – that is, protection from its own population of the regime whose acts have so awakened our humanitarian concerns – or for threats against Brazil's neighbours, in particular those neighbours who might choose to jeopardize the closely related economic interests of the Brazilian privileged elite and American investors. We are, I am afraid, reduced to the first objective: the protection and expansion of 'our' economic interests in the hemisphere.

Before we attribute this or that misadventure to 'blind anti-communism,' we would do well to distinguish several varieties of anticommunism. Opposition to indigenous movements that might pursue the so-called Communist model of development, extricating their societies from the international capitalist system, is not 'blind anticommunism,' strictly speaking. It may be 'anticommunism,' but it is far from blind. Rather, it is rational imperialism which seeks to prevent the erosion of the world system dominated by Western and Japanese capital. On the other hand, reference to a 'coordinated offensive directed by the Kremlin' against South-east Asia in 1949 (NSC 48/1) or to the 'militant and aggressive expansionist policy advocated by the present rulers of Communist China' (George Carver of the CIA; IV, 82; April 1966) is indeed blind anti-communism – or to be more precise, it is perhaps blind, but it is not anti-communism at all. Rather, it is pure imperial ideology, beyond the reach of evidence or debate, a propaganda device to rally support for military intervention against indigenous Communist-led movements. (The device is no doubt useful for the self-image of the policy makers themselves.) In Vietnam, the first form of anti-communism motivated United States intervention, while the second was called upon to justify it – as elsewhere, repeatedly.

It may be argued, with justice, that this view is no more than a first approximation to a general understanding of foreign policy, and that it omits many second-order considerations. Thus it would not be correct to claim that formation of foreign policy is in the interests of a monolithic corporate elite. On the contrary, there are conflicting interests. But we would expect to find – and do find – that those interests that are particularly concerned with foreign policy are well represented in its formation.[114] By similar dynamics, regulatory agencies tend to fall into the hands of industries that are particularly concerned with their decisions. It is, furthermore, no doubt true that at some point ideology takes on a motive force of its own. There are other interacting and for the most part mutually supportive factors: the interest of the 'state management' in the Pentagon in enhancing its own power;[115] the role of government-induced production of rapidly obsolescing luxury goods (largely military) as a technique of economic management, with a resulting need to secure strategic raw materials; the usefulness of an external enemy as a device to whip the taxpayer into line, in support of the production of waste and the costs of empire; the heady sense of power, to which academic ideologues in particular seem to succumb so readily. Such factors as these produce a fairly stable system to support the basic imperial drive, which is second nature to the men of power in the state executive in any event.[116] There are many specific factors that must be considered in a detailed examination of particular decisions, such as those that led us ever more deeply into Indochina. Nevertheless, it seems reasonably clear that American policy, like that of any great power, is guided by the 'national interest' as conceived by dominant social groups, in this case, the primary goal of maximizing the free access by American capital to the markets and human and material resources of the world, the goal of maintaining to the fullest possible extent its freedom of operation in a global economy. At the same time, ideologists labour to mask these endeavours in a functional system of beliefs.

It is interesting that such analyses of foreign policy, which incorporate the material interests of private or quasi-private capital as a central factor interacting with others, are often characterized as 'vulgar economic determinism' or the like when put forth by opponents of the system of private control of resources and the means of production. On the other hand, similar formulations receive little attention when they appear, as they commonly do, in official explanations of state policy. What is more, explanations that emphasize, say, vague emotional states, or ideological elements, or error, are not similarly characterized as 'vulgar emotional (ideological) determinism' or 'vulgar fallibilism.'

The term 'vulgar economic determinism' is particularly surprising, given that those segments of (quasi-) private capital that are particularly affected by foreign-policy decisions are generally well represented in the formation of state policy. One would therefore expect that the view mislabelled 'vulgar economic determinism' would serve as a kind of null hypothesis. Since it is, furthermore, quite plausible as an explanation for basic foreign policy decisions (and not infrequently, the justification offered for them), the reaction becomes still more curious. The label too often serves to deflect attention from the proposed explanations, which are much easier to ignore when misrepresented. This is a standard reaction to analysis that raises questions about prevailing ideology. Compare much of the response to 'revisionist' work on the cold war several years ago.[117] Many illustrations can be given; in fact, there is an interesting literary genre, worthy of investigation in itself, devoted to the refutation of nonexistent arguments attributed to 'radicals' – such as arguments that capitalism needs war to survive, or that the United States bears sole responsibility for the cold war.

It is possible to give some useful advice to an aspiring political analyst who wants his work received as thoughtful and penetrating – advice which surely applies to any society, not merely to ours. This analyst should first of all determine as closely as possible the actual workings of power in his society. Having isolated certain primary elements and a number of peripheral and insignificant ones, he should then proceed to dismiss the primary factors as unimportant, the province of extremists and ideologues. He should rather concentrate on the minor and peripheral elements in decision making. Better still, he should describe these in terms that appear to be quite general and independent of the social structure that he is discussing ('power drive,' 'fear of irrelevance,' etc.). Where he considers policies that failed, he should attribute them to stupidity and ignorance, that is, to factors that are socially neutral. Or he may attribute the failures to noble impulses that led policy makers astray ('tragic irony'), or to the venality, ingratitude, and barbarism of subject peoples. He can then be fairly confident that he will escape the criticism that his efforts at explanation are 'simplistic' (the truth is often surprisingly simple). He will, in short, benefit from a natural tendency

80 The Backroom Boys

on the part of the privileged in any society to suppress – for themselves as well as others – knowledge and understanding of the nature of their privilege and its manifestations.

In the particular case of Vietnam, anticommunism served as a convenient device for mobilizing the American people to support imperial intervention. After a time, they were no longer willing to bear the costs or were appalled at the consequences. At this point, the propaganda device, no longer effective, is discarded. We now hear laments about the cold-war myths that led us to a 'Greek tragedy' in Vietnam. But the war goes on.

The motive force for the American war in Indochina lies, it seems to me, where it was located in the earliest internal documents of the state executive: in the perceived significance of South-east Asia for the integrated global system that was to be organized by American power – and, under reasonable assumptions, dominated by American power for the primary benefit of those who possess that power. Although in the 1960s other and more irrational considerations may have come to predominate, nevertheless the continuing effort by the United States to achieve a Korean-type solution in Indochina, whatever the cost to its people, can still be traced in part to the same fundamental objectives.[118]

VI. THE MENTALITY OF THE BACKROOM BOYS

Perhaps the most significant contribution of the Pentagon study is the insight it provides into the mentality of the planners. Since there is no reason to expect changes in this regard in coming years, it is particularly important to examine the attitudes that are revealed by their decisions and debate.

1. THE BOMBING OF NORTH VIETNAM

The callous disregard of the planners for the victims of American terror is illustrated, in a fairly typical way, when one of the backroom boys explains that a programme of sustained bombing of the North 'seems cheap,' despite its higher cost in American casualties – particularly, since a reprisal policy 'demonstrates US willingness to employ this new norm in counter-insurgency.' Thus it will 'set a higher price for the future upon all adventures of guerilla warfare, and it should therefore somewhat increase our ability to deter such adventures.'[119] The importance of

Operation ROLLING THUNDER (RT), the analyst explains, was that 'breaking through the sanctuary barrier had been accomplished' (IV, 53). This was an important achievement, since the United States had previously been a staunch defender of the 'sanctuary barrier,' as when United Nations Ambassador Adlai Stevenson emphasized American disapproval of 'retaliatory raids, wherever they occur and by whomever they are committed' after the British raids against Yemen in reprisal for Yemeni attacks.[120]

But, it is important to add, though the 'sanctuary barrier' was effectively broken, the genocide barrier still remained,[121] for reasons that are most informative. A CIA analysis of March 1966 explicitly recommended intensification of RT, directed largely against 'the will of the regime as a target system.' But agriculture and manpower as target systems were 'not recommended at this time' – the genocide barrier stands. The sole reason is, 'the effects are debatable and are likely to provoke hostile reactions in world capitals.'[122] And John McNaughton urged:

> Strikes at population targets (per se) are likely not only to create a counterproductive wave of revulsion abroad and at home, but greatly to increase the risk of enlarging the war with China and the Soviet Union. Destruction of locks and dams, however – if handled right – might [perhaps after the *next* pause] offer promise. It should be studied. Such destruction does not kill or drown people. By shallow-flooding the rice, it leads after time to widespread starvation [more than a million?] unless food is provided – which we could offer to do 'at the conference table.' [IV, 43]

This was January 18, 1966. A report of the air war at that time states that only eight locks and dams were targeted as 'significant to inland waterways, flood control, or irrigation,' and one had been hit and heavily damaged (IV, 56). There is no further information here on the follow-up, if any, to McNaughton's proposal that the United States engage in explicit war crimes of the sort punished after World War II.[123] The DRV, however, reports attacks on dams in Thanh Hoa Province (April 4, 1965; the Pentagon history reports only attacks on Thanh Hoa bridges from April 2–8; IV, 285) and Nghe An Province (June 26–28, 1965, and many later occasions) and elsewhere.[124] These attacks increased sharply after 1965.[125] Eyewitness reports have occasionally appeared in the American press, and bombing of the irrigation and hydraulic system in South Vietnam has been frequently reported.[126] The Pentagon Papers contain no information on the latter, as on most aspects of the American war in South Vietnam.

What is interesting, in the present connection, is McNaughton's reason for not breaching the genocide barrier in the North. Much the same considerations are stressed by McNamara when he argues that bombing of population centres in the North should be avoided because of the risk that it might precipitate Soviet or Chinese direct intervention and 'appall allies and friends' (IV, 28–9), a most unfortunate consequence.

The analyst is under the illusion that 'populated areas were scrupulously avoided' in the North (IV, 18). This is nonsense, as any visitor to the DRV quickly discovers as soon as he leaves Hanoi. The CIA estimated that by 1966, after 161,000 tons of bombs had fallen, there had been almost 30,000 civilian casualties (IV, 136). Note also that the figure of 1,000 killed or seriously wounded a week, cited below, refers to the bombing of North Vietnam. As early as December 1965, Bernard Fall reported that 'at least one hospital [in North Vietnam] had been completely destroyed by bombers,' as 'verified by non-Communist outside observers,' and that 'Canadian officials who recently returned from North Viet-Nam also told me that the city of Vinh was 'flattened' – a city of 60,000, he notes.[127] I myself have seen the ruins of towns and villages not far from Hanoi and the remains of the hospital in Thanh Hoa city, destroyed, according to the North Vietnamese, in June 1965.[128] Testimony on this matter is by now so voluminous that it is amazing, a real tribute to the power of government propaganda, that one can still read that the bombing of the North scrupulously kept to military targets. The appalling destruction in the North, which has suffered less than 10 per cent of the total bombing through 1971 (and of course none of the still more destructive shelling, apart from naval bombardment), is small only in comparison with the accomplishment of our government elsewhere in Indochina.

United States government propaganda has tried to give the impression that aerial bombardment achieved near-surgical accuracy, so that military targets could be destroyed with minimal effect on civilians. Technical military documents give a different picture. For example, Captain C. O. Holmquist writes:

> One naturally wonders why so many bombing sorties are required in order to destroy a bridge or other pinpoint target. . . .

However, with even the most sophisticated computer system, bombing by any mode remains an inherently inaccurate process, as is evident from our results to date in Vietnam. Aiming errors, boresight errors, system computational errors and bomb dispersion errors all act to degrade the accuracy of the system. Unknown winds at altitudes below the release point and the 'combat degradation' factor add more errors to the process. In short, it is impossible to hit a small target with bombs except by sheer luck. Bombing has proved most efficient for area targets such as supply dumps, built-up areas, and cities.[129]

The American government claim that the bombing of North Vietnam was directed against military targets does not withstand direct investigation. But even if one were to accept it, considerations such as those mentioned by Captain Holmquist indicate that this was to a large extent a distinction without a difference.

Later, McNaughton and McNamara were to raise other objections to bombing.

The picture of the world's greatest superpower killing or seriously injuring 1000 non-combatants a week, while trying to pound a tiny backward nation into submission on an issue whose merits are hotly disputed, is not a pretty one. It could conceivably produce a costly distortion in the American national consciousness and in the world image of the United States – especially if the damage to North Vietnam is complete enough to be 'successful.' [IV, 172; 484]

The most important risk remains 'the likely Soviet, Chinese and North Vietnamese reaction.' The question whether there might conceivably be some other objection to killing or maiming 1,000 noncombatants a week, apart from its potential costs to us, is not raised.

The same logic underlies the CIA advocacy of an 'unlimited campaign' as 'the most promising' in January 1967 (IV, 139–40; analyst) but with the proviso that although 'bombing the levee system which kept the Red River under control, if timed correctly, could cause large crop losses,' nevertheless the military effects might be short-lived. A draft memo of the Clifford Group in March 1968 argued against 'a change in our bombing policy to include deliberate strikes on population centers and attacks on the agricultural population through the destruction of dikes' on the sole grounds that this 'would further alienate domestic and foreign sentiment' and might lose European and other support (IV, 251). For this reason, the genocide barrier must stand. Not that everyone agreed: see the proposals from CINCPAC (Commander in Chief, Pacific) and Air Force Secretary Harold Brown (IV, 261).

In an informative analysis of the management of the air war in the North, Ralph Stavins points out some differences, determined by interviews, among the planners. Paul Warnke 'opposed the bombing to the hilt' and sought to restrict targets. According to Alvin Friedman of the Pentagon, he came 'from a different geological age compared to the likes of McNaughton, M. Bundy, McNamara and Rusk.' McNaughton, in particular, was quite uncritical in recommending targets. 'Warnke himself said his disagreement with McNamara arose over the possibility that the bombing would draw the Communist superpowers into the war,' throughout, a major factor in deterring all-out bombing of the major population centres.[130]

2. MILITARY OPERATIONS IN SOUTH VIETNAM

South Vietnam, of course, has borne the brunt of the American attack in Indochina. As noted above, the facts of the American war in South Vietnam are barely discussed in the thousands of pages of documents and analyses, and, the record suggests, were not a matter of great interest or concern to the backroom boys. For example, from the analysis of United States ground strategy, the reader can learn that 'in the estimation of the MACV staff [Operation CEDAR FALLS] gained outstanding results, capturing large numbers of weapons, ammunition and other war materials, plus near a half-million pages of enemy documents' and destroying the Iron Triangle as a 'secure base areas.'[131] But he will have to look elsewhere to discover that for over a week before this operation, the windows of Saigon were rattling from concentrated B-52 raids in this settled area, or to learn the fate of the inhabitants of Ben Suc, forcibly evacuated from their demolished village to barren camps surrounded by barbed wire, with a sign at the entrance saying 'Welcome to Freedom.'[132]

On the rare occasions when questions were raised about the United States attack on South Vietnam, the moral level of the analysis is on a par with the occasional qualms expressed about RT. For example, William Bundy (June 30, 1965) advocated that 'our air actions against the South should be carried on a maximum effective rate,' including 'substantial use of B-52s against VC havens.' He recognized only one problem: 'we look silly and arouse criticism if these [B-52 raids] do not show significant results' (IV, 612). If the B-52 raids do show significant results, we may turn out to be mass murderers (since in the nature of the case, there could be at best partial information about the targets), but this appears to be no problem at all.[133]

As noted earlier, the Pentagon Papers contain virtually no record of the decision to bomb the South. Perhaps we are to infer that this, like the bombing of the North, was undertaken to raise the morale of the South Vietnamese population. The reader who finds this remark overly cynical may turn to II, 546, where a MACV monthly evaluation appears for February 1965: '*US/ GVN strikes against DRV and increased use of U.S. jet aircraft in RVN* has had a salutary effect on both military and civilian morale which may result in a greater national effort and, *hopefully, reverse the downward trend*' (emphasis in original). Not a word on the character of the bombing, which was improving morale in South Vietnam by 'literally pounding the place to bits' (see Bernard Fall, p. 24 above). So effective was this pounding that McNamara, in a generally gloomy analysis of July 20, 1965, could at least point to the fact that 'US/VNAF air strikes in-country have probably shaken VC morale somewhat' (IV, 620) an important matter given the high morale of the indigenous Viet Cong and the civilian society in which they were embedded.

This is not the place to review once again the bloodbath for which the United States is directly responsible in South Vietnam. To appreciate the scale, recall the estimates presented by Bernard Fall in April 1965 – prior to the outright American invasion, prior to the introduction of any regular units of the North Vietnamese so far as Washington was aware: 66,000 Viet Cong killed between 1957 and 1961, that is, before the large-scale combat involvement of American air and helicopter forces (see note 4); 89,000 between 1961 and April 1965.[134] McNamara estimated another 60,000 of the 'enemy' killed by mid-1966 (IV, 348), overwhelmingly South Vietnamese and probably including many civilians (see p. 96 below). 'The problem is that American machines are not equal to the task of killing communist soldiers except as part of a scorched earth policy that destroys everything else as well,' so that the task of United States technology must be 'to "bomb the hell out of Indochina," as one airman put it.'[135]

Furthermore, it became necessary to demolish the rural society, for reasons to which we return. The consequences are indescribable, and entirely missing from the Pentagon Papers.

The facts, of course, will be denied, no matter how strong the evidence. For example, Brigadier General W. A. Tidwell, chief of the Reconnaissance and Photo Intelligence Division in Vietnam and director of the Target Research and Analysis Center in 1964–5, writes that he developed many of the bombing techniques (including B-52 bombardment), and assures the reader that there was virtually no possibility that villages were attacked, except during ground combat.[136] And no matter what the facts may be, there will always be a Sidney Hook to claim that Bertrand Russell 'plays up as deliberate American atrocities the unfortunate accidental loss of life incurred by the efforts of American military forces to help the South Vietnamese repel the incursions of North Vietnam and its partisans'[137] One can imagine what the same commentator would write if the enemies of the state whose propaganda he so faithfully parrots[138] were to indulge in a small fraction of the savagery of the American attack on the population of South Vietnam.

In an era that has experienced good Germans and apologists for Stalinist terror, it is perhaps not surprising to find some who will depict the horrors inflicted by the United States on Indochina as 'unintended consequences of military action.' Still, even the most cynical might be somewhat taken aback when such apologetics are coupled with attacks on critics of the American war for overlooking the barbarism of the enemy. One can hear the voice of some party hack berating critics of the Russian intervention in Hungary because they fail to denounce the terror of the resistance. In fact, it was quite proper for Russell, whom Hook castigates for such 'omission,' to concern himself with atrocities for which Americans bear responsibility, either by their own actions or through their local agents. Consider in contrast Hook's practice: denunciation of Communist atrocities, absolute silence with regard to the far greater GVN atrocities (for which the United States bears a large measure of responsibility), and miserable apologetics with regard to the United States attack on the civilian population, incomparably greater in scale as well as foreign in origin.

In the Pentagon study, the Vietnamese appear only marginally, and then only as items to be controlled by the American-instituted regime, never capable of performing its assigned task; or as infrastructure to be rooted out; or as people who must be permitted to 'enjoy the inherent right to choose their own way of life and their own form of government' (John McNaughton, describing the 'national commitment' of the United States; IV, 393) within the framework of a constitutional system that 'opposes Communism in any form' and prohibits 'every activity designed to publicize or carry out Communism' (Article 4 of the 1967 Constitution, the proclaimed legal basis of such monstrosities as the Phoenix programme – see below, pp. 103–5).

There is occasional recognition that the creatures who inhabit Vietnam may be human, or at least animate. It is assumed, for example, that they have a threshold of pain that can perhaps be reached without too much danger to the United States – we have already noted the reasons why the bombing 'was too light, gave too subdued and uncertain a signal, and exerted too little pain' (IV, 20). The bombing of the North, that is.

As for the South, the careful reader can determine from the Pentagon study that it was being bombed. There are scattered statements referring to the fact, side comments in the review of the extensive debate over the American ground invasion, or in the course of the elaborate and detailed discussion of the vicious though far milder bombing of the North, which was the real 'attention getter' (III, 431). In comparison to this, the decision to land combat marines in March 1965 'created less than a ripple' (III, 433), although proposals for further build-up 'were the center of much private debate in the spring and early summer of 1965' ('behind the scene while the American public was in ignorance of the proceedings'; III, 445), and therefore merit a lengthy chapter in the Pentagon study. The build-up of United States combat forces, like the bombing of the North was expected to be costly to the United States and was uncertain and dangerous in its further consequences. Therefore, it was worthy of attention.

The decision to pound South Vietnam to bits was the subject of no internal debate, so far as the record indicates. In fact, the decision and its impact were so insignificant that even the lack of concern over it receives no comment (in contrast to the decision to land combat marines). A similar observation applies to 'responsible' segments of the peace movement, in large measure. On July 30, 1965, McNamara pointed out to the president, not inaccurately, that the 'hue and cry' over bombing relates primarily to the North (III, 387). There were, of course, those whom

McGeorge Bundy called the 'wild men in the wings,'[139] but their hue and cry over the destruction of the rural society of South Vietnam had not yet come to the attention of Washington, and would not, until it became considerably more strident and indecorous (see above, p. 43).

With regard to scale, we read that 'from the first, strike requirements in SVN had first call on U.S. air assets in Southeast Asia' (IV, 18). The analyst refers to 'recommendations that had been made previously by COMUSMACV [United States Commander in Vietnam], and especially insistently by CINCPAC, to expand the use of US airpower in SVN' (III, 337). He cites one example from each of these authorities. General Westmoreland, on February 25, 1965, thought that we could 'buy time' and reverse the decline in the South by adding three army helicopter companies, flying more close support and reconnaissance missions, and using ground combat troops. Admiral Sharp wrote to General Wheeler the following day that 'the single most important thing we can do to improve the security situation in South Vietnam is to make full use of our airpower.' These recommendations followed shortly after the initiation of regular and intensive aerial bombardment in South Vietnam (see above, p. 43, and note 140).

In the preceding months there had been a few references to the possibility of bombing the South, and some dispute over its advisability (see III, 562, 581, 587, 591, 618, 634). On January 27, as the political base of the American effort in the South appeared to be collapsing, McNamara agreed that Westmoreland should be authorized to use American jets in the case of 'emergencies in South Vietnam' (III, 687). This seems to exhaust the record prior to February, when the bombing of the North was undertaken in a mood of desperation, and American jets were 'authorized to support the RVNAF in ground operations in the South without restriction' (III, 391), with consequences already noted.

A cable from Admiral Sharp (CINCPAC) to the Joint Chiefs on February 24 recommended that a squadron of Marine F4s be deployed to Da Nang for close air support for the two marine battalions soon to be dispatched and 'for other missions along with primary mission' (III, 419). The 'other missions' are not specified. The GVN did not acquiesce in the deployment of a marine tactical fighter squadron until April 6 (III, 455). This reluctance of GVN officials was not unique (another instance of

'Vietnamese xenophobia,' no doubt). The general pattern through the 1960s was for the United States authorities to decide on appropriate measures of escalation and then to try to convince the GVN to go along. Finally, if agreement was obtained, a news release would be issued, stating typically that 'after consultation between the governments of South Vietnam and the United States, the United States Government has agreed to the request of the Government of Vietnam to...' (III, 423). The elaborate manoeuvring was necessary to maintain the pretence that the United States was responding to the request of the authentic indigenous government for help in resisting aggression. As the analyst states, in commenting on some proposals of President Diem in 1961 which probably caused 'the initial reaction... of surprise': 'The U.S. was not accustomed to GVN initiatives; it seldom sought them' (II, 446–7). In later years, as the facade disintegrated, the problem of gaining GVN acquiescence mounted. In one crucial case, the president's new programme of escalation in February 1965 was received 'with enthusiasm' by Ambassador Taylor in Saigon, but in his response to the president, 'he explained the difficulties he faced in obtaining authentic GVN concurrence 'in the condition of virtual non-government' [Taylor's phrase] which existed in Saigon at that moment' (III, 323). Compare Lyndon Johnson's recollection of Taylor's reply) *Vantage Point* p. 130): 'In his reply Taylor reported that our decision had been received in Saigon with "deep enthusiasm."'

On March 5, CINCPAC cabled to General Wheeler that 'the single most important thing we can do quickly to improve the security situation in SVN is to make full use of our air power' (III, 429). Four days later, restrictions on United States aircraft 'were lifted, permitting their use in combat operations in South Vietnam with USAF markings and without VNAF personnel aboard' (III, 334) – that is, without the deception of earlier years (see notes 4, 142; *For Reasons of State*, Chapter 1, note 14).

At the time that these restrictions on explicit use of United States air power were lifted, Army Chief of Staff Harold K. Johnson was leading a 'high-ranking team' investigating the situation in South Vietnam. He returned on March 12 with twenty-one recommendations, four relating to the use of air and helicopter forces in the South. The first three, approved by Secretary McNamara, proposed additional helicopters for troop mobility, aircraft for intelligence, and target research and analysis 'to utilize increased info effective' – how is not specified. The fourth recommendation, with a question mark in the margin added by the defence secretary, is: 'Evaluate effects of COMUSMACV's unrestricted employment of U.S. fighter-bombers within SVN' (III, 95; General Johnson's recommendations were approved by the president on April 1; III, 703). Directly below we read that 'on 17 March . . . refugee problems were mounting in I and II Corps' (III, 97) – perhaps, though nothing is said, a result of unrestricted bombing. So press reports would indicate. For example A. J. Langguth writes that in the spring of 1965 he 'watched while a tribe of hill people near Kontum [II Corps] trudged away from their village to escape the American bombing,' to be 'given a lecture by a Vietnamese officer on the evils of Communism' upon their arrival at a refugee camp.[140]

In a memo of February 18, William Bundy mentions an incident 'in which Communist agents stirred up a village "protest" against government air attacks' (III, 692). The incident is not further identified. Perhaps it was similar to one a few weeks later, when after South Vietnamese planes bombed a village, killing 45 (including 37 schoolchildren), villagers carrying coffins marched in protest to Da Nang but were turned back by Vietnamese troops.[141]

Maxwell Taylor, who can always be counted on to add just the right note of black humour, had apparently already completed the evaluation urged by General Johnson. He informed the president on March 11: 'The most encouraging phenomenon of the past week has been the rise in Vietnamese morale occasioned by the air strikes against North Vietnam on March 2, the announcement of our intention to utilize US jet aircraft within South Vietnam, and the landing of the Marines at Danang. . . . The press and the public have reacted most favorably to all three of these events' (III, 345; the marines at Da Nang were soon to learn differently – see below, p. 91). It is not recorded whether the ambassador's survey of public opinion included the inhabitants of five hamlets north of Saigon where fifty peasants had been killed in a napalm attack by American-piloted B-26s several months earlier – that is, well before the lifting of restrictions on United States aircraft.[142] We have already noted the February evaluation by COMUSMACV regarding the beneficial effect of United States air strikes in the North and South on Southern morale in February (see above, p. 85; also III, 424–5).

In a draft 'plan of action for South Vietnam' on March 24, McNaughton suggested 'US/VNAF air & naval strikes against

VC ops and bases in SVN' as one element in an elaborate 'program of progressive military pressure' (III, 697). General Westmoreland presented what he described as 'a classical Commander's Estimate of the Situation' two days later. In this extremely detailed analysis, he stated: 'If *basic strategy of punitive bombing in RVN* does not take effect by mid-year additional deployments of U.S. and 3rd Country forces should be considered' (III, 464; my emphasis). The reference to RVN – South Vietnam – rates a '*sic!*' from the analyst.

We know from other sources that the 'punitive bombing in RVN' did take effect in several respects. While 'literally pounding the place to bits,' it also succeeded in tripling the number of recruits for the Viet Cong. In 1966, unobserved strikes alone succeeded further in providing the 'enemy' with about 27,000 tons of dud bombs and shells, more than enough material for mines and booby traps which were the cause of death for over 1,000 American soldiers in that year – a year in which the number of Viet Cong and North Vietnamese killed by these strikes was estimated at probably less than 100.[143]

The tactic of massive bombardment must be labelled 'Counter-productive' in Pentagonese, and can be attributed only to advanced cretinism, *if* the United States goal had been to restrict American casualties or to win popular support for the Saigon government or to 'protect the population.' But it is quite rational as a device for demolishing the society in which a rebellion is rooted and takes refuge. Hearts and minds can be left to a later stage, when the population is driven to refugee camps or urban slums with (it is hoped) no way to survive outside of the framework established by United States terror. Then the gentle nation builders can appear on the scene to win the hearts and minds that are left, while the apologists for state violence speak of the 'unintended consequences of military action' (see section III, below).

In early March two marine battalions were deployed at Da Nang, joining the 1,300 marines already there (III, 402), the first overt deployment of United States combat forces. Their mission was to protect the Da Nang base, 'which was heavily supporting air activity over North and South Vietnam' and was therefore 'a lucrative target' for the Viet Cong (III, 424, 389). The mission, in short, was to prevent another 'outrageous act' of the Southern rebels such as the attack on the United States air base at Bien Hoa on November 1, 1964 (see p. 130). By April 1–2, the president decided 'to get US ground combat units involved in the war against the insurgents' (III, 394). At the Honolulu meeting of April 20 'it was agreed that tasks within *South* Vietnam should have first call on air assets in the area' (III, 359; McNaughton's minutes, his emphasis). According to the analyst, 'it seems apparent that Honolulu marked the relative downgrading of pressures against the North, in favor of more intensive activity in the South.' A May 4 assessment by Ambassador Taylor noted that North Vietnam might introduce 'additional PAVN units on order of several regiments [in the hope of] offsetting US/GVN application of air power' (III, 364). See below, pp. 121, 133–5.

'In line with the April decision to give priority to South Vietnam over North Vietnam in the employment of U.S. air power, a major administration decision was taken after the bombing pause [ending May 18] to assign saturation bombing missions in the South to SAC B-52 bombers . . .' (III, 383). This decision followed some complaints by General Westmoreland with Taylor's 'political endorsement') that massive air attacks on Viet Cong base areas (one on April 15, with 900 tons of ordnance dropped) were inefficient, the topography being 'more suitable for area carpet bombing.' The first B-52 raid was authorized on June 18. Air attacks 'increased significantly in *South* Vietnam' (III, 383–4).

There are occasional further references to proposed 'increased use of air in-country, including B-52's' (McNamara, July 20, 1965; IV, 298), but nothing about the scale and character of the air war, or the devastating helicopter and artillery war in the South, as there is virtually nothing said directly about the impact of United States ground operations on the Vietnamese. Thus we learn that 'Vietnam changed over from a rice exporter in the years through 1964 to a heavy importer from 1965 onwards' (II, 366), but the reasons remain a mystery, one of the many that did not have sufficient 'signal strength' to reach the higher circles of decision making.

One can deduce from the Pentagon study that the American war was not exactly a bed of roses for the Vietnamese. A Roles and Missions study of August 1966 recommended that 'the physical and attitudinal consequences of present air and artillery employment policies should be studied' (II, 385). But the follow-up, if any, is missing from this record, though it is presumably to be found in the secret RAND study mentioned above (see p. 25). The same report urged that ARVN Ranger units should be disbanded 'because of generally bad behavior,' that is, terrorizing the population, but COMUSMACV demurred on grounds that this 'would seriously reduce ARVN combat strength.'

To pick up the story of the air war in South Vietnam after the April 1965 decision to give priority to the South in employment of air power, we must again turn to other sources. By May 1965 huge sectors had been declared 'free bombing zones,' and 'tens of thousands of tons of bombs, rockets, napalm and cannon fire [were being] poured into these vast areas each week,' with heavy casualties, 'if only by the laws of chance.'[144] But the backroom boys were so bemused by China's aggressive expansionist policies and the like[145] that they could not spare the time for 'the heaps of dead in the battle zone includ[ing] many local villagers who didn't get away in time.'[146] The displacement of the brute facts by weird geopolitical delusions produces a tone of moral imbecility that is only enhanced when the planners occasionally express some reservations over the policies that they are recommending, invariably on grounds of the sort illustrated above.

Documentation of the air war prior to 1965 is also slight. A CIA report of July 1962 mentions 'extensive relocation Montagnards,' allegedly resulting from fear of Viet Cong, 'and new found respect for power GVN has manifested bombing attacks and use helicopters' (II, 687; in other cases, the CIA tactfully observes, 'movement has been at invitation GVN'). The CIA analyst shares the concern of the ambassador, 'fearing adverse political impact of bombing non-VC installations and concentrations of people.' In December 1962, State Department intelligence noted reports 'that indiscriminate bombing in the countryside is forcing innocent or wavering peasants toward the Viet Cong' (II, 706), and estimated that over 100,000 Montagnards had fled Viet Cong-controlled areas,

> due principally to Viet Cong excesses and the general intensification of the fighting in the highlands rather than to any positive measures taken by the GVN to appeal to the tribespeople. The extensive use of artillery and aerial bombardment and other apparently excessive and indiscriminate measures by GVN military and security forces in attempting to eliminate the Viet Cong have undoubtedly killed many innocent peasants and made many others more willing than before to cooperate with the Viet Cong . . . (II, 708–9).

The report further urged 'restriction of the tactical use of airpower' since extensive use of air power and crop destruction may provoke 'militant opposition among the peasants and positive identification with the Viet Cong' (II, 714), who recruit locally and are largely dependent on the local population. Their ability to regroup, intact, after GVN military clearing operations 'is considerably enhanced by the concealment afforded them, voluntarily or otherwise, by the local population' (696). It is left to the reader to imagine the effects of the use of artillery and air power 'to "soften up" the enemy' (II, 703), an enemy that is concealed by the local population.

Similar concerns were expressed shortly after by Michael Forrestal (II, 717–18), who reported that American advisers, helicopters, air support, and arms have led to 'increased aggressiveness' on the part of ARVN. The United States can hardly evade responsibility for the consequences, say, for the fact that 'no one really knows . . . how many of the 20,000 "Viet Cong" killed last year were only innocent or at least persuadable villagers,' in particular, because of the direct United States involvement (see note 4, and *For Reasons of State* Chapter 1, notes 14 and 15).

In April 1966, a task force was set up 'to establish a set of interagency priorities.' In its 'first rank of importance' the task force placed 'those activities that persuade the people that RVNAF is wholly on the side of the people and acting in their interests' (II, 580–3). At this point, words fail. For years, RVNAF – the South Vietnamese air force, trained, equipped, and advised by the United States – had been driving the people of South Vietnam from their homes and smashing their villages into dust; and now, in April 1966, it is a highest priority task for the United States Mission to persuade the people that RVNAF is on their side and acting in their interests. What kinds of thoughts must pass through the mind of a person capable of producing such a recommendation?

The Pentagon study terminates before the massive escalation of the air war in 1968, to reach its peak of fury in the early months of the Nixon administration, and before the concentrated air attack on Laos and then Cambodia, presumably under the direction of the amiable professor who is said to provide the president with his more profound strategic concepts. One of the final documents in the Pentagon study is a cable to United States ambassadors informing them of the decision to redistribute the bombing on April 1, 1968 (what the analyst describes – tongue in cheek, perhaps – as 'the decision to cut back the bombing,' IV, 275):

'air power now used north of 20th [20th parallel in North Vietnam] can probably be used in Laos . . . and in SVN' (IV, 595), a grim and accurate portent, as the peasants of South Vietnam, Laos, and later Cambodia would soon discover (see note 227).

In these documents, some policies are regarded as controversial, but not the policy of 'elimination of the Viet Cong from . . . the Saigon areas and the Mekong Delta,' for example. It is the task of United States troops to 'vigorously undertake' this programme of eliminating Viet Cong forces, known to be indigenous (IV, 301, 302; summer 1965). In the delta, a major centre of Viet Cong strength, few NVA forces were reported during the period covered by this study, though American air and later ground forces were heavily engaged in combat, once the United States invasion had reached a scale sufficient 'to take on the Delta.'[147] 'US Army units continued their work in the densely populated Delta provinces,' the analyst blandly reports (II, 399; early 1967). We must assume, from his silence, that the documents available to him do not describe 'their work.' When the United States units were deployed, one commanding officer told correspondent Peter Arnett that they hoped to 'drive the Viet Cong out of the area before they have to reduce the whole countryside to ashes.'[148] They failed. Another mistake, with more unintended consequences. By the end of 1969, officials were complaining that pacification efforts were hampered by the indiscriminate killings of civilians by American soldiers, and peasants were fleeing the dead grey-and-black fields and charred ruins of delta hamlets.[149]

By late 1966, the plan was to give 'increased emphasis . . . to identifying and eliminating the VC infrastructure,' for example, by armed river-patrol operations in the delta (IV, 379), which were to prove 'significantly successful in depriving the enemy of freedom and initiative in the population and resources-rich Delta areas' (IV, 539), where 'the VC effort is primarily indigenous' (IV, 487). McNamara explains that it 'has been our task all along' to 'root out the VC infrastructure and establish the GVN presence' (November 1966; IV, 376). The Combined Campaign Plan 1967 announces that 'the people are the greatest asset to the enemy,' providing him with 'food, supplies, money, manpower, concealment and intelligence.' Conclusion: 'During this campaign every effort will be made to deny these assets to the enemy' (IV, 380). We call this 'protection of the population,' just as 'identifying and eliminating the VC infrastructure' is defence of the South Vietnamese people against aggression.

It takes no military genius to predict what will happen to the people who are being protected in this way. On returning from a trip to Saigon in October 1966, McNamara informed the president: '*The one thing demonstrably going for us in Vietnam over the past year has been the large number of enemy killed-in-action resulting from the big military operations*' (IV, 348; his emphasis). On November 17, he reported that 'US forces in SEA have performed exceedingly well.' The enemy 'has lost 114,000 troops in the last year, including invaluable cadre' (IV, 368). But there is some question as to just who these enemy 'troops' really are: 'the VC/NVA apparently lose only about one-sixth as many weapons as people, suggesting the possibility that many of the killed are unarmed porters or bystanders' (IV, 371; see notes 146, 149). With no comment, the text cites the report by the marines in late 1966 of '5000 to 6000 NVA troops killed or disabled and 414 weapons lost' (II, 609). In the Tet offensive, 1968, when the United States command conceded that 'the enemy' were overwhelmingly NFL rather than NVA,[150] killed and captured outnumbered captured weapons by a factor of five (IV, 539). By the same criterion, figures presented in IV, 377, suggest that United states forces were killing far more civilians than ARVN forces were.

Without describing American military practices, McNamara further notes that 'about 30% of the reported gains [in population under GVN control] probably came from movement of refugees into cities and towns' (IV, 374). It was surely not the attractiveness of the GVN that enticed these refugees to flee the countryside. The same report notes the belief of the rural Vietnamese that 'the GVN is indifferent to the people's welfare; the low-level GVN officials are tools of the local rich; and the GVN is excessively corrupt from top to bottom' (IV, 374). This is one reason, no doubt, why the Viet Cong can replace current losses solely from within South Vietnam' (IV, 371), and why *pacification has if anything gone backward*' (McNamara's emphasis) while 'the VC political infrastructure thrives in most of the country, continuing to give the enemy his enormous intelligence advantage,' and full security exists nowhere, 'not even behind the US Marines' lines and in Saigon' (IV, 348). In fact, when the marines were deployed in spring 1965, they discovered 'to their own amazement' that 'the toughest war for them was the war in the villages behind them,' and they turned 'away from the enemy to a grueling and painfully slow effort to pacify the villages.'[151]

Their strategy was derived in part 'from their own traditions in the "Banana Republics" and China' in the 1930s, where many of the top officers had served. They were opposed even by the dominant right-wing political party of the area (II, 535–6).

The point was not lost on Robert Komer, who was in charge of 'the other war.' His recommendation, on leaving for Saigon in April 1967, was to '*step up refugee programs deliberately aimed at depriving the VC of a recruiting base*' (IV, 441; emphasis his). Translation into 'operational reality': drive the population into the American-controlled areas, thus depriving the enemy of his 'greatest asset,' namely, the people. Surely Komer understood this, in April 1967. Nicholas Katzenbach put it more delicately: 'We should stimulate a greater refugee flow through psychological inducements to further decrease the enemy's manpower base' (IV, 508; see pp. 24–6 and notes 7–9). Again, we must turn to other sources to learn about the 'psychological inducements' used, for example, the 26 billion leaflets that had been dropped over South Vietnam by summer 1971, warning villagers to move to GVN areas or 'be considered hostile and in danger'; to 'hurry to return to the righteous cause' or 'stay to die in suffering and horrible danger'; or warning that 'the US Marines will not hesitate to destroy, immediately, any village or hamlet harboring the Vietcong.'[152]

By the use of such psychological inducements, along with measures to drive home their reality, it was possible to deplete the recruiting base of the enemy. By the time McNamara visited Saigon in July 1967, army intelligence and General Westmoreland were able to inform him that the war was 'becoming more and more an NVA war' because the enemy had been 'denied recruits in the numbers required from the populated areas along the coast, thereby forcing him to supply manpower from North Vietnam' (IV, 520, 518). This was the primary reason for the infiltration, as COMUSMACV was aware (see pp. 133–5 below), though as the Tet offensive was to show, his calculations were the result of 'wishful thinking compounded by a massive intelligence collection and/or evaluation failure' (IV, 557).

Still, Komer's recommendation was to the point. He writes today that 'up through 1967 most of the forces arrayed against Saigon were southern Viet Cong, not regular troops from the North,' but 'today the VC recruiting base is attenuated.'[153] How it was attenuated he does not specify, nor does he recall his recommendation that this be done deliberately. Komer, like

McNamara, understands that it was not the attractiveness of the GVN that depleted the Viet Cong recruiting base. On the contrary, 'Saigon's record in dealing with the underlying causes of the Viet Cong revolution is still spotty at best,' though American firepower was an effective substitute.

In 1966 Komer felt that the growing number of refugees posed a problem, though in some ways it was 'a plus' since it helped to 'deprive VC of recruiting potential and rice growers.' Furthermore, it was 'partly indicative of growing peasant desire to seek security on our side' (II, 569). How significant and gratifying that the peasants should seek security on our side, joining the righteous cause, instead of remaining in their villages with the Viet Cong 'to die in suffering and horrible danger.'

The general problem was outlined in a force-requirement study in early 1967. In I Corps in the North, it is necessary to eliminate enemy forces and base areas 'and to remove his control over large population and food resources' in areas where 'the enemy has operated for years virtually unmolested' (COMUSMACV). 'The next most dangerous situation,' the analyst summarizes, 'appeared to be that in II Corps [where] the enemy, orienting himself on the population, presented a different problem. . . .' in III Corps it is necessary 'to expand security radially from the Saigon–Cholon area [with] an intensified campaign conducted to root out the VC infrastructure.' United States forces will 'provide a protective shield behind which the Revolutionary Development programs could operate,' conducting search-and-destroy operations against the indigenous VC forces and 'base area clusters' (IV, 433–5). Unless the Viet Cong infrastructure ('the VC officials and organizers') 'was destroyed, US–GVN military and pacification forces soon degenerated into nothing more than an occupation army,' a Systems Analysts study concluded. It was never asked 'whether or not US forces should be or even could be profitably engaged in pacification' (IV, 513). We know from many other sources, apparently not available to the analyst, that United States forces were profitably engaged in the destruction, massacre, and forced population concentration that was a necessary preliminary for 'revolutionary development.'

The United States command found itself 'fighting a war of attrition in Southeast Asia,' in accordance with Westmoreland's concept of 'a "meatgrinder,"' – kill[ing] large numbers of the enemy but in the end do[ing] little better than hold[ing] our own' (IV, 442). 'Essentially, we are fighting Vietnam's birth rate,' states an official quoted in a 'startlingly accurate' newspaper account (IV, 587). Specifically in North Vietnam, 'the bombing was unable to beat the birth rate' (IV, 227). There is only one way to beat the birth rate, in North Vietnam but more crucially in the South, where the primary enemy of the United States, the South Vietnamese peasant, permits the NLF to 'orient himself on the population.' The method is that succinctly described by General Westmoreland's chief planner: 'The solution in Vietnam is more bombs, more shells, more napalm . . . till the other side cracks and gives up.'[154]

3. NATION BUILDING AND CRIMES OF WAR

In the South, the task faced by the United States was to build a nation while rooting out the infrastructure of the organization that had captured the nationalist movement. A difficult task, but perhaps not impossible, given sufficient force and terror. Robert Komer, always an optimist, thought it could be done. He advocated 'increasing erosion of southern VC strength' (IV, 391), and cheerily reported to the president (February 1967) that although 'few of our programs – civil or military – are very efficient,' still 'we are grinding the enemy down by sheer weight and mass' (IV, 420). Later, Komer was to explain that 'thanks to massive US intervention at horrendous cost,' a favourable military environment was created 'in which the largely political competition for control and support of the key rural population could begin again' in this 'revolutionary, largely political conflict.'[155] The constructive aims' of pacification, Komer explained, are to protect the rural population from the insurgents, 'which also helps to deprive the insurgency of its rural popular base,' and to generate support for the Saigon regime – not easy, given the character of this regime, as noted by McNamara (see p. 96 above) and others. It was far easier to fulfill the constructive aim of depriving the insurgency of its rural popular base by stepping up the programs of deliberate refugee generation, as Komer proposed.

Komer finds it difficult to comprehend why some regard him as a possible candidate for a war-crimes trial. The issue was raised by Eqbal Ahmad, with reference to a speech in which Komer explained that Vietnam had proved the inefficacy of 'gradual escalation' which permitted the 'guerillas to make adjustments'; the lesson of Vietnam, he said, is to escalate ruthlessly and rapidly, to 'snow them under.' In an outraged reply to Ahmad, Komer reviews his career as special assistant to the president from April 1966 and as 'chief pacification adviser to the GVN' from May 1967 to November 1968. The charge, Komer claims, must seem strange to any familiar with the post-1966 programme, which he helped develop, 'one of the more sensible and constructive endeavors which the US belatedly supported in Vietnam.' Its first phase 'was essentially a nation-building effort, an attempt to help build a viable socio-economic fabric in the middle of a shooting war.' From May 1967, when CORDS was set up under Komer's direction, the pacification programme *was wholly Vietnamese manned and commanded*' (his emphasis), his role being only 'to provide advice and logistic/financial help' to the GVN effort. The programme did not rely on 'bombing, napalm, defoliation, and other technological means' and the 'pacifiers' opposed and sought to minimize generation of refugees; 'the stress was on local self-government, political checks and balances, and rule of law.'[156]

In general, Komer explains, his task was clean, bloodless, and constructive: to help the Saigon regime 'build a nation.' Surely, then, only the ill-informed or malicious could possibly accuse him of complicity in criminal acts.

Noting Komer's laudable concern that 'the record of US pacification support and advice need not be hidden behind a classified screen,' let us compare his presentation with the record that is available now that the classified screen has been partially lifted.

The 'pacifiers,' he tells us, did not seek 'the displacement and dispossession of the rural population' and sought to minimize refugee generation. As already noted, Komer is one of the few administration officials on record with the explicit recommendation to '*step up refugee programs deliberately aimed at depriving the VC of a recruiting base*.'

Komer states that after the establishment of CORDS, the pacification programme was '*wholly Vietnamese manned and commanded*.'

He fails to mention the fact, documented endlessly by the press, the Pentagon Papers, and others, that rooting out the Viet Cong infrastructure and 'denying the villages to the Viet Cong' was primarily an American responsibility. American armed force was to 'provide the shield' behind which ARVN could undertake 'pacification' (Westmoreland, August, 1966; II, 588). Discussing the CORDS programme, headed by Komer as deputy to COMUSMACV, the analyst remarks that the structure of CORDS was 'so massive that the Vietnamese were in danger of being almost forgotten' (II, 622). McNamara proposed in September 1966 that COMUSMACV be assigned responsibility for pacification. Komer, supporting this proposal, noted that 'the military are much better set up to manage a huge pacification effort,' since 60–70 per cent of the 'real job of pacification is providing local security [which] can only be done by the military' (II, 590). As Komer explains elsewhere,[157] 'Given the massive military support required, it made good sense on the US side to put the new unified US advisory structure [CORDS] under military command.'

In an announcement drafted by Komer in May 1967, Ambassador Bunker stated that support of RD is 'to be neither exclusively a civilian nor exclusively a military function, but to be essentially civil–military in character,' involving 'both the provision of continuous local security in the countryside – necessarily a primarily military task [—] and the constructive programmes conducted by the Ministry of Revolutionary Development [of the GVN], largely through its 59 member RD teams,' trained by the CIA (II, 616–17; 567–8). Bunker reported that General Westmoreland would undertake 'the responsibility for the performance of our US Mission field programs in support of pacification or Revolutionary Development,' with Komer serving as 'the single manager for pacification' (II, 428). The Combined Campaign Plan for 1967 of the United States and Saigon military forces (MACV/JGS; II, 495–6) assigned to ARVN regular forces the task of 'operations to destroy VC guerillas and infrastructure in specified hamlet or village areas' in conjunction with provincial military forces and civil intelligence and police. US–FW military forces were to conduct combined operations with the Saigon military and police forces 'to destroy VC guerillas and infrastructure in specified hamlet or village areas,' though it was left to the provincial forces and the National Police to carry out 'population and resources control' directly. US–FW military forces were also to conduct 'military and civic action to help win the support of the people for the government with emphasis to ensure that credit is given to the GVN,' a directive observed by Komer in the remarks cited in his 'Epilogue.'

Komer's remarks on the '*wholly Vietnamese manned and commanded*' programme should also be read in the light of his recommendation that 'leverage' must be applied 'always in such manner as to keep the GVN foremost in the picture presented to its own people and the world at large' (II, 503–4). We are 'applying more leverage in Pacification,' he adds. His view was that 'increased use of US leverage . . . must be done discreetly' (II, 430; analyst). Perhaps it might be more accurate to say that the United States must pretend that the GVN exists, to ourselves, to the world at large, and to the population that we are trying to win for it.

Komer always emphasized the central military component in pacification: 'we must dovetail the military's sweep operations and civil pacification' so as to 'secure and hold the countryside cleared by military operations.' Komer 'put everyone politely on notice' that he had no hesitation in calling on 'military resources, which are frequently the best and most readily available' (II, 570). Pacification 'demands a multifaceted civil-military response' to provide security, for '*breaking the hold of the VC over the people*,' to '*systematize the flow of refugees*,' and so on (II, 572–3; his emphasis). The most important problem in pacification, in his constantly reiterated view, is security, a military-police problem. In comparison, his position on land reform, though he pressed for signs of progress and urged that it be accelerated 'to consolidate rural support behind the GVN,' was that 'it was not an important issue in Vietnam.' 'Far more important was the matter of security in the countryside' (II, 400, 569, 392; IV, 441).

A CORDS report from Bien Hoa Province for the period ending December 31, 1967, gives a bit more insight into the wholly Vietnamese programmes that Komer and his American colleagues merely advised. Because of the corruption and inefficiency of the GVN officials (whose 'primary interest . . . is money'). 'CORDS has had to increasingly rely on the resources, skills and capabilities of resident US military units.' 'CORDS Bien Hoa (as well as the GVN itself) owes a great deal to these units and their commanders who have unselfishly devoted themselves to furthering pacification.' The 'disturbing truth' is that 'it still remains for the government [of South Vietnam], with forceful and meaningful direction from above, to begin to assume the responsibility for prosecuting this war and the pacification effort' (II, 407). The Pentagon study terminates at this point, but we know from many other sources that in the following months the reliance on the United States military in preparing the ground for 'pacification' increased, the My Lai massacre being only the best-known and most grotesque example (see note 149). Allan Goodman writes: 'Whatever else the introduction of [American combat troops] may have achieved it is now clear that their participation in the conflict (particularly in the twelve months after the Tet offensive of 1968) seriously weakened the ability of the VC/NVA to conduct effective mobile warfare within South Vietnam.'[158] Forced population removal and massive devastation intensified, laying the groundwork for Komer's programme of constructive nation building.

The same period marked the implementation of another of Komer's important recommendations: *'Revamp and put new steam behind a coordinated US/GVN intelligence collation and action effort targeted on the VC infrastructure at the critical provincial, district, and village levels'* (IV, 441; his emphasis). The problem, he related, is that 'we are just not getting enough payoff yet from the massive intelligence we are increasingly collecting. Police/military coordination is sadly lacking both in collection and in swift reaction.'

Two months later, on June 14, 1967, in a memorandum for General Westmoreland entitled 'Organization for Attack on V.C. Infrastructure,' Komer recommended 'consolidation, under his direction, of US anti-infrastructure intelligence effort,' and expressed his desire for a 'unified GVN/US, civil/military "management structure targeted on infrastructure."' In response, the ICEX (Intelligence Coordination and Exploitation) structure was developed in July 1967, under Westmoreland and Komer (II, 429, 585). ICEX, involving CIA, American military and civilians, and the GVN military-police-intelligence apparatus, was the immediate predecessor of the Phoenix programme, other sources indicate. Early internal directives describe the Phoenix programme as an American programme of advice, support, and assistance to the GVN *Phung Hoang* programme. Later modifications delete reference to 'Phoenix' and refer merely to the GVN *Phung Hoang* programme again in line with the approach of 'keep[ing] the GVN foremost in the picture presented to its own people and the world at large.'

On March 4, 1968, the secretary of defence recommended that 'Operation Phoenix which is targetted against the Viet Cong must be pursued more vigorously in closer liaison with the US,' while 'Vietnamese armed forces should be devoted to anti-infrastructure activities on a priority basis' (IV, 578).

After Westmoreland and Komer's ICEX became Phoenix, the co-ordinated US–GVN intelligence–military police programmes succeeded in 'neutralizing' some 84,000 'Viet Cong infrastructure' with 21,000 killed, according to reported 'official figures.'[159]

According to the same UPI report, Komer is indeed correct when he states ('Epilogue') that United States advisers criticized excesses. One reports that local officials in the delta decided to kill 80 per cent of the suspects, but American advisers were able to convince them that the proportion should be reduced below 50 per cent. Another American adviser concedes that 'naturally, we kill and torture many Vietcong. . . . The only way to combat these people who act like animals is to kill them.' We treat them just as they treat us, he adds, failing, however, to list the American towns in which cadres assisted, trained, and paid by the NLF have conducted murder and torture missions. According to the same report, the actual assassinations are largely carried out by former criminals or former Communists recruited and paid by the CIA, which also organizes the provincial interrogation centres where prisoners are tortured. Other reports indicate that CIA-directed teams drawn from ethnic minorities are widely used; that American military men often conduct operations; and that the units often include Nationalist Chinese and Thai mercenaries. An American IVS volunteer reports picking up two hitchhikers in the Mekong Delta, former criminals, who told him that by bringing in a few bodies now and then and collecting the bounty, they can live quite handsomely.[160]

The 'pacification' programme was reportedly accelerated substantially in March 1971, its 'top priority' being neutralization of the political apparatus of the Viet Cong, at a reported cost of considerably more than $1 billion to the United States and an undisclosed amount to the Saigon regime (hence indirectly, the United States).[161] A rare statistic for April 1971 reveals that in that month, of 2,000 'neutralized' more than 40 per cent were assassinated,[162] possibly the firstfruits of the accelerated terror programme. A United States intelligence officer attached to the Phoenix programme in the Mekong Delta states that when he arrived in his district, he was given a list of 200 names of people who were to be killed, and when he left six months later, 260 had been killed, but none of those on his list.[163]

As in other cases of 'body count,' the numbers given and the identity of the victims raise various questions. There is ample evidence that the operatives and intelligence collectors (heavily infiltrated, quite probably, by the NLF) often avoid the difficulties and hazards of trying to tangle with the NFL infrastructure, meeting their quotas in other ways.[164] As a device for terrorizing the political opposition, however, the Phoenix programme may well be effective. Although the actual assassinations, torture, and imprisonment are conducted by operatives trained, advised, and paid by the United States, it would be 'double think,' Komer insists ('Epilogue'), to criticize the 'GVN *Phung Hoang* program' too harshly.

We have noted Komer's insistence that his 'pacifiers' are devoted to the rule of law. That may well be true, though the significance of this noble commitment only becomes clear when we explore the system of laws that they uphold. 'Security offenses' can be tried by military field courts, and the laws are so severe that virtually any form of overt dissent might be regarded as a violation of national security: undermining public morale, or acts in furtherance of communism or procommunist neutralism, or acts to undermine the anticommunist spirit of the country, all punishable by five years to death.[165]

The problem that Komer always regarded as the most important, namely, 'security in the countryside,' has been approached by the methods just indicated. Among the most savage were the programmes of deliberate refugee generation and 'swift reaction' by the military and police under the 'coordinated US/GVN intelligence collation and action effort,' as explicitly recommended in both cases by Komer, who tells us that he was concerned merely with the constructive taks of nation building, after United States military force had provided a 'favorable military environment' for these benign activities. He is quite right, incidentally, in emphasizing that in the full spectrum of American activities in Vietnam, those that he directed are the least criminal.

4. THE ASIAN MIND – THE AMERICAN MIND

So far as the bombing of the North was concerned, the analyst concludes that the idea was based 'on a plausible assumption about the rationality of NVN's leaders,' namely, that they would want to bear its cost (IV, 57). But the guerrillas were 'supplying themselves locally, in the main' (IV, 57), and, as McNamara rather prissily explained to a Senate committee, the North Vietnamese leaders' 'regard for the comfort and even the lives of the people they control does not seem to be sufficiently high to lead them to bargain for settlement in order to stop a heightened level of attack' (IV, 202). Any Nazi could have said the same about Winston Churchill.

This line of thinking has been extended since by a number of thoughtful commentators. William Pfaff, liberal-in-residence at the Hudson Institute, explains that 'ours has been a reasonable strategy,' but it was 'the strategy of those who are rich, who love life and fear "costs."'[166] For us, 'death and suffering are irrational choices when alternatives exist.' 'We want life, happiness, wealth, power. . . .' But we failed to comprehend 'the strategy of the weak,' who 'deal in absolutes, among them that man inevitably suffers and dies.' The enemy 'stoically accept[s] the destruction of wealth and the loss of lives'; 'happiness, wealth, power – the very words in conjunction reveal a dimension of our experience beyond that of the Asian poor.' The weak thus invite us to carry our 'strategic logic to its conclusion, which is genocide,'[167] but we balk, unwilling to 'destroy ourselves . . . by contradicting our own value system.' As Hoopes formulated it, we hesitate because we realize 'that genocide is a terrible burden to bear.' Thus we fail. Neither Pfaff nor Hoopes tells us how he has determined that the Asian poor do not love life or fear costs or seek wealth and happiness. Perhaps this is demonstrated in a classified research study of the Hudson Institute.

Pfaff and Hoopes are rivalled in their understanding of the Asian mind by several secretaries of state. Byrnes, in December 1946, alluded to the problems caused by the 'almost childish Vietnamese attitude and knowledge of economic questions and vague groping for "independence,"' which was causing all sorts of troubles, citing Abbot Moffat (*DOD*, bk 8, p. 89). These childish attitudes and vague gropings were perhaps still more pronounced because the Vietnamese had 'been thoroughly indoctrinated with the Atlantic Charter and other ideological pronouncements' and thus foolishly expected American help (Richard Sharp, reporting remarks of General Philip Gallagher; *DOD*, bk 8, p. 56). Secretary Marshall, more practical and realistic than the Vietnamese, understood the need for 'a continued close association between newly-autonomous peoples and powers which have long been responsible their welfare,' as France had been responsible for the welfare of the Vietnamese;[168] and he recognized that 'for an indefinite period' the Vietnamese would require not only French material and technical assistance but also 'enlightened political guidance,' under a voluntary association (*DOD*, bk 8, pp. 100–1). Still another secretary of state commented that 'as with most Orientals Diem must be highly suspicious of what is going on about him' (Dulles, April 1955; *DOD*, bk 10, p. 909); though apparently Diem was not suspicious enough, as events were to prove in mid-1963.

The National Security Council, equally astute, explained the favourable prospects of the Soviet Union in Asia in part on the grounds that 'its protégés deal with Asiatic peoples who are traditionally submissive to power when effectively applied' (*DOD*, bk 8, p. 239; December 1949) – an insight that has been corroborated so conclusively by the effective application of force to the Vietnamese in the past quarter-century.[169]

Similar perspicacity is exhibited by United States Ambassador Maxwell Taylor, who has been described elsewhere as the 'chief adviser, if not *éminence grise*' of the Kennedy administration.[170] He bemoans the 'national attribute' which 'limits the development of a truly national spirit' among the South Vietnamese, perhaps 'innate' or perhaps a residue of the colonial experience. And he then proceeds to speculate about 'the ability of the Viet Cong 'continuously to rebuild their units and to make good their losses' – 'one of the mysteries of this guerilla war' – and their remarkable morale and recuperative powers and continued strength, for which 'we still find no plausible explanation' (III, 668; November 27, 1964). The only explanation he can conjure up is the dispatch to the South of 'trained cadre and military equipment' and the flow of radio messages. It did not, apparently, occur to him that US–GVN operations in North Vietnam somehow did not have a similar impact. It is, of course, completely beyond his comprehension that the true source of Viet Cong resilience may be precisely a 'national attribute,' deeply rooted in the peasant society that we have systematically destroyed, an 'attribute' that arouses the Vietnamese peasants to continued resistance to colonial domination – the attribute that is repeatedly characterized as 'xenophobia' in these documents. The same remarkable foolishness is revealed when overflights for dropping leaflets in North Vietnam were recommended in May 1961 'to maintain morale of North Vietnamese population,' as though the people of North Vietnam, enslaved by their Communist masters, were prayerfully awaiting salvation by American bombers, or perhaps by the 'networks of resistance, covert bases and teams for sabotage and light harassment' to be formed in North Vietnam, 'using the foundation established by intelligence operations' (II, 641).

It would perhaps be unfair to quote the various contributions of the Joint Chiefs, for example, their suggestion that a firm declaration of intent by the United States to block 'aggression originating outside of Indochina . . . would in general raise the morale of all peoples in Southeast Asia and in particular would increase the determination of the Indochinese to fight the war to a successful conclusion' against the 'Soviet Communist campaign in Southeast Asia' (January 15, 1954; *DOD*, bk 9, pp. 214, 216).

In comparison, Eisenhower appears a model of profundity 'in commenting philosophically' on the low morale among 'democratic forces in Laos' and wondering aloud 'why, in interventions of this kind, we always seem to find that the morale of the Communist forces was better than that of the democratic forces' (II, 637). 'His explanation was that the Communist philosophy appeared to produce a sense of dedication' not matched among those 'supporting the free forces.' The problem had been noted much earlier, as in a National Intelligence estimate of June 1953 pointing out the gloomy prospects for the 'Vietnamese government' given 'the failure of Vietnamese to rally to [it],' the effective Viet Minh 'control,' the fact that the population assist the Viet Minh more than the French (making it difficult 'to provide security for the Vietnamese population'), the inability of 'the Vietnam leadership' to 'overcome popular apathy and mobilize the energy and resources of the people,' and so on (I, 391–2). With hardly more than a change of names, this analysis might be taken for the despairing report from pacification specialists (MACCORDS) on December 31, 1967, cited above, deploring the corruption of the GVN,[171] the 'ever-widening gap of distrust, distaste and disillusionment between the people and the GVN,' and its growing weakness. With these words, the record of US–GVN relations ends (II, 406–7). *Plus ça change* . . .

Somehow, the United States never managed 'to influence the GVN to do the things we believe they must do to save their own country' (II, 623). In October 1966, McNamara lamented 'that the US had not yet found the formula for training and inspiring the Vietnamese' (II, 388; analyst): '*the discouraging truth is that, as was the case in 1961 and 1963 and 1965, we have not found the formula, the catalyst, for training and inspiring them into effective action* (IV, 349; McNamara'a emphasis; Carver of the CIA disagreed, II, 598). All we seem to be able to do is kill, he adds.

Not that ideas were not put forth as to the proper formula, or catalyst. A memorandum of October 20, 1954, to the director of the CIA suggested that 'a psychological operations concept entitled "Militant Liberty"' might do the trick. The concept was later endorsed by General Bonesteel of the NSC Planning Board (*DOD*, bk 10, pp. 777, 975), but it then disappears from the record. The Joint Chiefs, in February 1964, while recommending increased crop destruction and other measures, added that it would be helpful to 'create a "cause" which can serve as a rallying point for the youth/students of Vietnam.' A 'National Psychological Operations Plan' might help, they thought (III, 45).

The technical intelligentsia were also rallied to the effort of finding the proper formula to inspire the Vietnamese to effective action. The journal *Army* (December 1966) discusses a meeting of

> a group of physicists in the so-called Jason division of the Institute for Defense Analyses (IDA), a think factory that works closely with the Department of Defense. . . . Although they concentrated upon such matters as night vision for detecting guerrillas, improved communications, and vulnerability of aircraft to guerrilla gunfire, the scientists finally concluded that the compelling research need was not in the 'hard' sciences but in 'softwares' – the social sciences.
>
> 'We found that it was a very different problem from what we encountered in dealing with strategic weapons which are generally removed from human factors,' said Dr. Jack Ruina, former president of IDA and now a vice president at the Massachusetts Institute of Technology. 'In nuclear weapons it's machine versus machine. When we started thinking about counterinsurgency we quickly realized that you cannot isolate these problems from people. What did we know about these people – the Viet Cong and the Vietnamese generally? We felt we needed to know a great deal more from the anthropologist, from the social scientists. The greatest insight we have obtained about the Vietnam situation comes from anthropologists who can speak Vietnamese.
>
> 'What we concluded at the Jason session was that social and political and cultural knowledge was very important. A systematic and scholarly study of these areas of the world was clearly necessary. There would be serious difficulties in this type of research, some false starts, and some obstacles, but it should be done.'

The report goes on to cite some results, for example, a RAND study of the effects of American bombing, 'finding that such raids in North Vietnam improved morale in South Vietnam; that raids in South Vietnam damaged Viet Cong morale and that hostility toward the US did not grow materially in the bombed areas' (see note 8).

Another RAND study 'showed Viet Cong recruits in the villages are lured by the promise of their own rifle and a uniform. As a result the Saigon government decided to try to attract youths with flashy uniforms, jaunty with red, yellow or other lively scarves and berets.' This idea does not seem to have been quite the answer. Apparently some component is missing; further research is necessary.

Still another RAND study observed: 'The communication of a charisma (miraculously acquired powers) or a set of sympathetic symbols has received attention as an effective leadership device to arouse responsiveness in populations of underdeveloped societies. Charisma or similar symbolism is parsimonious of administrative skill, but also unstable and difficult to use in accomplishing complex social cooperation.' No doubt the Pentagon is still puzzling over how to translate this advice into an effective catalyst.

One should not laugh at this sort of inanity. When intelligence fails, there is plenty of force in reserve. As the insights from the social scientists proved inadequate, the United States simply extended and intensified its war of machines against people.

American ambassadors in Saigon were in no position to await the results of the research by government intellectuals, and therefore proposed programmes of their own for creating a 'cause' that would 'accomplish complex social cooperation' on the part of the Vietnamese. Ambassador Bunker suggested that the United States should use its influence to get the GVN to 'adopt a program and identify it with that of a former national hero' – in his words, 'so as to give the new governmnt an idealistic appeal or philosophy which will compete with that declared by the VC' (August 1967; II, 403). But this ingenious proposal met with no better results than the Ten Point Programme for Success proposed by Ambassador Lodge two years earlier. The first point: 'Saturate the mind of the people with some socially conscious and attractive ideology, which is susceptible of being carried out' (II, 530). Apparently, it didn't matter much what the ideology was. At least, nothing further is said. Somehow, these far-reaching concepts never succeeded in overcoming the 'idealistic appeal' of the Viet Cong.

Since the United States never succeeded in 'saturating the

minds of the people' with a sufficiently attractive ideology, it turned to the easier task of saturating the country with troops and bombs and defoliants. A State Department paper observed: 'Saturation bombing by artillery and air strikes . . . is an accepted tactic, and there is probably no province where this tactic has not been widely employed . . .' (IV, 398). The only objection raised is that it might be profitable to place greater emphasis on 'unconventional war,' specifically on winning popular support for the Saigon regime. That United States force should be devoted to winning support for its creation, the Saigon government, apparently seemed no more strange to the author than that the United States should be conducting saturation bombing of all provinces of South Vietnam.

5. 'THE PARTIES TO ANY DISPUTE SHALL SEEK A SOLUTION BY PEACEFUL MEANS' (UNITED NATIONS CHARTER)

1. Geneva, 1954

Given its inability to win popular support for the regime it imposed in South Vietnam, the United States government took a dim view of international conferences, negotiations, elections, and other peaceful means for resolving the conflict. The American attitude towards the Geneva Conference of 1954 foreshadowed a policy that still persists, in essence. Every effort was made to sabotage the Geneva Conference. When agreements were nonetheless reached, the United States government undertook at once to subvert them. The head of the French delegation at Geneva, Jean Chauvel, concluded that the 'only purpose of the Geneva agreements, as [the Americans] see them, is to provide a cover for the political, economic, and military preparations for the conquest.'[172] The documentation now available gives dramatic confirmation to this conclusion.

Immediately after the Geneva Conference, the National Security Council met and adopted NSC 5429/2 on August 20, 1954 (*DOD*, bk 10, pp. 731–2). This document, which appears only in the government edition and is misrepresented beyond recognition in the Pentagon Papers history, begins by recognizing the disastrous consequences of the Geneva Conference. One major problem is the Communist 'appearance of moderation,' which gives them 'a basis for sharply accentuating their "peace propaganda" and "peace program" in Asia in an attempt to allay fears of Communist expansionist policy and to establish closer relations with the nations of free Asia.' The 'loss of Southeast Asia,' apparently regarded as a serious prospect in the light of these Communist successes, 'would imperil retention of Japan as a key element in the off-shore island chain.' As we have already seen (section V above), the linkage of Japan to South-east Asia was a central element in over-all American planning in this period.

The document then outlines a variety of proposals for clandestine operations and other pressures. The key passage, repeated verbatim in NSC policy statements of December 1954 and June–July 1959 (*DOD*, bk 10, pp. 844, 1203), is the following (my emphasis):

> If requested by a legitimate local government which requires assistance to defeat local Communist subversion or rebellion *not constituting armed attack*, the U.S. should view such a situation so gravely that, in addition to giving all possible covert and overt support within Executive Branch authority, the President should at once consider requesting Congressional authority to take appropriate action, which might if necessary and feasible include the use of U.S. military forces either locally or against the external source of such subversion or rebellion (including Communist China if determined to be the source).

This doctrine is in clear and explicit violation of the law (see section III above). In effect, NSC 5429/2 and subsequent elaborations announce that the United States is not bound by its fundamental obligations under the United Nations Charter, and make nonsense of the subsequent appeals to article 51 of the charter, farcical in any event, as we have already observed. Since the 'legitimacy' of a local government is a matter of unilateral United States decision, the statement implies that the United States will intervene as it sees fit in the internal affairs of other countries, constrained only by the need to obtain congressional authorization (as it did, by fraud, after the Tonkin Gulf incident of 1964) for its illegal use of force, and will prepare to use military force against any state that it regards as responsible for local subversion or rebellion against a government designated by the United States as 'legitimate.' In keeping with this principle, the statement – in a section 'to be considered as a basis for further consideration,' not reported in the subsequent record – recommends policies to 'reduce the power of Communist China in Asia even at the risk of, but without deliberately provoking, war,' for example, 'support for Chinese Nationalist harassing actions' and efforts to 'create internal division in the Chinese Communist regime and impair Sino-Soviet relations by all feasible overt and covert means.'

The NSC policy statement proposes further that Japan be remilitarized and Thailand developed 'as the focal point of US covert and psychological operations in Southeast Asia.' With respect to Indochina, the United States will proceed to 'make every possible effort, not openly inconsistent with the US position as to the [Geneva] armistice agreements, to defeat Communist subversion and influence, to maintain and support friendly non-Communist governments in Cambodia and Laos, to maintain a friendly non-Communist South Vietnam, and to prevent a Communist victory through all-Vietnam elections.' The United States should undertake 'covert operations on a large and effective scale' in support of these policies throughout Indochina, including North Vietnam, where it should 'exploit available means to make more difficult the control by the Viet Minh of North Vietnam.'

Goodbye Geneva. August 1954.

This NSC statement formulates in outline the policies then pursued by the United States government in violation of its commitment to 'refrain from the threat or use of force to disturb' the Geneva settlement, and in violation of its more fundamental commitment to the United Nations Charter, The basic content of this highly significant document is omitted from the Pentagon Papers history. Worse still, the history cites the document with a fairly detailed exposition of its alleged content, little of which actually appears in the document cited (I, 204). In another chapter, the historian discussing the consequences of the Geneva settlement states that 'read in context,' the formulation of 'the corollary objective (stated by the NSC in August and approved by the President) "to prevent a Communist victory through all-Vietnam elections" did *not* connote American intention to subvert the accords,' but 'meant that American influence would aim at assuring that the Communists not gain an electoral victory through deceitful, undemocratic methods' (I, 177). He omits the context, cited above, which reveals clearly that the NSC statement approved by the president connotes precisely an American intention to subvert the accords, as part of a general campaign of intervention throughout East Asia. The director of the Pentagon study, summarizing, states only that 'almost at once [after

Geneva] US policy began to respond to military urgency' (I, 181).

This misrepresentation, it should be noted, is fully in accord with the general failure of the Pentagon history to inquire into the United States role as an agent of subversion and aggression, its tendency to regard the United States as a victim merely responding to situations created by others (see pp. 29–30; and section IV above).[173] It should also be noted that the Lansdale report on covert operations in North and South Vietnam in 1954 and 1955 (I, 573–4; also II, 643–4, a few years later) was not part of the Pentagon Papers, and was apparently obtained by the *New York Times* in some other manner. Making no reference to Lansdale's sabotage and subversion missions in the North, the Pentagon historian further states, falsely: 'Athough American policy spoke of taking steps to prevent the complete absorption of the DRV into the Soviet bloc, those steps amounted to nothing more than maintenance of a US consulate in Hanoi' (I, 213). The failure of the Pentagon historian to mention documented examples of subversion and sabotage – indeed, his denial of their existence – leaves us with no further information here with regard to the report by Bernard Fall that small saboteur groups were parachuted or infiltrated into North Vietnam, with small success and high casualties, 'at least since 1956.'[174] The combination of omissions and falsification, leading to a complete misrepresentation of the origins of the American war in Indochina, reveals in a striking way the effectiveness of the ideological controls that govern the Pentagon Papers history.

As the records of the International Control Commission make clear, the United States and the GVN during the 1950s attempted to make use of the Geneva Agreements selectively, relying on the ICC to protect the fragile Saigon government while obstructing the ICC at every turn in its efforts to implement the agreements, conducting a vast campaign of terror in the South, and excising the most important provision of the agreements, namely, the elections provision for reunifying the country.[175] Virtually everyone expected the DRV to win the elections, and therefore the United States and the GVN 'seemed determined from the outset to scuttle the Geneva Agreements,' much to the annoyance of Nehru, for example, who pointed out that 'the question is of giving effect to the Geneva Agreements [specifically, the elections provision] or of putting an end to them and facing the consequences,' namely, a return to armed struggle. By early 1956, the Western powers 'disclaimed responsibility for the most important clause of the Geneva Agreements,' the elections provision; and the ICC (Canada abstaining) declared that the explicit opposition of the GVN to the Geneva Agreements 'naturally amounts to revocation.' The British role was particularly ugly.[176] The ICC reported in 1956 that 'while the Commission has experienced difficulties in North Vietnam, the major part of its difficulties has arisen in South Vietnam.'[177] All discussions that even attempt to be serious note the difference in degree of compliance, easy to explain, given the general expectation that Vietnam would be unified under Communist rule if the accords were observed.

A DOD study of April 1955 concluded that should the Communists permit elections under international supervision, 'there is no reason to doubt at this time that they would win easily in the 1956 elections' (*DOD*, bk 10, p. 936), and the same fear was voiced, with various qualifications, throughout this period (*DOD*, bk 10, pp. 692, 806, 867, 883), though it was later hoped that it would be possible to weaken the Communists in the North and strengthen the government in the South so that the whole country might ultimately be unified under anticommunist leadership (p. 1131; April 1958). In April 1955 Dulles proposed (p. 892) that the Western powers insist on certain 'safeguards' that would be 'probably unacceptable to Communists because of provisions for strict compliance to ensure genuinely free elections' (such as those held under the United States aegis in Asia), and as is well known, the United States backed Diem in his refusal to hold elections or even enter into preliminary discussions, as required by the Geneva Agreements, which of course stipulated that the 17th parallel was merely a provisional military demarcation line, not a political or territorial boundary. Diem consistently took the position that this goverment was not bound by the Geneva Agreements (p. 1077).

It is interesting that none of these facts have prevented Washington, in later years, from claiming that its only wish is to restore the 'essential provisions of the Geneva Accords of 1954' (William Bundy, June 1967; IV, 502). The contents of the Geneva Accords have been so thoroughly forgotten that even Chester Cooper, who took part in the Geneva Conference and has remained active in Indochina affairs since, is able to say blandly that the United States' Vietnam aid programme was governed by 'a strong desire to maintain for the South Vietnamese the independence they were granted at Geneva' (discussing the 'basic philosophy of

American aid to Vietnam,' so 'naive and idealistic').[178] Thus are myths created.

2. Elections and democracy

In the late 1960s, the United States backed elections within the GVN, so long as they were held under laws that excluded Communists and neutralists who work directly or indirectly for the Communists or 'whose actions are advantageous to the communists.'[179] A Vietnamese commentator points out: 'The election laws in the Republic of Vietnam are laws designed to exclude all those patriotic people who have made the greatest contribution toward protecting their country and their villages and who will never be cowed by the foreigners.'[180] He is elaborating the views of a South Vietnamese judge who had written shortly before: 'In a whore-house society [Vietnam, under allied occupation] if the prostitutes were forced to organize elections to choose their leader, the house's madam can always have them vote for a pimp who can effectively carry out her orders.'

Since the publication of the Pentagon Papers and the one-man 'election' of October 1971, it has become fashionable to point out that the United States of course never really intended to bring democracy to Vietnam. But it should be recalled that while the illusion could still be popularly maintained, American intervention was consistently justified on just these grounds, to the public and internally as well. See, for example, John F. Kennedy's remarks cited above (p. 58), or the remarks of William Bundy on the 'courageous and extremely difficult effort [of South Vietnam] to become a true democracy during a guerrilla war' and the United States commitment to prevent any solution not 'aceptable voluntarily to the South Vietnamese Government and people.'[181] Such ideas are still expressed, for example, by Sir Robert Thompson, one of Britain's gifts to the Vietnamese people, who writes that 'giving the people of South Viet Nam a free choice' is the cornerstone of American policy.[182]

Sir Robert's concept of 'free choice' provides a good insight into the colonialist mentality. It is explained by Roger Hilsman in discussing Thompson's concept of strategic hamlets, which were to 'create the physical security the villager must have before he could make a free choice between the Vietcong and the government.' The plan failed, Hilsman explains, because Diem's brother Nhu did not follow a careful programme 'in which the loyalties of each area were assured and all Vietcong agents eliminated before the troops and civic action teams moved on to the next.' Thus 'Vietcong agents remained in place,' and a free choice was impossible. For a true 'free choice,' it was necessary to physically eliminate the opposition. Then the villagers could choose freely between the government and the Viet Cong, in their encampments surrounded by barbed wire and occupied by American-backed government troops.[183]

In a survey of the strategic hamlet programme, which the GVN claims resettled a third of the population of South Vietnam by summer 1962,[184] the Pentagon Papers analyst (II, Chapter 2) records Thompson's 'input,' in particular his belief that the programme should be 'clinical,' not 'surgical' – emphasizing police rather than military – and that it failed because the Viet Cong infrastructure was not eliminated. The analyst observes that the 'physical aspects' of the programme were 'similar if not identical to earlier population resettlement and control efforts practiced by the French and by Diem'; 'all failed dismally because they ran into resentment if not active resistance on the part of the peasants, at whose control and safety, then loyalty, they were aimed.' This was evident from the start, when the majority of the peasants refused to co-operate and had to be 'herded forcibly from their homes' in Operation SUNRISE. Another way of putting it is that the peasants, unaccountably, refused the free choice so generously offered them.

The form of 'democracy' envisioned by Americans who were intervening most extensively in the internal affairs of Indochina is revealed in some comments by General Lansdale. Discussing the situation in Laos in 1961, he writes: 'There is also a local veterans' organization and a grass-roots political organization in Laos, both of which are subject to CIA direction and control . . .' (II, 647). The concept of a grass-roots organization under CIA direction and control is symbolic of American aims in Indochina, and brings out the reality behind the rhetoric in which they are masked.

The conception of democracy advanced by our various ambassadors also makes interesting reading. Ambassador Durbrow, for example, thought that a liberal press code would be a good idea: 'it would be most beneficial to a better understanding of the fruitful efforts being made by your [Diem's] Government on behalf of the people. . . .' Under the system he envisioned, 'the Government should only intervene if articles are flagrantly dishonest, inaccurate, or favorable to the Communists' (*DOD*, bk

10, p. 1354; December 1960). Interchanging a few names, what commissar could disagree?

Ambassador Lodge's contributions are along similar lines. He opposed Diem when it appeared that Diem could not 'gain the support of the people who count, i.e., the educated class in and out of government service' (II, 738; August 1963). A few months later, he recognized that the Vietnamese generals obviously 'are all we have got' (II, 304), but was undeterred by this insight. In his second tour of duty, Lodge came to support elections, which he felt should be as fair as possible 'so as to gain a maximum improvement in the image of the GVN in the United States and internationally.' They should 'bring together' all noncommunist groups committed to receiving American help (to defend 'their country's independence'). With his concurrence, 'the approved electoral law gave the Directorate [the Ky regime] ample scope to exclude unwanted candidates, and prevent the Buddhists from putting their symbol . . . on the ballot.' Lodge further 'unreservedly backed' the exclusion of Buddhists of the Struggle Movement as 'moderate measures to prevent elections from being used as a vehicle for a Communist takeover.' Lodge regarded the Buddhists 'as equivalent to card-carrying Communists,' the analyst reports (II, 376-8, 384). Any democracy, after all, must take special measures to exclude communists from the electoral process if they have a chance to win, and also to defend itself from criminal elements; and the Buddhists of Hue and Da Nang, in Ambassador Lodge's considered judgment, were responsible for 'criminal violence operating under political, economic and social guise.' Their actions demonstrated to him that the Vietnamese are obviously not ready for self-government, and raised the possibility that 'we may have to decide how much it is worth to us to deny Viet-Nam to Hanoi and Peking – regardless of what the Vietnamese may think' (IV, 99–100). Lodge also opposed a 'constituent assembly' (a 'pernicious French phrase') which 'stays around and makes trouble for an indefinite period,' preferring a 'constitutional convention,' which 'would meet, adopt the constitution and disband' (II, 371).

Perhaps a fair indication of how the United States actually viewed Vietnamese politics is given by the reaction to the elections to the National Assembly of September 27, 1963, 'with predictably high turnouts and majorities for Government candidates' (II, 215). At just this period, as the analyst reports, 'we variously authorized, sanctioned and encouraged the coup efforts of the Vietnamese generals and offered full support for a successor government' (II, 207), for the reason that the government had so 'alienated popular support' that victory over the Viet Cong under Diem was thought to be virtually impossible (II, 201–2).

It might be added that the attitude towards American democracy was not too different (see note 39). This is revealed in a striking way during the deliberations of 1964. Plans for the February 1965 escalation were undertaken in 1964 with awareness of the necessity for waiting until the president had a congressional mandate and a popular mandate.

> Mid-1964 was not an auspicious time for new departures in policy by a President who wished to portray 'moderate' alternatives to his opponents' 'radical' proposals. Nor was any time prior to or immediately following the elections very appealing for the same reason. . . . President Johnson had neither a congressional nor a popular mandate to Americanize the war or to expand it dramatically by 'going north.' [III, 2–4; cf. NSC 5429/2, discussed in sub-section 5.1 above]

By June 1964, it was recognized 'that only relatively heavy levels of attack on the DRV would be likely to have any significant compelling effect,' but most of the president's advisers 'recognized the necessity of building firmer public and congressional support for greater US involvement in SEA before any wider military actions should be undertaken' (III, 107). After the Tonkin Gulf incident and the resulting congressional endorsement, and President Johnson's 'smashing victory at the polls,' his 'feasible options increased.' He was now 'armed with both a popular mandate and broad Congressional authorization' and could therefore proceed (III, 4–6). By September, 'there was little basic disagreement among the principals on the need for military actions against the North.' At an important meeting of top-level officials (Rusk, McNamara, Wheeler, Taylor, McCone), this view was advanced 'with a sense that such actions were inevitable.' But 'tactical considerations,' among them the ongoing election campaign in which the president 'was presenting himself as the candidate of reason and restraint,' prevented action 'for the time being' (III, 111). During the September deliberations, 'unity of domestic American opinion' was regarded as a precondition to escalation, but during the November debates, this was 'no longer an important factor,' though the president remained 'cautious and equivocal.' In the interim, he had been elected 'with an overwhelming mandate' (III, 113–16). Decisions to escalate or to carry out deliberate provocation to justify United States response were to be postponed 'probably until November or December.' Throughout the deliberations, December or January 1 was regarded as 'target D-day' (III, 198–200, 207), that is, after the elections.

It is remarkable that nowhere does the analyst see fit to mention that the popular mandate was *not* to escalate, or that the congressional support was obtained in a rather dubious fashion.[185] It was sufficient that congressional approval was obtained, and that there was a smashing victory at the polls. The obvious conclusion to draw from this history is that peace-minded people should have voted for Goldwater, so that the 'mandate' would have been less overwhelming, since apparently it was only its scale and not its character that mattered. The whole affair is a remarkable example of the totalitarian instincts of the planners, accepted as natural by the historian.[186]

3. Negotiations

A major reason why the president was 'cautious and equivocal' was the fear that a Communist response to American escalation would topple the unstable GVN and that international pressures would bring about 'premature negotiations' – that is, negotiation that might lead to a political settlement, hence a Communist victory, given the political strength of the opposing forces. Recall that this was a period when, as Douglas Pike puts it, the noncommunists in South Vietnam, with the possible exception of the Buddhists, could not risk entering a coalition, 'fearing that if they did the whale would swallow the minnow.'[187]

These fears were expressed early in the year, when plans for direct military action against the North were under serious consideration. Secretary McNamara informed the president that such operations were of an 'extremely delicate nature': 'There would be the problem of marshalling the case to justify such action, the problem of communist escalation, and the problem of dealing with the pressures for premature or "stacked" negotiations' (III, 504; March 16, 1964). A few days later, the president informed Ambassador Lodge in Saigon that the immediate task must be 'to strengthen the southern base.' 'For this reason,' he went on, the plans for overt military action against the North must be 'on a contingency basis at present, and the immediate problem in this area is to develop the strongest possible military and political base for possible later action' (III, 511). Further deliberations remained within this framework until the elections.

It has been argued that there was no real deception during the presidential campaign of 1964, since the plans to escalate were only 'contingency plans.' The record excludes this interpretation. True, the plans were 'on a contingency basis,' for the reasons just noted: the need for a popular and congressional mandate, the weakness of the Southern base, the dangers of premature negotiations. To place these deliberations in the category of plans to bomb Moscow or invade Brazil, if circumstances warrant, is patently absurd.

Throughout the fateful year of 1964, planning continued on the assumptions noted. After the election, there was little doubt that escalation would be undertaken. As Ambassador Taylor explained rather neatly on November 27, if the GVN falls, 'we should be prepared for emergency military action against the North if only to shore up a collapsing situation'; and 'if, on the other hand . . . the government maintains and proves itself, then we should be prepared to embark on a methodical program of mounting air attacks' (III, 241). In short, whatever the situation, bomb. He also added, 'Do not enter into negotiations until the DRV is hurting.'

The latter assumption was unchallenged, through 1964. McNamara's fear of premature or 'stacked' negotiations was reiterated throughout the detailed planning. The DRV might respond with some military action of its own to a direct bombing attack, which 'may have to continue through substantial levels of military, industrial, and governmental destruction in the DRV' (III, 620). Such Communist perfidy might topple the collapsing GVN. It might also spur international efforts to achieve a solution by peaceful means. But negotiations, seriously undertaken, would lead to a political solution, hence an American defeat. We have already noted the refusal of the planners to accept the likely outcome of a Vietnamese-negotiated deal leading to a unified Communist Vietnam hostile to China (see p. 51 above).

The insistence on using force prior to any negotiations should be read in the light of the legal obligation, under the United Nations Charter, to refrain from the threat and use of force and to employ peaceful means (such as negotiations) for settling disputes. In a parody of the supreme law of the land, the cabal insisted that 'after, *but only after*, we have established a clear pattern of pressure' could peaceful means be considered (William Bundy,

August 11, 1964: III, 526; his emphasis). The same wording was repeated a few days later in a message from State to Saigon under the heading 'Essential Elements of US Policy' (III, 535). First force, then talk.

One finds no discussion of the legal obligations of the United States.[188] Rather, all agencies 'saw negotiations as something that should not be entered into until the pressures were hurting North Vietnam' (III, 204). As Taylor put it in February, we must 'convey signals which, in combination, should present to the DRV leaders a vision of inevitable, ultimate destruction if they do not change their ways'; 'degree of damage and number of casualties inflicted gauge the impact of our operations on Hanoi leadership and hence are important as a measure of their discomfort' (III, 316). Consistently, United States policy was to avoid being trapped[189] into reliance on peaceful, legal means until the proper signals had been conveyed by sufficient damage, casualties, and a credible threat of ultimate destruction.

Subsequent policy adhered to the principle: First force, then talk. President Johnson's speech of April 7, 1965, according to the analyst, 'was in accord with the "pressures policy" rationale that had been worked out in November 1964, which held that US readiness to negotiate was not to be surfaced until after a series of air strikes that had been carried out against important targets in North Vietnam' (III, 356). For this reason, 'significantly,' there had been particularly intensive bombing for the two weeks prior to the president's 'initiative.' The cynicism of this approach entirely escapes the analyst. Nor does he, in a later section, draw any connection between the general 'pressures policy' and the odd fact that, repeatedly, apparent DRV peace feelers and negotiations opportunities were undercut by sudden escalation of bombing (IV, 135, 205). To the analyst, the bombing escalation at these moments was 'inadvertent' or an 'unfortunate coincidence' (though he admits that the DRV leaders must have had 'the strong impression they were being squeezed by Johnsonian pressure tactics'). He attributes the failure of negotiations to 'North Vietnam's bruised ego,' a degree of sensitivity revealed as well by his reference to the 'cries of civilian casualties . . . heard long and loud from Hanoi' when the Hanoi power plant was bombed in May 1967 (IV, 153).

Historians who do not unthinkingly accept the framework of government propaganda have taken note of the 'unfortunate coincidences,' and have suggested possible explanations that need not concern us here.[190] It is possible that all of these instances merely reflected the 'pressure policy' rationale of Washington, the general assumption that, in explicit contradiction to the supreme law of the land, threat and use of force must precede efforts at 'peaceful settlement' of disputes.

This is not to deny that the consensus of the planners in late 1964 was realistic. It was. There was simply no basis for negotiations, given the balance of political forces. A predominant United States role in determining the economic and social structure of Vietnam is not negotiable as long as nationalist forces that oppose such an outcome are sufficiently strong to continue their resistance. Hence all negotiations are doomed to failure, apart from those leading to a true United States withdrawal, or ratifying the surrender of those who had 'captured' the nationalist movement to the United States and its local associates.

The volumes of the Pentagon Papers dealing with negotiations are not yet available to the public, but in the record presented here there are some interesting curiosities. Throughout 1964 and early 1965 there are repeated references to various negotiations efforts, but one is conspicuously missing, namely, the effort by U Thant that was probably the most promising of all. In October 1964, U Thant told United Nations Ambassador Stevenson that Ho Chi Minh had apparently agreed to negotiations in Rangoon. The proposal seems to have been concealed internally until U Thant threatened to 'blow' the story in January, when the United States rejected the proposal.[191] On January 6, 1965, William Bundy reported to the secretary of state that the Soviet Union, China, and the DRV had 'called for a Laos conference without preconditions but have refrained from mentioning a conference on Vietnam' (III, 684), and went on to suggest an explanation for the latter omission. Apparently Bundy was unaware of the proposal (as was his brother, according to Cooper). Without further information, it appears that there was a conspiracy within a conspiracy, in this instance.

6. INITIATIVE AND RESPONSE: AGGRESSION AGAINST SOUTH VIETNAM

In its official propaganda, the United States government, like most others, presents itself as a status quo power attempting to uphold a stable international order in the face of violence and aggression. As we have seen, the Pentagon historians generally operate within this ideological framework. The documentary record that they were examining, however, reveals that exactly the opposite was the case. At every point, the United States resorted to force to disrupt social and political arrangements that it regarded as detrimental to its global policies. A response by indigenous forces was then labelled 'aggression,' and presented to the public as a justification for further American escalation.

The essence of the United States position is revealed by public statements explaining the concept of 'aggression.' Consider, for example, the fairly typical remarks by Adlai Stevenson to the United Nations Security Council, May 21, 1964 (III, 715–16). He observed that 'the point is the same in Vietnam today as it was in Greece in 1947.' In both cases, the United States was defending a free people from 'internal aggression':

> I would remind the members that in 1947, after the aggressors had gained control of most of the country, many people felt that the cause of the Government of Greece was hopelessly lost. But as long as the people of Greece were prepared to fight for the life of their own country, the United States was not prepared to stand by while Greece was overrun.

Similarly, 'The United States cannot stand by while South-east Asia is overrun by armed aggressors.'

Stevenson's historical analogy is more or less to the point. In Vietnam as in Greece, the United States was seeking to block 'internal aggression,' that is, 'aggression' by a mass-based indigenous movement against a government protected by foreign power, where the 'internal aggression' has the kind of outside support that few wars of liberation have lacked (for example, the American Revolution, to cite a case where far greater outside support was decisive; cf. *For Reasons of State*, Chapter 1).

In both cases, in utter defiance of available evidence, the United States executive has sought to mask the absurdity of its claims by pretending that the 'internal aggressors' were merely agents of a global conspiracy directed by Moscow or 'Peiping.'[192] As the United States undertook to overthrow the status quo of 1945–1946 by attempting to restore French influence and control over Indochina, the State Department solemnly informed the French government, in June 1949, of the 'inevitable intention' of the Viet Minh 'to subvert the nationalist cause in the end to the requirements of international Communism.' The benighted Vietnamese, unable to comprehend this fact, are impressed by 'its effective leadership of the nationalist movement.' But the

United States understands full well, and therefore takes the 'paramount question in Indochina' to be 'whether the country is to be saved from Communist control,' all other issues being 'irrelevant,' given the need 'to preserve Indochina from a foreign tyranny' (*DOD*, bk 8, pp. 208–9). Dean Rusk went on to inform the press that the French and the 'independent' Associated States are firmly holding the line in 'defense of Indochina against communist colonialism,' spearheaded by the Viet Minh (p. 397).

The National Security Council (February 1950) held that the French army, along with native troops, 'is now in armed conflict with the forces of communist aggression,' and is 'attempting to restore law and order' (I, 361). The president's Special Committee on South-east Asia, in early 1954, explained further that the French had demonstrated, by their grant of independence to the Associated States, that 'the Viet Minh are not fighting for freedom.' The French are fighting 'to defend the cause of liberty and freedom from Communism in Indochina.' 'The cause of Viet Minh,' in contrast, is 'the cause of colonization and subservience to Kremlin rule as was the cause in China, in North Korea[193] and in the European satellites' (*DOD*, bk 9, p. 342).

The Viet Minh are the colonialists; the French defend Vietnamese independence.

In his first State of the Union message, President Kennedy warned that 'in Asia, the relentless pressures of the Chinese Communists menace the security of the entire area – from the borders of India and South Viet Nam to the jungles of Laos, struggling to protect its newly-won independence.'[194] A draft report of the Gilpatric Task Force (May 1961), discussing the deployment of 'US battle groups,' stated that their purpose would be to deter '*further* Communist aggression from North Vietnam, China, or the Soviet Union, while rallying the morale of the Vietnamese' (II, 48; emphasis mine). On the eve of the escalation of February 1965, John McNaughton, with the agreement of McNamara, described the 'US objective in South Vietnam' as 'to contain China' (III, 686, 267), and two months later stated a major objective as 'To keep SVN (and then adjacent) territory from Chinese hands.'[195] A more profound misunderstanding of the content of Vietnamese nationalism, and its Communist leadership, could hardly be imagined. And George Carver, speaking for the CIA in April 1966, proclaimed the objective 'Demonstrating the sterile futility of the militant and aggressive expansionist policy advocated by the present rulers of

Communist China' (IV, 82; cf. note 145). Essentially the same view was developed further by McGeorge Bundy, in mid-1967, when he stated that whatever Eastern intellectuals may think, most Americans and 'nearly all Asians' know that the domino theory is correct; thus United States intervention 'has already saved the hope of freedom for hundreds of millions,' no less (IV, 159). Robert McNamara added that the objective of 'draw[ing] the line against Chinese expansionism in Asia' had already been attained (IV, 174).[196] And so on.

The notions of the Kennedy intellectuals and the CIA are hardly different from some of the weird views of American military experts. For example, General Van Fleet, reporting on his mission to the Far East in October 1954, charged that 'since the end of World War II, the Chinese Communist regime has waged a relentless war against the free world, specifically the United States.' 'Peace with freedom cannot be restored to Asia as long as the Chinese Communist regime continues to exist' (*DOD*, bk 10, p. 794). It would be interesting to explore further General Van Fleet's ideas about 'restoring' freedom to Asia.

Internal documents quite generally refer to the 'VC aggression in the South' (e.g., IV, 58, October 1965). Similarly, a Pentagon memorandum described 'the obvious and not wholly anticipated strength of the Viet Cong infrastructure' after the Tet offensive of 1968, adding that this 'shows that there can be no prospect of a quick military solution to the aggression in South Vietnam' – the aggression, that is, organized by the Viet Cong infrastructure (IV, 581).

On the character of 'aggression,' there are also interesting comments by the Joint Chiefs. In February 1955, they foresaw 'three basic forms in which aggression in Southeast Asia can occur: (*a*) Overt armed attack from outside of the area. (*b*) Overt armed attack from within the area of each of the sovereign states. (*c*) Aggression other than armed, i.e., political warfare, or subversion' (*DOD*, bk 10, p. 885). The concept of 'overt armed attack from within' a sovereign state is Stevenson's 'internal aggression.' In defining 'political warfare' as a form of aggression, the Joint Chiefs reveal that they comprehend with precision and insight the fundamental position of the United States executive.

Notice that it is the same concept of 'internal aggression' that Sidney Hook employs in the remarks cited earlier, when he refers to the application of American military force in repelling the 'incursions' of the NLF (mere 'partisans' of North Vietnam), for example, by B-52 raids in the Mekong Delta with their 'unfortunate accidental loss of life' (p. 86 above).

In January 1959, the Operations Coordinating Board published an 'Operations Plan for Viet-Nam,' to be implemented by member agencies. As the plan was developed within the Defence Department, the Joint Chiefs of Staff were assigned responsibility to 'deter the Viet Cong (formerly called Viet Minh) from attacking or subverting Free Viet-Nam or other neighboring states.' They were also to 'probe weaknesses of the Viet Cong and exploit them internally and internationally whenever possible' (*DOD*, bk 10, p. 1186; May 1959). The Pentagon, in short, was to deter 'internal aggression' by the nationalist movement of Indochina.

According to the same plan, the Pentagon was to 'encourage US training and orientation visits' for Vietnamese, expanding existing programmes, and to 'encourage fullest assimilation into Vietnamese life (military, economic, social, political and cultural) of returned exchanges, participants and trainees,' thus 'help[ing] them exercise a pro-Free World influence among fellow Vietnamese.' Or, to use the terminology favoured by American propagandists, the United States military was to step up its programme of infiltrating trained regroupees into South Vietnam to subvert South Vietnam and to place it more firmly under foreign domination. The Operations Plan for Vietnam does not deal with the problem of deterring ongoing 'aggression from the North,' there being none. Rather, its concern is to implement American intervention in the South, that is, military and other actions against the indigenous 'Viet Cong.' At the same time the United States military command was to increase its efforts to bring South Vietnam within the American orbit, in accordance with the long-term objectives laid down years earlier.

There is a certain irony in the fact that both the propaganda apparatus of the United States government and independent scholars have given much attention to a meeting that took place in Hanoi in the same month, May 1959, when the Communist Party of North Vietnam – as government spokesmen would have it – set in motion its effort to subvert and conquer its free Southern neighbour. At this meeting, the party is reported to have granted Southern cadres permission to take up arms to defend themselves against the terror of the United States-imposed regime, which had decimated the Southern Viet Minh during the period when Hanoi was urging restraint and abstention from force and violence.[197] The same meeting reportedly authorized Southerners who had regrouped to the North in accord with the Geneva Agreements to return to their homes in the South to participate in the ongoing Southern rebellion. Not even the most extreme advocate of United States intervention claims that the party did more in May 1959 than initiate programmes of the sort that the American Joint Chiefs of Staff were given responsibility to *expand* at the same moment. All of this, to be sure, overlooks a fundamental asymmetry: those who were implementing the Operations Plan for Vietnam could hardly be classed as Vietnamese, and the border they were crossing was most assuredly a political and territorial boundary.

The same concept of 'internal aggression' was employed with regard to Laos. The president justified the initiation of low-level armed reconnaissance (that is, bombing and strafing) in Laos in May 1964 as a reaction to 'new acts of communist aggression in Laos' (III, 720). The 'aggressors,' in this case, were left-leaning neutralists and Pathet Lao who restored the status quo as of April 1963, possibly responding to a right-wing coup attempt in Vientiane and an effort to integrate left-neutralist forces into the rightist army.[198] In Laos as in South Vietnam, the United States had for many years trained right-wing military forces abroad, then returned them to take part in rebellion and domestic repression. For example, in late 1960 the United States handed over 200 Laotian paratroopers who had been training in Thailand (the 'focal point' for American operations in South-east Asia – see p. 113 above) to Phoumi Nosavan, the favourite of the CIA and the American military, who was then in open rebellion against the Souvanna Phouma government,[199] pro-Western but not sufficiently reactionary to enlist United States support. This was a period when American correspondents reported that 'if free elections were held today in Laos, every qualified observer, including the American Embassy, concedes this hermit kingdom would go Communist in a landslide,' that the Pathet Lao political party 'controls the countryside [and] the odds [in any election] are heavily in favor of that party, which has diligently built up an organization controlling most of the country's ten thousand villages.'[200] The dispatch of Lao paratroopers in an effort to overthrow the centrist regime which itself could not withstand the Pathet Lao in open political competition is not regarded by the United States government or the Pentagon historians[201] as aggression or armed intervention, though the return of Southern regroupees to their homes from 1959 was an 'armed attack' against South Vietnam which justified United States 'response' under article 51 of the United Nations Charter.[202]

In these and many other cases, the concept of aggression employed by the United States executive gives the game away. Indigenous forces are carrying out 'internal aggression' against regimes chosen to rule by the Western powers, and protected from their own populations by outside force (acting in 'collective self-defense' against this 'aggression').

The Pentagon historian traces the 'US awareness of the requirement to promote internal stability' to the late 1950s, noting in particular the contribution of the Draper Committee (The President's Committee to Study the US Military Assistance Programme) in 1958-9. The Draper Committee distinguished clearly between two tasks of the military forces assisted by the United States: 'countering external aggression' and countering 'internal aggression' (II, 435). Perhaps this is the origin of the interesting phrase 'internal aggression,' later adopted by Adlai Stevenson and others. The Draper Committee's papers also 'sought to popularize military civic action programs and to link them to politically acceptable precedents – such as the US Army's role in the development of the American West.' The reference is suggestive. The United States Army was protecting the developers of the American West from the internal aggression of the Indians who were being swept off their lands. Taking this as a 'precedent,' who plays the role of the American Indians in the 'military civic action programs' advised and assisted by the United States military in some foreign land? And to whom is the precedent, or its contemporary analogue, 'politically acceptable?' Pursuing these questions, we achieve some interesting insights into counterinsurgency doctrines that developed out of the deliberations of the Draper Committee and that so entranced the Kennedy intellectuals.[203]

Occasionally, explicit notice is taken of the fact that 'in South Vietnam, the Communists are clearly embarked on a "national liberation war" of insurgency and subversion from within rather [than] on overt aggression.'[204] The distinction is fundamental. It undermines any appeal to the United Nations Charter or to the SEATO treaty, as has frequently been noted. The facts, however, did not prevent President Kennedy from asserting that 'the systematic aggression now bleeding that country is not a "war of liberation" – for Viet Nam is already free' (II, 806; January 1962), as they have never prevented his advisers from saying that the United States was throughout engaged in defending a free people from aggression, or that in 1962 'aggression [was] checked in Vietnam.'[205] Misrepresentation becomes absurdity when we realize that in that same year, 1962, American forces were directly engaged in combat operations against the insurgents in South Vietnam.[206] Throughout, the United States, exactly like France, is fighting to preserve the freedom of the Vietnamese from the colonialist Viet Minh and their successors in aggression. On this assumption it is quite proper for Ambassador Maxwell Taylor to sputter with indignation over the 'outrageous acts of the Vietcong in South Vietnam, such as the attack on Bien Hoa,' the American air base, damaging or destroying 27 of 30 United States B-57s and killing several Americans. To 'repay' such outrageous acts, 'we could engage in reprisal bombings' against North Vietnam, which we have determined to be responsible (III, 669; II, 341; III, 288; October–November 1964).

On other occasions, administration spokesmen were placed in a position where reference to 'internal aggression' would appear too cynical or unconvincing, and they therefore simply asserted that there had been overt aggression by the North Vietnamese prior to United States escalation in February 1965. Secretary Rusk, testifying before the Senate Foreign Relations Committee in January and February 1966, stated that the 325th Division of the North Vietnamese army had entered South Vietnam by January 1965, an act that constituted 'aggression by means of an armed attack' and entitled the United States to respond under article 51 of the United Nations Charter. The public record sufficed to disprove this contention, as Theodore Draper demonstrated in a careful analysis at the time.[207] The Pentagon Papers now demonstrate conclusively that when the United States undertook the February escalation, it knew of no regular North Vietnamese units in South Vietnam. In fact, in early July 1965, the assistant secretary of defence was still concerned with the *possibility* that there might be PAVN forces in or near South Vietnam; and a few weeks later, the Joint Chiefs included one regiment of the 325th PAVN Division in their estimate of 48,500 'Viet Cong organized combat units' (the only PAVN unit identified). For comparison, note that the Honolulu meeting of April 20 had recommended that American forces be raised to 82,000 supplemented with 7,250 Korean and Australian troops (2,000 Koreans had been dispatched on January 8, 1965). By June, the United States decided 'to pour US troops into the country as fast as they could be deployed' (II, 362), and in mid-July the president approved the request that the United States troop level be raised to 175,000.[208] In the light of these facts, the claim that the United States was defending South Vietnam from an armed attack is merely ludicrous.

Conceivably, one might argue that Secretary Rusk's testimony is not inconsistent with the record presented in the Pentagon Papers and elsewhere. One might speculate that information obtained prior to his testimony, but after the summer of 1965, revealed that the PAVN 325th Division had in fact infiltrated into South Vietnam by January 1965, as Rusk maintained in his Senate testimony.

There are two difficulties in this defence, the only possible one. In the first place, there is no evidence that the speculation is correct. Second and more important, even if it were correct it would be irrelevant. Rusk's testimony was an effort to justify the United States escalation of February as collective self-defence against armed attack. Putting aside a variety of other objections, the justification would have force only if it had been known at the time of the escalation that an armed attack had taken place. The record makes it absolutely clear that this was not the case. Hence the justification fails under any assumption with regard to unknown facts.

Suppose, for example, that after invading Czechoslovakia the Russians had discovered that, unknown to them, some armed attack had taken place against Czechoslovakia, say, by West German forces. They could not have argued that this 'discovery' justified their armed intervention on the grounds of article 51. It is therefore clear that Rusk's testimony consisted of either false statements or fraudulent representations, and hence was technically criminal (see note 41). It may also be recalled that the fraudulent nature of Rusk's testimony (and not his alone) was known and demonstrated at once (cf. Draper, *Abuse of Power*), even without the far more extensive confirmation now possible. And finally, we may take note of the homilies on 'the rule of law' that are delivered from the judicial bench or in the pages of journals of opinion when citizens undertake minor acts of non-violent civil disobedience in protest against aggression and mass murder: the fabric of society will dissolve and we will fall into anarchy and barbarism if the law is not uniformly applied.

The Pentagon Papers reveal that United States policy makers believed the NLF to be a creature of Hanoi, and Hanoi to be an agent of 'international communism.' Under law, they were entitled to express these beliefs and to request the Security Council of the United Nations to determine the existence of a threat to peace. That they did not do so is significant, and self-explanatory. But it is worth mentioning that there is a logical gap between the demonstration that American policy makers expressed (and perhaps even held) such beliefs and the demonstration that the beliefs were correct. The matter has no bearing on the issue of American aggression, but it might be considered nonetheless. It is interesting, for example, that the Soviet Union had virtually cut off aid to North Vietnam from 1962 to 1964 (IV, 116), when this agent of international communism was allegedly engaged in aggression against the free people of South Vietnam. So marginal was the Soviet interest in South-east Asia prior to the American escalation of 1964 that the NSC working group (November 1964) expressed the view that 'Moscow's role in Vietnam is likely to remain a relatively minor one' (III, 215). But the 'period of nearly three years of diligent detachment' came to an end; 'the Soviet Union . . . reentered Southeast Asian politics in an active way' with a 'reported Soviet pledge in November [1964] to increase economic and military aid to North Vietnam,' and subsequent warnings that it would support the DRV in the face of the naval attacks on the coast and United States air attacks in Laos, then approaching the DRV border (III, 266–7). As to the Chinese menace, the United States White Paper of February 1965 was able to report the discovery of three 75-millimetre recoilless rifles of Chinese Communist origin (more is claimed in internal documents – cf. III, 502). The only Chinese directly engaged in Indochina, so far as is known, were the 'few Chinese nationalists' involved in covert operations in North Vietnam (III, 500), and those reportedly engaged in clandestine operations under CIA direction in South Vietnam and Laos.[209]

The Pentagon historian observes that Chinese Communist activity in South-east Asia appeared 'ominous' to Washington in late 1964 (III, 267), but he is able to cite as factual basis only 'Sukarno's abrupt withdrawal of Indonesia's participation in the UN,' which led to various speculations. We have already noted the determined efforts, always unavailing, to demonstrate the link to 'international communism' in earlier years, and the significance of this quest see above, pp. 66–70). See also Lyndon Johnson's ludicrous account of the pattern of Communist aggression in Asia in 1964–5 (*Vantage Point*, pp. 134–6).

As to the matter of the assumed North Vietnamese control over the NLF, it is relevant that the Commander-in-Chief, Pacific (CINCPAC), also believed that Hanoi furnished 'support and direction' to the 'insurgency in Thailand' (IV, 124), exactly as claimed with regard to the NLF. When pressed, however, United States officials are unable to present evidence that the Thai insurgency was directed by or received more than minimal support from China or North Vietnam, even long after the use of Thailand as the 'focal point' for United States covert and direct military operations (including the air war) throughout Indochina.[210] There have been efforts to demonstrate that the Pathet Lao is hardly more than an agency of the DRV, but they are not very impressive. The United States did attempt to prove North Vietnamese aggression in a White Paper of February 1965. But as Chester Cooper observes, this 'proved to be a dismal disappointment' because 'the actual findings seemed pretty frail.'[211] His statement takes on added interest when we learn that Cooper was in charge of preparing the evidence on infiltration for publication (III, 255, 681).

The Pentagon history refers to intelligence estimates allegedly demonstrating North Vietnamese control over the NLF, but no evidence is actually presented.[212] It is useful to recall that United States intelligence is not the only source of information on Indochina and has not been remarkable for its insights. Others with a more intimate understanding of the affairs of Indochina have consistently been more successful in interpreting, explaining, and predicting events there. Turning to such sources, we find considerable scepticism with regard to the belief that the NLF are well-behaved puppets of North Vietnam. 'Even a summary acquaintance with Vietnamese realities,' two such experts write, 'excludes the possibility that the insurrection in the South is directed or even inspired by the North Vietnamese. If Vietnam is one, still regional differences remain and the members of the resistance are too well-informed to fail to take account of this.'[213]

Surveying such evidence as exists, United States government claims with regard to DRV control of the NLF prior to 1965 are not compelling, though as DRV forces were drawn into the war by American aggression, and as South Vietnamese society crumbled under the massive American attack, the degree of influence and control exercised by Hanoi undoubtedly increased, as had been anticipated by American planners.

It was, in fact, always understood that heightened American intervention might lead to 'DRV ground action in South Vietnam or Laos' in 'retaliation' (III, 616; William Bundy, November 1964). The same assumptions underlie the analysis of the 'fast/full squeeze,' the most aggressive option under consideration in November 1964 (III, 633–4). This analysis considers the possible 'serious Communist responses to increased military pressures' by the United States against the DRV: 'a VC offensive in South Vietnam; DRV or Chicom air attacks in South Vietnam; DRV ground offensives into South Vietnam; and Chicom/DRV offensives into South Vietnam or Laos.' These are identified as the possible forms of Communist 'retaliation' in response to 'a systematic program of military pressures against the north, meshing at some point with negotiation, but with pressure actions to be continued at a fairly rapid pace and without interruption until we achieve our present objective of getting Hanoi completely out of South VN and an independent and secure South VN reestablished.' In the event of a DRV ground offensive into South Vietnam in response to the United States attack on the North, the United States would implement CINCPAC OPLAN 32–64, Phase III, which 'envisages further an early ground attack northward to seize, liberate and occupy North Vietnam.' In the event that Chinese troops join in 'retaliation' against American escalation of the war, then the United States would 'employ massive US naval and air power against Communist China and her satellites [not further identified] at times and places of our choice to force termination of the aggression [sic], including liberation and control of North Vietnam and reunification of Vietnam under a government aligned with the Free World . . . and the curtailment of communist influence in Southeast Asia.'

Consider the reasoning of the American planners. The United States initiated a 'fast/full squeeze' against the DRV. If the DRV 'retaliates' by sending troops to the South (where more than 20,000 American forces are deployed, and American troops have been engaged in combat and combat support against Southern rebels for three years), then the United States will 'liberate and occupy North Vietnam.' If China joins the DRV in responding to the American aggression then the United States will attack Communist China and her 'satellites' at will, 'to force termination of the aggression.' Here we see exposed, with full clarity, the thinking of a gang of international outlaws.

Similar fears are expressed by Ambassador Maxwell Taylor in May 1964. He submitted a United States Mission 'Assessment of DRV/VC Probable Courses of Action During the Next Three Months,' which argued that Hanoi might expand its military action in the South, 'including covert introduction of additional PAVN units on order of several regiments,' a course that offers 'the prospect of achieving major military gains capable of offsetting US–GVN application of air power' (III, 364; on American estimates of PAVN strength in the South at the time, see reference of note 208). An intelligence estimate of July 23, 1965 warned that it was 'almost certain' that 'additional PAVN forces [would be] employed in South Vietnam on a scale sufficient to counter increased US troop strength' (IV, 25). In July 1967, McNamara was informed by Westmoreland in Saigon that 'the enemy' was forced 'to supply manpower from North Vietnam' to compensate for the fact that he 'has . . . been denied recruits in the numbers required from the populated areas along the coast' in the South, as a result of United States military actions (IV, 518; cf. also III, 397, 621: IV, 484 ff.). In short, United States authorities were well aware that their escalation would probably draw the North Vietnamese army into combat in the South. When the expected happened, every hypocrite in Washington would howl in protest, to the accompaniment of much of the press (and with nuances, parts of the 'intellectual community' as well), over the infamy of the North Vietnamese aggressors, launching an unprovoked attack against the peace-loving South Vietnamese people and their staunch American allies. With minor variants, the same record has been replayed in response to events elsewhere in Indochina.

7. POLITICAL FORCE VERSUS MILITARY FORCE

Whatever the facts may be about North Vietnamese influence over the NLF, existing sources of information leave little doubt, that the NLF was the major political and social force within South Vietnam. The sources of its success, as a nationalist and revolutionary movement with constructive programmes and considerable appeal to the overwhelmingly rural population, have been explored at length in valuable studies.[214] There is, furthermore, no question that the successive governments backed by the United States were quite incapable of competing with the indigenous political forces mobilized by the NFL. In Vietnam, as in Laos, this was a constant problem for the United States, another of those ethically neutral dilemmas of counterinsurgency.

In the early years, 'the Viet Minh was the main repository of Vietnamese nationalism and anti-French colonialism' (I, 42; cf. State Department analysis, cited on pp. 27, 47, 50). Acheson noted in March 1950 that the French appear to 'understand that success of [military] operation . . . depends, in the end, on overcoming opposition of indigenous population' (*DOD*, bk 8, p. 301). Recall that these are the same French who are defending Indochina from 'foreign tyranny' – or, as Acheson put it here, who 'are determined to protect IC from further COMMIE encroachments by [political], [economic] as well as [military] measures.'

As noted earlier, it was a similar estimate of Communist political strength that led the United States-imposed regime to reject the elections provision of the Geneva Agreements in 1955–6 (see note 176), and to resort to a campaign of terror and repression to destroy the Viet Minh political structure and other potential opposition groups in the late 1950s, thus precipitating renewed resistance.

By March 1961, intelligence estimated that 'VC controlled most of countryside' (II, 417), despite their limited military force.[215] As in the next few years, it was recognized that 'vast majority of Viet Cong troops are of local origin' and there was 'little evidence of major supplies from outside sources' (II, 72). As to infiltrators, intelligence warned of 'experienced guerilla forces from North Vietnam in guerrilla operations in territory long familiar to them' – that is, South Vietnamese returning to their homes (II, 77; October 1961).

Towards the end of the Diem regime, the analyst concludes that 'only the Viet Cong had any real support and influence on a broad base in the countryside' and that the army was 'the only real alternative source of political power' (II, 204–5). The 'clear and growing lack of legitimacy of GVN' (II, 278, January 1964) is a constant refrain, reiterated as the situation was seen progressively to 'deteriorate' through 1964–5. Offensive action against the North was undertaken partly in the hope that it 'might provide at least a partial antidote against the willingness of country boys to join the VC' (III, 95; analyst, referring to the situation as of March 1965). John McNaughton explained: 'Action against North Vietnam is to some extent a substitute for strengthening the government in South Vietnam. That is, a less active VC (on orders from DRV) can be matched by a less efficient GVN' (III, 599; November 6, 1964). Therefore the terms for settlement (under the favoured option) should be that 'we will stop squeeze on DRV (no promise to withdraw from SVN)' if the DRV not only stops support and direction for the insurgency, but also 'must order the VC and PL to stop their insurgencies' (III, 603). As Ambassador Taylor perceived the situation, even in the unlikely event that an effective government were established in the South, to attain United States goals it would not suffice to 'drive the DRV out of its reinforcing role'; rather, we will not succeed unless we also 'obtain its cooperation in bringing an end to the Viet Cong insurgency.' We must 'persuade or force the DRV to stop its aid to the Viet Cong and to use its directive powers to make the Viet Cong desist' (III, 668–9).[216]

As the United States prepared to extend the war to the North, intelligence concluded that 'the basic elements of Communist strength in South Vietnam remain indigenous' (III, 653; November 24, 1964), though the 'high VC morale' is sustained in part by 'receipt of outside guidance and support.' The question why far greater outside guidance and support fails to sustain GVN morale remains unanswered, even unasked (nor is there an effort to explain why guerilla operations in the North were such a miserable failure). The fact nevertheless was noted, and dominated discussion as the United States prepared to take over the war. The principals (Rusk, McNamara, Wheeler, McCone, McGeorge Bundy, Ball) agreed 'that the struggle would be a long one, even with the DRV out of it,' and, of course, the United States in it (III, 237; November 24). The preceding August, Taylor had reported from Saigon that the Khanh government 'has not succeeded in building any substantial body of active popular support in the countryside' and 'has about a 50–50 chance of lasting out the year' (III, 82). By the end of the month Vietnamese paratroopers with bayonets had to be called out to restore order in Saigon (III, 86). On September 6 Taylor explained that the politicians in Saigon and Hue feel that 'the conflict with the VC belongs to the Americans.' The United States must therefore 'actively assume . . . increased responsibility for the outcome following a time-schedule consistent with our estimate of the limited viability of any South Vietnamese government.' The only alternative would be a political settlement, that is, 'development of a popular front, knowing that this may in due course require the U.S. to leave Vietnam in failure,' with consequences that would be 'disastrous' throughout the third world (II, 336). 'He went on to recommend that escalating pressures on the DRV begin around December 1' – that is, a decent interval after the peace candidate had been re-elected.

By the beginning of the next year, the situation was desperate. William Bundy wrote on January 6 that 'the situation in Vietnam is now likely to come apart more rapidly than we had anticipated in November . . . the most likely form of coming apart would be a government of key groups starting to negotiate covertly with the Liberation Front or Hanoi,' sooner or later asking us to leave (III, 685). The problem, as the analyst explains, was that 'there was no sense of dedication to the GVN comparable to that instilled in the VC' (III, 94). Bundy felt that actions against North Vietnam 'would have some faint hope of really improving the Vietnamese situation, and, above all, would put us in a much stronger position to hold the next line of defense, namely Thailand.' Therefore we should not accept the present situation, 'or any negotiation on the basis of it,' but should move 'into stronger actions.' In early 1965 'the GVN was seen to be well on its way to complete collapse. The most optimistic estimate was that the VC would take over within a year' (III, 390; analyst).

Given its indigenous political strength and the lack of legitimacy of the GVN, the NLF was able to pursue the strategy of gaining a political settlement, that is, one that would reflect indigenous political forces. Or, as Ambassador Taylor expressed the same thought on August 10, 1964: 'The communist strategy as defined by North Vietnam and the puppet National Liberation Front is to seek a political settlement favorable to the communists . . . passing first through "neutralism," using the National Liberation Front machinery, and then the technique of a coalition government' (III, 531). Intelligence reports, shortly after, 'estimated that it was the Communist intention to seek victory through a "neutralist coalition" rather than by force of arms' (III, 207). McNaughton warned in mid-October that the United States must 'watch for Saigon and Vientiane hanky panky with Reds' (III, 582) – that is, moves towards a political settlement. But a political settlement could no more be considered by the United States than by the French, since it would mean a victory for the Communist-led nationalist movement, so it was always assumed. The president had clearly excluded any peaceful settlement when he explained to Ambassador Lodge that his mission was 'knocking down the idea of neutralization wherever it rears its ugly head' (III, 511; March 20, 1964). Neutralism, as Ambassador Taylor noted, 'appeared to mean throwing the internal political situation open and thus inviting Communist participation' (W. Bundy, memorandum of meeting of November 27, 1964; III, 675). According to the analyst's report of this meeting, George Ball 'observed that a neutralist state could not be maintained unless the VC were defeated and that the GVN must continue to be free to receive external aid until that occurred' (III, 242) – an interesting concept of 'neutralism,' expressed by the administration's official dove. It is possible that 'Saigon hanky panky with Reds' was a factor in the removal of Diem (see note 223). There can be little doubt that the administration was aware of the publicly announced position of the National Liberation Front in 1962 calling for neutrality of South Vietnam, Laos, and Cambodia.[217] But neutrality and moves towards peaceful settlement were obviously incompatible with the long-term objectives of the United States, as clearly outlined in 1948 and never significantly modified.

The analyst regards it as 'ironic' that the NSC working groups 'considerations of a negotiated settlement did not include the problems of a political settlement in the South' (III, 225). This might appear ironic to someone who takes seriously government propaganda about the American role in world affairs and the commitment to the rule of law and international peace. To a more realistic observer, this is nothing ironic in the oversight. The political weakness of the American-imposed regimes as compared with their indigenous rivals ruled out a political settlement or the reliance on pacific means as prescribed by law. This is no more ironic than the Russian unwillingness to permit free elections in Czechoslovakia. The United States 'had few bargaining points,' the analyst notes, and 'it was primarily to fill this lack that many group members and Administration officials favored initiation of direct military pressures against North Vietnam.' Quite true. The impending NLF victory in the South compelled the United States to move to a wider confrontation, in the hope that somehow North Vietnam would use its alleged 'directive powers' to 'make the Viet Cong desist.' Furthermore, within this wider confrontation the imperial aggressor could undertake a far more effective war against South Vietnam, with massive aerial and artillery bombardment and a direct invasion by American ground troops to destroy the indigenous NLF and, as proved necessary, the rural society in which it was based. All of this, of course, to protect the free people of South Vietnam from the 'aggression from the North' that had for several years been a major theme of government propaganda and most of the mass media. Use of such terms as 'ironic' in describing these developments reveals a complete incapacity to comprehend American policy, not only in Vietnam.

We have already noted a certain similarity between the situation of May 1972 and that of late 1964 (see note 217). Furthermore, the United States administration still rejects the concept of a political settlement among Vietnamese, in the South or in Vietnam as a whole (cf. references of note 61). The reasons are those of 1964, of 1962, of 1954, and of 1948. Furthermore, as in 1964–5, the administration in the spring of 1972 moved to a still more devastating attack on Vietnam within the context of the broader international confrontation it constructed. Only the internal collapse of the American-imposed regime in the South, or some form of domestic or international pressure that does not at the moment seem very likely, will bring about a modification of policies that have not substantially changed, apart from scale, in twenty-five years.

From other sources, we know that the general opinion in Washington and in the United States Mission in Saigon regarding the political viability of the American-backed regimes was about the same as that revealed in the Pentagon Papers. Chester Cooper, who was close to the centre of planning for many years, speaks of 'the hope [in 1965] that a South Vietnamese government could be organized that would eventually be able to compete politically with the National Liberation Front.'[218] American spokesmen in Saigon outlined the problem of utilizing our vast military power, with its weak political base, to defeat an enemy with enormous political force but only modest military power.[219] In almost the same words, captured documents speak of the 'absolute superiority over the enemy in the political field,' in contrast to the military superiority of the US–GVN.[220] Western scholars have generally come to the same conclusion. Few would disagree with John McAlister's explanation as to why the pro-Western, urban-oriented (and to be fully honest, Western-imposed) governments have had 'no choice but to rely on military force' – foreign military force at that: 'Without a means of transforming control over territory into popular political loyalties, these governments have simply not been able to compete on the same plane with their Communist adversaries,' who were 'successful in mobilizing political power' primarily because of 'the relevancy of their values to the lives villagers must lead.'[221] Hence the inescapable necessity for the United States to demolish the rural society.

In the same vein, Mieczyslaw Maneli reports a discussion in 1964 with an anticommunist Vietnamese intellectual who chose to support the NLF, regarding its victory as 'inevitable,' since the Communists 'were the only ones to fight for national liberation and meaningful social reforms' and the only possible alternative is 'the corrupt regime kept in power by the Americans.'[222] A highly placed member of the Lao ruling elite spoke to me in almost exactly the same terms in April 1970 in Vientiane.

To complement the extensive documentation revealing United States opposition to neutralism and a political settlement in the South, we must again turn to sources beyond the Pentagon study, sources which take cognizance of the position of the NLF and the DRV. The official position of the NLF since 1962, with constant DRV backing, has been that South Vietnam, 'independent and sovereign,' should be nonsocialist and should constitute a neutral zone together with Laos and Cambodia. Reunification of Vietnam is to be a gradual evolutionary process (see note 47). George Chaffard presents considerable evidence that the NLF and DRV hoped that the 1962 Geneva Agreements on Laos would serve as a model for South Vietnam as well, with a tripartite government (as in Laos) in which the NLF would constitute one element. The United States rejected any such idea – not surprisingly, given its estimate of the relative strength of political forces in the South (see note 218). For the United States, the Laos settlement was intended to 'permit the isolation of the Vietcong infection so that it could be better treated.'[223] Chaffard concludes, quite plausibly, that by adopting this attitude the United States and its British ally destroyed any possibility for the success of the 'Laotian experiment,' while of course never even considering the possibility of neutrality and political settlement in South Vietnam.[224]

In later years, the problem faced by the United States remained basically unchanged. By January 1966, McNaughton reported that 'the GVN political infrastructure is moribund and weaker than the VC infrastrcture among most of the rural population' (IV, 47); or in simpler words, the NLF is the dominant political force in the rural society of Vietnam. A few months earlier, McNamara reported Prime Minister Ky's estimate that 'his government controls only 25% of the population' (IV, 622). In April 1966, McNaughton noted a report from Saigon that 'we control next to no territory' and 'people would not vote for "our side"' (IV, 84). After Tet, 1968, General Wheeler reported that 'to a large extent the VC now control the countryside,' the situation being particularly bad in the delta (IV, 548);[225] and Systems Analysis concluded that 'our control of the countryside and the defense of the urban areas is now essentially at pre-August 1965 levels' (IV, 558). And so on.

But these matters were of no concern, apart from the technical difficulties they created. To the imperial mentality, it is perfectly comprehensible that the best-organized political forces in some country are engaged in 'internal aggression' against the incumbent government installed and maintained in power by the imperial master who is responsible for the welfare of the misguided and backward population. The assumption is not only expressed constantly by planners, advisers and administrators, and political leaders, but is even implicit in the judgments of the 'intelligence community.' For example, an intelligence estimate of October 1955 could, with a straight face, speak of Diem's progress 'toward establishing the first fully independent Vietnamese government' (I, 297) – namely, the government accurately described by the analyst as 'essentially the creation of the United States' (II, 22). Naturally, intelligence discounted the DRV, a mere agency of Communist colonialism.

It is interesting that the PRG position today, with DRV backing, is hardly different from that of ten years ago. Correspondingly, the United States continues to reject any thought of a coalition government in the South incorporating the PRG, and insists rather on a 'cease-fire,' that is, a surrender by the indigenous revolutionary forces to the massive military and police structure established by the United States, which will continue to maintain 'law and order' by the 'GVN *Phung Hoang* program' (see above, subsection 3) and other similar devices, under the terms of a cease-fire. The American position is based on the reasonable grounds that if the American-backed army and police apparatus are neutralized, there will be no organized force to oppose the Communists; the generals are still 'all we have got,' as Ambassador Lodge pointed out in January 1964.

The United States proposal is what Henry Kissinger calls 'leav[ing] the determination of the political future to the Vietnamese' (press conference, May 9, 1972). Perhaps, like their predecessors, administration officials will announce their willingness to accept a Communist victory in elections, so long as these elections take place within the legal and constitutional framework described earlier (cf. above, subsection 5.2), and with the country in the firm grip of the apparatus of terror and repression installed by the United States. If, on the other hand, this apparatus is neutralized and a coalition regime of South Vietnamese political groupings is established, the Communists are likely to emerge as the dominant political force within South Vietnam, contrary to long-term United States objectives.

'That is the only issue on which negotiations have broken down,' Kissinger explains. 'That is what we call the imposition, under the thinnest veneer, of a Communist government.' The demand for a tripartite coalition government including the PRG is what the president (May 8) calls the Communist 'ultimatum . . . that the United States impose a Communist regime on 17 million people who do not want a Communist government' – a statement worthy of a man who can announce that 'the United States has exercised a degree of restraint unprecedented in the annals of war.'

As in the past, the conflict in South Vietnam pits a foreign-created military force against an indigenous political force, now weakened (perhaps, as American spokesmen claim, decimated) by the 'semi-genocidal counterinsurgent strategy' that is responsible for such 'successes' as the United States has achieved in its war in South Vietnam,[226] and now backed by the armed forces of the DRV that were introduced in response to the American aggression in the South and the bombing of North Vietnam.

When Kissinger speaks of 'the constant delusion that there is just one formula that has somehow eluded us,' he is perhaps being somewhat disingenuous. Averell Harriman is surely correct in stating: 'While negotiations have been going on, this Administration has never accepted the concept of a neutral non-aligned south nor has it given up its futile attempt to maintain a pro-American government in Saigon.[227] In fact, the formula of a political settlement among South Vietnamese continues to 'somehow elude' Henry Kissinger because of the unresolved dilemma of 1948 (see above, pp. 49–50). An accommodation based on existing political forces, whether in South Vietnam, in Vietnam as a whole, or throughout Indochina, is inconsistent with the long-term United States objective of maintaining Western dominance. Therefore the people of Indochina must continue to massacre one another under a hail of American bombs.

Perhaps a word should be added on the interpretation of this record by numerous American commentators, John Roche criticizes the Pentagon study for a 'serious gap':

> There is no examination of the 'neutralization' option, which flourished in the aftermath of the 1962 Geneva Agreement on Laos. In retrospect, the notion of the neutralization of all Indochina under great power auspices was doubtless a fantasy – Hanoi simply would not cooperate. But at the time a number of serious men, both inside and outside the government, took the possibility seriously.[228]

He suggests, as a general corrective to the Pentagon study, that the 'conscientious analyst' must turn to 'existing commentaries on our Vietnam policy, particularly Lyndon B. Johnson's *The Vantage Point*, with its careful documentation of what occurred in the president's inner circle.'

The conscientious analyst will find little of significance in Johnson's self-serving account, with its many examples of distortion and misrepresentation, but he will find a few remarks on the neutralization option.[229] Johnson quotes McNamara's 'gloomy' appraisal of December 1963: 'Current trends, unless reversed in the next two or three months, will lead to neutralization at best and more likely to a Communist-controlled state.' Johnson confirms that '"neutralization" of Vietnam was in many people's minds at the time, and it had a particular meaning.' Namely, it meant the proposal of de Gaulle 'that North and South Vietnam be unified and neutralized, and that all foreign forces be withdrawn.'[230] But, Johnson continues, 'Most thinking people, I believe, recognized that the De Gaulle formula for "neutralization" would have meant the swift communization of all Vietnam, and probably of Laos and Cambodia as well.' He then cites approvingly President Kennedy's sharp response to the de Gaulle proposal, which Kennedy interpreted as the demand that 'we all just go home and leave the world to those who are our enemies' – unthinkable, of course. The Kennedy–Johnson view clearly implies that we must, if we can, conquer and reorient any part of the world where indigenous forces pursue a path inimical to 'our interests.' It was with this 'particular meaning' of 'neutralization' in mind that Johnson explained to Ambassador Lodge his mission and that the backroom boys expressed their fears about neutralism and political settlement, as outlined above.

In the light of the existing record, it is astonishing that a political scientist can write that 'serious men' in Washington 'took the possibility [of neutralization] seriously,' but that the option was 'a fantasy' because 'Hanoi simply would not cooperate.' As we have seen, the option was indeed a fantasy, but not quite for this reason.

American observers on the scene have hardly been more accurate. To cite one case, not untypical, Robert Shaplen writes that the present (June 1972) outlook in South Vietnam is not 'altogether bleak – that is, perhaps the North Vietnamese will settle for half a loaf, including some territorial adjustments, resumed trade and other relations with the South, and an emerging political process that might keep the rest of South Vietnam from going Communist in the immediate future.'[231] In short, perhaps the North Vietnamese will settle for considerably more than they have ever demanded ('territorial adjustments' have never been mentioned). As for the NLF–PRG–DRV positions from 1962, it is as if they do not exist. It is the same cheery dismissal of fact that permits the American press, in case after case, to speculate that 'Hanoi, scenting military failure, might resume negotiations in a few weeks,'[232] while the news columns report that Hanoi continues to press for reconvening of the Paris talks, while the United States continues to refuse.

Reviewing the ample documentary record on the topics surveyed here, and contrasting it with journalistic and 'scholarly' commentary, one has the impression of living in a madhouse.

8. WE MUST BUILD A NATION

When the United States took over from the French, a National Intelligence estimate noted perceptively that 'the energy and resourcefulness necessary' for 'building national states' in the noncommunist areas of Indochina 'will not arise spontaneously among the non-Communist Indochinese but will have to be sponsored and nurtured from without' (*DOD*, bk 10, p. 695). On May 1, 1967, the director of Systems Analysis in the Pentagon pointed out: 'We are facing the strongest political current in the world today: nationalism.' Hence, 'we must match the nationalism we see in the North with an equally strong and patient one in the South'; we must 'build a nation in South Vietnam' (IV, 463). Typically, he overlooked the nationalist forces in the South that the United States was then attempting to crush. To recognize the true character of the American war in South Vietnam was, as always, beyond the capacity of the commentator.

We must build a nation in the South, to counter the Communist Vietnamese, who seem to be alone in their ability to mobilize the people of Vietnam, North or South, in pursuit of nationalist and revolutionary goals. *We* must 'establish an adequate government in SVN' (Maxwell Taylor; III, 668). *We* must undertake activities to 'add to GVN's strength and image of concern for all its citizens.'[233] 'I think we're up against an enemy who just may have found a dangerously clever strategy for licking the United States,' the director of Systems Analysis warns. 'Unless we recognize and counter it now, that strategy may become all too popular in the future' (IV, 466). The strategy was to wage a war of national liberation based on the aspirations of the Vietnamese for independence and social justice.

Somehow, the outside power was never able to compete. The United States could kill and maim, drive peasants from their homes, destroy the countryside and organized social life, but could not build a nation in the approved image. Apparently, only the Vietnamese can govern Vietnam. The United States had taken on a society and a culture that was simply not fit for imperial domination. Therefore, it had to be destroyed. This was worse than a crime; it was a blunder, as the realistic experts soberly explain.

People who are personally acquainted with the individuals whose deliberations are reported in the Pentagon study describe them as humane, liberal, gifted, and sometimes even sincere opponents of the war. Knowing none of them personally, I have no comment on this judgment. Assuming it to be accurate, the Pentagon study serves as a dramatic record of the impact, on anyone, of participation in an odious venture. Decent young men were made into vicious murderers by the circumstances of Vietnam, and many of them have spoken of the process and its consequences with courage and sensitivity.[234] There has been nothing similar from the backroom boys, whose responsibility was incomparably greater and who were, of course, in a far better position to think about what they were doing than a soldier in a village where any ten-year-old child might try to kill him.

Congressman Robert Drinan, on a tour of Vietnam, was told by a Vietnamese lawyer:

> ... long after you have left we will conduct our own Nuremberg trials. You will brush these trials off as Communist or

Asian propaganda,[235] but you shoud remember that by one-half of the population the Americans will be thought of as barbarians.[236]

It will be unfortunate for American society if we must await the judgment of the victims.

VII. FINAL COMMENT

To my mind, one of the more depressing paragraphs of the Pentagon study is in the epilogue, where the analyst comments on the change of tactics after the Tet offensive in early 1968 (IV, 603). He reports that 'large and growing elements of the American public had begun to believe the cost [of the war] had already reached unacceptable levels and would strongly protest a large increase in that cost.' If the analyst is correct, then the public is at one with the executive in its almost exclusive concern with the costs to us of continued aggression. I doubt the accuracy of this assessment, but it seems that the Nixon administration is counting on it, and is hoping that a less costly technological war, with automated fire-control systems and mercenaries in place of GIs, with helicopter gunships and smart bombs in place of Westmoreland's 'meatgrinder,' may still succeed in destroying the infrastructure of the enemy and guaranteeing to the people of Indochina that particular variety of independence that United States global strategy will tolerate. If the analyst is correct in his assessment, the revelations of the Pentagon Papers will have little impact on public attitudes towards Vietnam, or on the global policy of which Vietnam was a particularly disastrous episode. If he is correct, then the McNamara study might just as well gather dust in the vaults of the Pentagon.

TWO

Endgame: The Tactics of Peace in Vietnam

The Paris Agreements signed on January 27, 1973, are entitled 'Agreement on Ending the War and Restoring Peace in Vietnam.' Whether this will prove an apt designation remains to be seen. The historical precedents are not encouraging. Nor is the White House response to the settlement.

There are two very different versions of the Agreements signed in Paris. The first is the text itself. The second is the commentary on the Agreements presented by spokesmen for the United States government. The text itself is very close to the position of the 'enemy' for more than a decade. Washington's version, which differs in fundamental respects, reflects the long-standing position of the United States government. We may ask whether the United States government version is merely rhetoric for home consumption or whether it is the framework for policy. It is probable that Nixon and Kissinger themselves do not know the answer to this question. They will feel their way, determining just how far they can go on the basis of the domestic and international response. One factor of no small importance will be the manner in which the United States intervention of the past twenty-five years is perceived within the mainstream of opinion in the United States and in the countries that generally support United States international policies.

The Paris Agreements state: 'Foreign countries shall not impose any political tendency or personality on the South Vietnamese people' (Chapter IV, Article 9C). The official White House 'summary of basic elements of the Vietnam agreement' states: 'The government of the Republic of (South) Vietnam continues in existence, recognized by the United States, its constitutional structure and leadership intact and unchanged.' This government (GVN) has the right to 'unlimited economic aid' and 'unlimited military replacement aid.' The latter will maintain in existence one of the more powerful military forces in the world (in terms of equipment at least) and a vast police apparatus. Furthermore, as Kissinger remarked in his press conference of January 24 outlining the Agreements, the United States maintains the right to provide 'civilian technicians serving in certain of the military branches.' He did not add that the United States will continue to train pilots and other personnel in the United States and elsewhere, but this will undoubtedly be the case.

Kissinger further explained that the United States has adhered to its principle of refusing to 'impose a coalition government or a disguised coalition government on the people of South Vietnam.' The Paris Agreements, however, are broader. They require as well that the United States refrain from imposing on the people of South Vietnam a right-wing autocracy based on the military and a narrow urban elite and consisting largely of former collaborators with French imperialism – namely, the Saigon regime. No serious observer can doubt that 'South Vietnam . . . was essentially the creation of the United States,' in the wording of the Pentagon Papers,[1] or that this regime has been maintained in existence through United States force. To take one crucial moment of recent history, it is generally conceded that the US-imposed regime was on the verge of succumbing to a South Vietnamese revolutionary movement by late 1964, despite massive United States aid and direct military participation in combat and combat support for at least three years. General Thieu, for one, understands the present situation quite well. He observed, in a recent interview, that 'The French abandoned us in 1954, and because of that, half of Vietnam fell to the Communists. If the United States does the same thing now, the other half of Vietnam will go.'[2] In 1954 the French abandoned the quisling regime it had established, and half of Vietnam fell to what the United States government had ruefully conceded, years before, was the nationalist movement of Vietnam. General Thieu and his colleagues, most of whom fought with the French against the nationalist movement of Vietnam, quite naturally fear that their future is dim if they are abandoned by the imperial power that replaced France in 1954.

Washington, however, has now served notice that it intends to continue to impose the 'political tendency' and 'leading personalities' of the GVN on the people of South Vietnam. Given the historical circumstances and the context of the Agreements, it is evident that for the United States to 'impose' the rule of the GVN can mean nothing other than to recognize, supply, and directly support this regime, instituted and maintained in power by the United States military might, as the sole legitimate government of (South) Vietnam. If words have any meaning, the military and police forces of the United-States-imposed regime are quasi-mercenary forces, assembled, trained, supplied and paid by the United States. These forces could not have existed in the past, nor could they now, without United States direction and massive support, just as the Saigon regime itself has always been entirely dependent on the imperial power that created it and kept it alive.

Kissinger once explained 'what we call the imposition, under the thinnest veneer, of a Communist government' (May 9, 1972). This he equated with acceptance of the Communist proposal that the United States permit the formation of a government excluding Thieu which would disband the 'machinery of oppression,' free political prisoners, renounce United States aid, and negotiate with the PRG. If such measures constitute 'imposition of a Communist government,' as Kissinger argues, then surely support for the GVN as the sole legitimate government under the conditions just outlined constitutes 'imposing a political tendency or personality' on the South Vietnamese people.

The central issue of the war since the early 1960s has been the question of sovereignty in the South. The United States government is announcing that, in violation of the Agreements it has just signed, it will continue to impose the regime it created on the people of the South. In obvious defiance of fact, Thieu asserts that the Paris Agreements identify his government as the 'one legal government' in the South.[3] Washington agrees.

The announced intentions of the United States government become still more significant as we look further into what is implied by recognition of the GVN, 'its constitutional structure and leadership intact and unchanged.' Consider first its constitutional structure. Article I of the GVN Constitution, which is unamendable, states that 'Viet-Nam is a territorially indivisible, unified and independent republic'; the GVN 'represent[s] the people of Viet-Nam,' North and South. This might be dismissed as bluster, but not so Article V, which proclaims: 'The Republic of Viet-Nam opposes communism in every form. Every activity designed to propagandize or carry out communism is prohibited.'[4] This Article provides the 'legal basis' for the Phoenix program and for the various laws of the past years that outlaw not only communism but also 'pro-communist neutralism', for example, 'All plots and actions under the false name of peace and neutrality according to a Communist policy . . .' including 'diffusion, circulation, distribution, sale, display . . .' in any form of material 'aimed at spreading Communist policies, slogans and instructions,' and so on. Nixon and Kissinger must be aware of this when they announce that they will continue to recognize and support the GVN, under its existing constitutional structure, as 'the sole legitimate government of South Vietnam,' in Nixon's phrase.[5]

Consider now the leadership which remains 'intact and unchanged,' with full United States backing. Its intentions are no secret. 'According to the semi-official newspaper *Tin Song*, South Vietnamese President Thieu has issued shoot-to-kill orders to his troops and police that would take effect with the announcement of a cease-fire. The report said the orders cover Communist demonstrators, rioters, and sympathizers; deserters; anyone who raises the Viet Cong flag or takes part in Communist propaganda campaigns.'[6] Thieu has 'reminded the commanders' that 'police and armed forces are authorized to shoot on the spot people who incite riots and "applaud the communists,"' to 'arrest summarily anyone who distributed Communist propaganda' or who 'urged others to move to Communist-controlled areas.' Furthermore, 'anybody engaging in political activities as "neutralist or pro-Communists" or issuing currency to the Communists [sic] are subject to arrest.' These tactics, according to *Tin Song*, 'will remain in effect in Government-controlled areas after a cease-fire goes into effect,' under 'the authorities and powers granted by the Constitution and laws' of the GVN.[7] 'Saigon troops and police have been ordered to restrain the refugees – forcibly if necessary' if they attempt 'to return to their homes after a cease-fire is declared.' According to articles planted by the GVN in the press, 'half a dozen actions considered "pro-Communist" are also punishable by death.'[8] 'Saigon radio said troops and police had orders to shoot on sight anyone tearing down flags and banners or creating disturbances for the Communists.'[9]

Shortly after the peace scare of late October, government-backed groups in Danang began distributing leaflets which 'called on South Vietnamese to "exterminate the Communists"' before, during and after a cease-fire.'[10] General Thieu made it plain that in his view there can be no peace until all Communists are killed. According to United States officials, the Thieu regime has 'drawn up long lists of opposition political figures who would be arrested when an accord is signed.'[11] Thieu's closest adviser, Hoang Duc Nha, stated in an interview that with Thieu in power, communists 'are afraid of an Indonesian-style coup even in a coalition. They are afraid we would cut their throats.'[12] Nha is referring to the massacre of hundreds of thousands after the military takeover in the fall of 1965. The Thieu regime proudly boasts that the CIA-directed Phoenix programme has been assassinating civilians at the rate of better than 1000 a month.[13] After an abortive anti-Sihanouk coup in 1959, the Saigon government diplomatic representative in Phnom Penh told British reporter Michael Field: 'You must understand that we in Saigon are desperate men. We are a government of desperadoes.'[14] It is all the more true today. It is not unreasonable to suppose that the United States-imposed regime means exactly what it says.

The Paris Agreements state that the 'two South Vietnamese parties,' namely, the GVN and the PRG, will 'Achieve national reconciliation and concord, end hatred and enmity, prohibit all acts of reprisal and discrimination . . .' and will insure 'democratic liberties' including freedom of speech, press, meeting, organization, political activities, movement and residence, and so on (Chapter IV, Article 11). Article 2 of the Protocols on the Cease-Fire states that 'All regular and irregular armed forces and the armed police of the parties in South Vietnam shall observe the prohibition of the following acts: . . . Armed attacks against any person, either military or civilian, by any means whatsoever . . . [and] All acts endangering lives or public or private property.'

In short, the United States supports as the sole legitimate government a regime which has been informing the world that it has not the slightest intention of observing the Agreements it has just signed. Its constitutional structure, which remains intact with full United States backing, is inconsistent with fundamental provisions of the Agreements and serves as the 'legal basis' for subverting them. The announced intentions of this regime also clearly reveal its own analysis of the degree of its popular support.

Though direct reports from South Vietnam are scanty, the pattern that is evolving appears to be about as one would expect, given the statements of the various parties. One correspondent explains 'the reasons that the ceasefire has not worked well' primarily in these terms:

> The PRG planned to move into surrounding areas from its base camps and spread propaganda, put up PRG flags and otherwise seek to demonstrate that large areas were actually under communist control. Saigon usually responds with military action, sending in artillery or air strikes and soldiers to re-establish or re-assert South Vietnamese Government control.[15]

Of course, the PRG actions are legal under the Agreements, while the response violates their provisions in the most flagrant manner. The Saigon government claims to have taken 400 villages, more than 10 per cent of the total number of villages in Vietnam, in the first six weeks following the cease-fire.[16] In a few cases, Western correspondents have been present. Daniel Southerland reported from Long Khanh Province that a few days after the cease-fire, 'government forces did not hesitate to use the heaviest weapons at their disposal, including bombs, artillery shells, and helicopter rockets' in retaking 12 hamlets that Communist troops had 'penetrated'; 'the brutal manner in which the government forces blasted their way back into the hamlets has hardly won friends.'[17] A Western cameraman who spent twenty-five hours in a 'Vietcong-controlled zone' reported that 'a South Vietnamese helicopter gunship sprayed a village in a raid lasting more than half an hour' and that villagers predicted, to within five minutes, the onset of the regular evening artillery bombardment.[18] A few weeks later, Southerland reported from Trung Lap village that the government was forcibly preventing people from returning to the hamlets from which they had been driven by United States Army forces several years before, burning down houses in their old hamlets and confiscating identification papers in an effort to discourage resettlement and 'as a means of keeping a hold on villagers.' In the way of further 'discouragement,' those who nevertheless return are 'constantly being harassed by government artillery fire.' 'Each day they picked up shell casings and fragments from the napalm cannisters and helicopter rockets which continue to shatter the countryside here.' Villagers complained that 'The soldiers beat us up if we go to our fields.' Police and army officers stated that they knew nothing of the Peace Agreements and had orders not to let villagers 'go over to the other side.' 'When people ask us about the peace agreement, we tell them that this is nothing more than a cease-fire in place, and the people are supposed to stay in place.'[19] According to an AP report the same day, 'big guns fire into the [Batangan] peninsula as they have again and again over the eight years that American, South Korean and South Vietnamese forces have been trying to make it safe [sic].' This region was a free-fire zone for five years, and the scene of numerous United States-Korean atrocities, including My Lai, which 'is still not safe for the living.'[20]

'Significantly,' Stanley Karnow reports from Saigon, 'the North Vietnamese have distributed millions of copies of the Paris agreement, and have broadcast its contents in detail. Only a few Saigon newspapers have been authorized to publish excerpts from the document.'[21] The most significant feature of the immediate post-ceasefire period is that the GVN is living up to its word, systematically calling upon its military and police forces to violate the agreements, employing the ample means of violence provided for it by the United States.

All of this recalls the behaviour of the Diem regime in the mid-1950s. The 1954 Geneva Accords, which Diem publicly renounced by January 1955, guaranteed democratic liberties and prohibited reprisals or discrimination (Article 14c). Diem instituted 'pacification' programmes which the correspondent for the London *Times* and *Economist*, David Hotham, described in these terms: 'They consist of killing, or arresting without either evidence or trial, large numbers of persons suspected of being Viet-Minh or "rebels".'[22] The Diem army conducted 'massive expeditions' to peaceful Communist regions, arresting tens of thousands and killing 'hundreds, perhaps thousands of peasants,' destroying 'whole villages . . . by artillery' in operations that were 'kept secret from the American public.'[23] Diem's forces were trained, equipped and advised by the United States. His secret police 'was largely the brainchild of a highly respected, senior United States Foreign Service professional.' General Lansdale reported secretly in 1961, adding: 'I cannot truly sympathize with Americans who help promote a fascistic state and then get angry when it doesn't act like a democracy.'[24] These methods were temporarily successful in crushing the Viet Minh and others in the South, in direct and immediate violation of the Geneva Accords, although as the United States Military Assistance Advisory Group (USMAAG) warned in July 1957, 'the Viet Cong guerrillas and propagandists, however, are still waging a grim battle for survival' and still attempting to form groups 'seeking to spread the theory of "Peace and Co-existence",'[25] along with other similar crimes against the state.

As in the 1950s, the United States commitment to the Thieu regime signifies an intention to violate the central provisions of the Agreements that had just been signed. It is easy to conjure up some unpleasant 'scenarios.' Suppose that refugees attempt to return to their homes or that PRG supporters or neutralists of the wrong type try to make use of the freedoms theoretically granted them by the Agreements; the GVN proceeds with its announced intention of preventing this by force, shooting to kill if necessary;

there is resistance to government terror; Nixon appears on TV to announce that the United States will not tolerate such communist violence and lawlessness – the bombers are now on their way; the liberal press denounces both the 'communist atrocities' and the 'retaliatory bombing.' Whether or not something of the sort takes place, it is clear that Nixon and Kissinger have laid the basis for it in their response to the Paris Agreements.

In past years, when American bombing was temporarily halted in some area of Indochina, the planes were simply directed to other areas. Thus the bombing of Laos and South Vietnam was intensified with each restriction of bombing in North Vietnam in 1968. These were not 'bombing halts,' but 'bombing redistributions.' The January 1973 cease-fire is, so far, no exception. United States bombing of Indochina in February was 70,000 tons, close to the average for the war since 1966. Excluded from this total is the unknown tonnage of bombs dropped by the air force of the Saigon regime.

Virtually the sole 'progress' achieved by Kissinger between October and January was that the 'question of the return of Vietnamese civilian personnel captured and detained in South Vietnam' is left unresolved in the Agreements, whereas the 9-point plan of October indicated that they were to be released (Point 3). The Protocol on prisoners now states that 'All Vietnamese civilian personnel captured and detained in South Vietnam shall be treated humanely at all times, and in accordance with international practice. They shall be protected against all violence to life and person . . .' There have been numerous reports of torture and murder in the prisons.[26] On December 29, 1972, two Frenchmen who had been imprisoned in Saigon for over two years were released. They report beatings, torture and assassinations, with names and dates, adding that 'all of this is under the control of American advisers who, we are convinced, are aware of everything that happens in the Vietnamese prisons.'[27] They also report that a few days before their release, 'there were massive deportations to the Poulo Condor prison camp,' the scene of numerous reported atrocities in the past. They speculate that their sudden release may have been motivated by concern that they might witness what they expect will now take place: 'a liquidation operation which might begin in the prisons.' Amnesty International has since cited 'evidence that selective elimination of opposition members had begun' in the prisons, and reports that '267 political prisoners were sent from Chi Hoa national prison in

Saigon to the notorious prison on Con Son Island, home of the 'tiger cage' detention cells,' adding that '300 prisoners travelling on a boat from Con Son to the mainland are reported to have been killed.'[28] That United States officials are well aware of what goes on in the prisons that are maintained with United States aid is hardly in doubt. The Chief of the Public Safety Division in Saigon, Frank E. Walton, who publicly described Con Son as 'like a Boy Scout Recreational Camp,' signed a report on October 1, 1963 which stated that:

> In Con Son II, some of the hardcore communists keep preaching the 'party' line, so these 'Reds' are sent to the Tiger Cages in Con Son I where they are isolated from all others for months at a time. This confinement may also include rice without salt and water – the United States prisons' equivalent of bread and water. It may include immobilization – the prisoner is bolted to the floor, handcuffed to a bar or rod, or legirons with the chain through an eyebolt, or around a bar or rod.[29]

A significant element of United States 'aid' to the people of South Vietnam.

In his press conference of January 24, Kissinger attempted to show that the United States government had achieved its long-term objectives. His reasoning deserves careful attention. He distinguished the following issues: 'one, is there such a thing as a South Vietnam even temporarily until unification; secondly, who is the legitimate ruler of South Vietnam? This is what the civil war has been all about. Thirdly, what is the demarcation line that separates North Vietnam from South Vietnam.'[30] Noting that the January Agreements have 'specific references to the sovereignty of South Vietnam' and 'the right of the South Vietnamese people to self-determination,' Kissinger alleged that 'we have achieved substantial changes from the October 9-Point plan announced by Radio Hanoi.' This justifies the United States refusal to sign in October – and, by implication, United States military tactics since.

All of this is blatant deception. The October 9-Point plan explicitly provided for 'the South Vietnamese people's right to self-determination' and stated that 'the South Vietnamese people shall decide themselves the political future of South Vietnam' through free elections (Point 4). The January Agreement introduces no changes, substantial or otherwise, in this regard. Furthermore, the two plans are identical with respect to eventual reunification, 'carried out step by step through peaceful means' (Point 5, October; Chapter V, Article 15, January). As for the status of the demarcation line, the Paris Agreements of January merely reiterate the wording of the Geneva Accords of 1954, in accordance with consistent public statements of the DRV and PRG.

Kissinger was attempting to confuse the issue of self-determination of South Vietnam (his issue one) with sovereignty within South Vietnam (issue two), bringing in the irrelevant matter of the DMZ (issue three) merely to becloud the matter further. The 'enemy' has consistently taken the position with respect to issues one and three that Kissinger falsely claims that the United States has now succeeded in introducing into the Agreements. The second issue, as Kissinger perceives, is what the war has been 'all about': namely, who is to be sovereign in South Vietnam.

Kissinger is pretending that by recognizing the right of the South Vietnamese people to self-determination without external interference (in accordance with the DRV–PRG position), the Agreements grant the United States the right to recognize the sovereignty of the GVN as the 'sole legitimate government' in the South. The Agreements, however, speak only of the 'two parties' in the South, which are equivalent in status and must reach agreement as to sovereignty within South Vietnam. The 9-Point plan of October names the two parties as the GVN and the PRG, and these are the two Southern parties that signed the four-party version of the January Agreements. When Kissinger speaks of the 'civil war,' he presumably intends his audience to understand 'the war between North and South Vietnam.' Similarly, in his news conference of December 16, 1972, he presented the United States government position as 'that the two parts of Vietnam would live in peace with each other and that neither side would impose its solution on the other by force,' and he claimed that this 'modest requirement' was rejected by the other side.[31] He slips easily from the notion of self-determination for the South Vietnamese people to the entirely different notion of sovereignty of the GVN as their sole legitimate government. He is attempting to give the impression that the 'two parties' that must peacefully resolve their differences are North Vietnam and South Vietnam, whereas the Agreements make it plain that these two parties are the GVN and the PRG. To the extent that there is a 'civil war,' it is between these two parties. Having reached agreement, they are to move towards reunification with the North, peaceably, with no external interference, removing the provisional demarcation line at the 17th parallel, which is 'not a political or territorial boundary.'

There is no evidence to support Kissinger's contention that his 'modest requirement' has ever been a bone of contention. As I have already indicated, his identification of the GVN as the sole legitimate government in South Vietnam is not only without support in the texts, but is in plain violation of their provisions. The original and always primary source of external interference in the internal affairs of South Vietnam has been the United States, and apparently this will continue to be the case. One might dismiss Kissinger's evasions as merely a childish display, were it not for the fact that they may represent official policy. Furthermore, the mass media seem to be taken in, and continue to present Kissinger's conclusions as though they had something to do with the facts, a matter to which I return.

Exactly the same charade was enacted in October. On October 26, 1972, Kissinger stated that the Radio Hanoi broadcast of the 9-Point programme gave 'on the whole a very fair account.'[32] He then offered the following paraphrase: 'As was pointed out by Radio Hanoi, the existing authorities with respect to both internal and external politics would remain in office.' Although there is a studied ambiguity, the natural interpretation of his statement, made still more clear by the context, is that the GVN ('the existing authorities') will remain 'in office' as the government of the South, and will deal somehow with the other 'party', whose status remains mysterious. But this is not what 'was pointed out by Radio Hanoi,' which stated, rather, that 'the two present administrations in South Vietnam will remain in existence with their respective domestic and external functions,' and went on to identify these as the GVN and the PRG.[33]

On the issue which Kissinger now correctly identifies as what the war has been 'all about,' he was offering a 'paraphrase' which was sharply at variance with the broadcast that he conceded was accurate. Having rejected the central principle in the 9-Point programme, he then went on to say that 'peace is at hand.' The reason for the deception was quite obvious at the time. On the eve of the election, Nixon was not willing to reject publicly an agreement which offered return of the POWs and a cease-fire. He preferred to delay any response to the DRV initiative until after the election, when he would have more leverage. The mass media, with characteristic docility, chose to believe that peace was at hand and to overlook the fact that Kissinger was clearly rejecting the central provision of the 9-Point plan. Now apologists lamely argue that Kissinger's statement that 'peace is at hand' was a 'signal' to the DRV that United States intentions were serious. A telephone call would have achieved the same result, without any mysterious 'signals,' had this been the intention.

In mid-December Kissinger announced that negotiations had broken down, blaming DRV intransigence and overlooking the fact that the DRV was publicly calling for signing of the 9-Point agreement. Typically, the mass media repeated this nonsense, and depicted poor Kissinger as caught between two irrational adversaries, Hanoi and Saigon.[34] The terror bombing of urban centres in North Vietnam ensued. Though severe damage was caused, the tactic failed. The United States Air Force suffered substantial losses, and there were clear signs of resistance among B-52 pilots. Furthermore, there was an unanticipated and threatening international reaction. Nixon and Kissinger then formally accepted an agreement which is virtually identical to the 9 Points of October. But they continue to misrepresent the central terms of this Agreement in exactly the way they misrepresented the October plan, though more blatantly. The press remains obedient and silent.

The significance of these manoeuvres becomes still more clear if we recall a little history. In 1962 the NLF announced its official programme, which has not materially changed until this day. It proposed that South Vietnam, Laos and Cambodia form a neutral zone, and that 'South Vietnam will follow an independent, sovereign foreign policy' with internal democratic freedoms and no external interference. Negotiations between the leaders of the 'two zones' temporarily separated at Geneva in 1954 would lead to 'step-by-step reunification,' taking into account the different character of the two zones and observing the principle of 'equality' and 'nonannexation of one zone by the other.'[35] The United States government has been fighting for ten years to prevent the realization of this programme, which it has now, in essence, formally accepted at Paris, while continuing to reject it in the Washington version of these Agreements.

It is quite obvious why the United States could not consider the NLF Programme of 1962. Internal freedom in South Vietnam would have led to a political role for the NLF, in fact, a dominant role, if one accepts the assessment of high officials in the United States Mission in Saigon in 1962 that about half the population supported the NLF, while virtually no one supported the GVN.[36]

The United States government expert on the NLF, Douglas Pike, who gives the same estimate of NLF support in 1962,[37] notes that 'in September 1963 the NLF asked the United Nations for help in establishing a coalition government in South Vietnam similar to the one established in Laos' by the Geneva agreements of 1962. 'The NLF in mid-1964 put forth feelers for a proposal for what appeared to be an authentic coalition government.'[38] But, Pike continues, nothing came of these efforts. It was absurd to propose a coalition because the GVN feared that if it entered into a coalition with the NLF, 'the whale would swallow the minnow.'

We know from the Pentagon Papers that the great fear of American planners was that the NLF would achieve victory through the strategy of neutralization and political settlement.[39] They understood that there was no way to nourish the minnow, so they undertook to destroy the whale with the systematic bombardment of South Vietnam, the outright invasion and occupation, and the 'pacification' programmes. North Vietnam was bombed in the hope that it would use its alleged 'directive powers' to compel the NLF to desist. United States terror programmes in the South continued with mounting ferocity through the Nixon Administration, which also substantially extended these efforts in Laos and then Cambodia.

For ten years Washington has struggled to prevent the realization of the NLF programme, demolishing the society of South Vietnam in the process. Now it has signed the Paris Agreements that incorporate the essential features of this programme. What has led to this renunciation – formal at least – of long-established policy?

The primary factor is the local situation in South Vietnam. United States ground combat forces have been withdrawn and the local forces organized by the United States military (RVNAF) seem to be in fairly poor shape. Desertions have been reported to be more than 20,000 a month, the highest level of the war.[40] The Saigon army has never found much enthusiasm for the American war, and the United States is in no position to undertake another post-Tet accelerated pacification programme, this time without General Ewell and his 9th Division on hand to conduct Operation Speedy Express and the like to impose the control of the Thieu regime on rural areas.[41]

A second factor is the likely domestic and foreign response to further United States escalation. Pitifully slight in view of the circumstances, it has nevertheless always been an operative factor in constraining state violence.

Thirdly, the United States government may believe – rightly or wrongly – that its local affiliates are better prepared for a political confrontation than heretofore. The reasons are two-fold. There is, in the first place, an extensive police apparatus that has been effective in crushing dissidence. Though the Saigon government, in its enthusiasm, may have exaggerated the figures for Phoenix assassinations, there is no doubt that it has the capacity to conduct campaigns of repression and extermination. Secondly, though the minnow remains a minnow, Washington still believes, perhaps correctly, that it has severely wounded the whale. It believes that the political base of the NLF has been severely weakened in the course of the American war against the rural society – what is described in the West as the defence of South Vietnam against aggression. The success of the NLF, as such careful observers as Jeffrey Race have shown, resulted from the appeal of its constructive programmes to the population. The United States command may believe that these programmes will not appeal in the same measure to a generation of refugees and 'Saigon cowboys.' For years, the primary goal of the American effort has been to ensure that there do not exist any prospects for social and economic development that are rooted in the domestic society of South Vietnam itself, for if such prospects exist, they will be pursued and exploited by indigenous forces and the United States will lose control. United States policy was therefore directed to the destruction of the existing society, a process that is called 'modernization' by the more cynical academic ideologues. This policy had to guarantee that the only hope for survival lies in a foreign-based economy, dominated by local associates of foreign powers, with social and cultural patterns oriented towards the needs and interests of the industrial societies. United States planners may believe that this goal has been partially attained through the massive terror of the past eight years. If so, this would be another factor that would lead them to risk a shift to the political arena, revising long-standing policy.

There is a final reason, of some importance, I believe. United States planners may feel that their international goals have been largely attained. Shortly after Geneva, 1954, Dulles explained that 'investment [in] Viet-Nam justified even if only to buy time [to] build up strength elsewhere in area.'[42] The dominoes might topple if Vietnam were lost. Why was Vietnam regarded as so vital? Obviously, not as a military threat. United States planners did not expect Ho Chi Minh to set out in a sampan to conquer Indonesia and Japan. Nor did they fear that a Communist victory in Vietnam would enhance the 'militant and aggressive expansionist policy' attributed to China by CIA spokesman George Carver. On the contrary, the top-level analysis in late 1964, when United States escalation was being planned, predicted that a unified Vietnam under Communist leadership would have no ambitions beyond Indochina and would resume its 'traditional hostility' towards China. What then was the mysterious mechanism by which 'the rot would spread,' if not by military conquest? How would the dominoes topple, if not by military force?

As noted in chapter 1, section V, what the planners feared, in their more rational moments, was the 'ideological threat' – more accurately, the demonstration effect. Successful social and economic development in Vietnam under Communist leadership might provide a model that would be adopted by indigenous mass movements elsewhere, toppling the dominoes, spreading the rot, leading to Japanese accommodation, etc. This version of the domino theory was not implausible, though naturally one must discount the version that was used effectively to terrorize United States public opinion: the Communists (or in LBJ's version, the poor people of the world) would soon be landing in San Francisco if we did not stop them in Vietnam – or as Eugene Rostow once explained, if we lose South Vietnam, an inexorable process will begin that will reduce the United States to the status of Finland, almost the status of Poland, vis-à-vis the Soviet Union.[43]

Now, however, the threat of successful social and economic development is lessened. The devastation of Indochina by United States terror has reduced the prospects for successes that would be quite meaningful for the Asian poor. Furthermore, the 'second line of defense' has been strengthened – in the case of Japan, it has been strengthened a bit too much to suit some elements of the United States corporate elite. The belief that the American investment has paid off may or may not be accurate, but it is widely held.[44]

Whether the second line of defence will hold is, of course, another question. Recent events indicate that the local associates of the United States are none too secure about the matter. In the oldest United States satellite in the region, President Marcos declared martial law and rammed through a new constitution that gives him the authority to rule indefinitely. He explained that he had declared martial law in September 'after consulting God and receiving "several signs" from Him to act'; 'It seems as if I was being led and guided by some strange mind above me,' Marcos announced.[45] Earlier speculation had been that the 'strange mind above him' was located in the American Embassy, but apparently it was God, or perhaps Marcos cannot distinguish between the two. It might be noted that God has taken a special interest in the Philippines for many years, since McKinley requested divine guidance in 1898. He reported that he had received divine authorization to proceed with the invasion of the Philippines, to fulfil his duty 'to educate the Filipinos, and uplift and *civilize* and *Christianize* them, and by God's grace do the very best we could by them, as our fellowmen for whom Christ also died.'[46] Seventy-five years later, the true character of this enterprise is plain enough, just as the true meaning of the Truman Doctrine – 'to support free peoples who are resisting attempted subjugation by armed minorities or by outside pressures' – is revealed by the state of freedom in Greece and Turkey today.

The Philippines followed a few weeks behind South Korea, where Park Chung Hee was granted an unlimited grant of virtually absolute power in another country that is almost entirely in the hands of United States and Japanese capital, and locally, in the hands of the Korean CIA, rather firmly, it appears. Discussing the domestic terror, Elizabeth Pond concludes that 'the society at large is too honeycombed with Korean CIA informers – and too impregnated with fear – for any spontaneous movement [of resistance] to develop' – for the moment, at least. Dissidents were reduced to the two-word underground joke: 'Marcos, Parkos.'[47]

The pattern is evident. It grows directly from the 'Nixon-Kissinger doctrine,' the principle that a conservative coalition of great powers will enforce global order, repressing movements of liberation or social change, operating through domestic collaborators who are provided with the most efficient tools of repression that can be devised.

Surveying the situation in East Asia, United States planners may feel that the investment in Vietnam has paid off, as Dulles and others hoped, and that they can risk abandoning Vietnam to its people.

The October 9-Point programme, now in effect signed in Paris, differed in one significant respect from earlier PRG–DRV proposals; namely, it incorporated the United States demand that a cease-fire precede a political settlement. The reason for the change seems clear. After the 'successes' of such post-Tet pacification programmes as Operation Speedy Express (cf. Chapter 1, note 149), much of the countryside was under the effective control of the United States-imposed regime. For the PRG to have accepted a cease-fire in which the military and police forces of this regime could operate freely would have been to surrender. By October, the situation in the South was quite different. The offensive had succeeded in drawing United States–ARVN force away from settled areas, permitting the resistance to reconstitute its 'infrastructure.' The Saigon army was severely battered, and military forces of the PRG–DRV were in a position to give some protection to the indigenous political movement of South Vietnam. More generally, all military forces were undoubtedly weakened by the savage fighting and the colossal United States bombing attack. But it has always been clear to both sides that the conflict pits a massive United States-controlled military force with little political backing against an opponent that is politically powerful but relatively weak in military strength. As military forces are weakened, political strength – the comparative advantage of the 'enemy' – becomes a more critical factor. Correspondingly, the PRG and DRV have much to gain if United States military force is effectively withdrawn and the terms of the Paris Agreements are more or less applied.

It has been widely argued that the PRG–DRV shift was motivated by Russian–Chinese pressure, a result of the successful Nixon–Kissinger great power diplomacy. Naturally, spokesmen for the Administration will offer this view, but although an argument can be constructed, it seems to me rather implausible. Whatever the intentions of China and Russia may be, the fact seems to be that supplies continued to flow relatively unimpeded to the DRV. Recent visitors and journalists in the DRV report no signs of shortages. McNamara's analysts had predicted that mining of the harbours would have little effect on the flow of supplies, and it appears that they were correct. The changed situation in South Vietnam provides adequate gounds to explain the shift in negotiating position noted in the Hanoi radio broadcast of October 26 announcing the 9-Point plan.

While there is little reason to suppose that Russian–Chinese pressure impelled Hanoi to accept the Paris Agreements, nevertheless one should not mistake the intent of the Nixon–Kissinger diplomacy. The goal, plainly, is a coalition of great powers that will institutionalize the cold war system of imperial domination with more rational controls, reducing the freedom of weaker states within the 'spheres of influence' established by great power agreement. There is little novelty in this doctrine. In essence, it amounts to an agreement by the United States to accept the programme advocated by Stalin at the end of the Second World War. It is possible that the PRG may suffer from the 'successes' of this policy. The great powers may support or tolerate the Washington version of the Paris Agreements. It is important to recognize that in a sense, every state is a 'satellite' of the United States, in that it must recognize and somehow come to terms with the enormous power, military and economic, that the United States commands. The Vietnamese people exert no such international influence. Russia and China may determine, for their own reasons, that their best interests require them to adopt tacitly the American view that further efforts by the PRG to realize the actual terms of the Paris Agreements are a violation of the 'status quo.' It would be a romantic illusion to discount this possibility, though it may prove to be the case, once again, that the amazing resiliency of Vietnamese revolutionary nationalism will be the decisive factor.

The crucial question, at the moment, is whether the United States will adhere to the Paris Agreements or whether it will act in accordance with its expressed intention of violating them. It is interesting that a propaganda basis is being established to justify the inevitable claim that the Communists are responsible for violations of the cease-fire. Walt Rostow suggests that the present situation is similar to that in Laos in 1954, when Communist forces regrouped in Sam Neua and Phong Saly provinces. He asserts categorically that 'The International Control Commission created in 1954 was never permitted to enter these two provinces'; 'A unified independent Laos was never created as a result of Communist political and military actions.'[48] Robert Shaplen comments that the ICC was 'usually prevented by Indian doubts and Polish vetoes from taking any substantive action,' suggesting that this was a primary cause in the breakdown of the Geneva arrangements for Indochina in 1954.[49]

The facts are rather different. Within two months of its formation in October 1954, the ICC in Laos was conducting on-the-spot investigations at Nong Khang, the provisional capital of Sam Neua province.[50] A United States MAAG was illegally introduced into Laos under the cover of the aid programme staffed by military officers in civilian clothes under the direction of the former chief of United States MAAG in Pakistan. It controlled most of the 'aid' funds and had direct channels of communication to Washington through the Pacific military command (CINCPAC). 'A unified independent Laos was never created' because of United States subversion. The United States Ambassador admitted that he had struggled for sixteen months to prevent a coalition, and when the Pathet Lao and its allies won an unexpected election victory in 1958, the government was quickly overthrown by CIA-backed right-wing groups after United States aid had been terminated, in accordance with the policy laid down in NSC 5612/1 of September 1956. By the fall of 1960, the United States was denying aid to the Souvanna Phouma government recognized by the United States, and the CIA and United States military were supporting extreme right-wing forces that were in open rebellion against this government. 200 Lao paratroopers trained in Thailand were dispatched to the rebels. This was a period when anti-Communist Western journalists were reporting that the Pathet Lao would surely emerge victorious in anything resembling a free election.[51]

As for Shaplen's claims, they hardly give an adequate picture of the complicated story of the ICC, which repeatedly cited United States–GVN violations through the 1950s, noting also that it was receiving considerably more co-operation in the North than in the South. The Canadian role, which Shaplen pointedly omits, often reached levels that can only be described as grotesque. For example, an investigating team of the ICC reported unanimously that ARVN forces entered Cambodia in May 1957, causing damage and casualties, but Canada argued that the ICC was 'not competent . . . to take any further action,' or even to forward a copy of the report, since the report 'makes it clear that the incursion was carried out by regular troops of the South Vietnamese Army' and the ICC must limit itself only to violations of Cambodian territory by the DRV (of which there were none reported by the ICC).[52]

These misrepresentations are important, just as it is important that in the mainstream of opinion in the United States, there is virtually no challenge to the official United States government propaganda line that the United States intervention, originally noble in intent, was an effort to secure the self-determination of the people of South Vietnam in the face of Communist aggression – wrongly, the doves allege, since no United States interest was involved, the costs were too high, and the means used out of proportion to the ends sought. As in the past, such historical fantasies may provide the basis in American public opinion for support of new United States military intervention.

The role of the press as an agency of state propaganda is illustrated, once again, by news commentary on the Paris Agreements. The press lauds Kissinger for his brilliant manoeuvring, failing to observe that in his genius he has succeeded in signing the NLF programme of 1962, in effect. Worse still, the press – in particular, the liberal press – presents the Nixon–Kissinger misrepresentation of the Agreements as if it were the text signed in Paris. Thus on the crucial matter of 'the South's political status,' *Newsweek* asserts that Hanoi has now

> accepted the provision that north and south are divided by a sacrosanct demarcation line, thus tacitly acknowledging the legitimacy of the Saigon regime . . . Equally vital to the Nixon Administration was specific mention of the 'sovereignty' of the Saigon government, and on the point, too, the U.S. had its way. Hanoi finally conceded that, in Kissinger's words, 'there is an entity called South Vietnam'. In one important sense, the dispute over that question was what the war in Vietnam was all about.

In the same issue Stewart Alsop proclaims that if the 'marvelously elaborate' Nixon–Kissinger settlement 'survives more or less intact, we will have won the war.'[53]

All of this is plainly false. Recognition of the status of the demarcation line in the terms of Geneva 1954 implies nothing, tacitly or otherwise, with regard to the legitimacy of the Saigon regime. It does imply that 'there is an entity called South Vietnam' in the precise sense that has been advocated, with no modification, by the NLF–PRG from the outset. Hanoi has 'conceded' nothing by signing an agreement that expresses the position that it has always backed. There is no specific mention in the Agreements of the 'sovereignty' of the Saigon government, though Washington pretends otherwise. The war was 'all about' the right of the major political force within South Vietnam to participate in governing this 'entity,' not about its existence. The 'enemy,' never departing from its insistence on the right of the South Vietnamese people to self-determination without external interference as now provided by the Paris Agreements, has demanded the right to participate in a democratic political process in South Vietnam. The United States, in contrast, has always insisted on imposing the rule of the GVN by force, with a constitutional structure that outlaws the major organized political force in South Vietnam. The Paris Agreements, with their two-party formula, express the unwavering position of the 'enemy' in the light of present conditions. It is quite true that the United States 'will have won the war' if the Washington misrepresentation, as repeated by *Newsweek*, 'survives more or less intact.' It is also true that the text of the Agreements signed in Paris represents a capitulation to the long-held programme of the 'enemy.'

It is interesting that as the liberal press dutifully proceeds to present state propaganda as fact, the state executive continues to denounce it for its occasional departures from total servility and demands that this 'imbalance' be rectified. If there were an honest and independent press, the headlines in January would have read: 'U.S. announces intention to violate Paris Agreements.' Instead, the mass media, once again, merely serve as a state propaganda agency.

It is a matter of some importance that even those political commentators who have been most outspoken in criticism of the war are reinforcing the illusions that the government is seeking to convey. For example, Tom Wicker writes that

> American policy, which never accepted the Geneva agreement, came to insist, instead, that South Vietnam was a legally constituted nation being subverted and invaded by another power; and that view is implied even in the documents that finally produced the cease-fire.

He adds that 'this implication' may have been designed 'more nearly to serve Saigon's political needs than to reflect actual American policy in the 1970's.'[54] For the reasons already noted, his account of the documents is incorrect. The Paris Agreements merely reiterate the position of the NLF and its North Vietnamese backers with regard to the status of South Vietnam, although the Washington version continues to express the contrary United States view. More important, by promoting such illusions, critical voices in the American press are contributing to the outcome that they most fear: the adoption of Administration rhetoric as 'policy for the 1970's.'

The point deserves emphasis. It might be asked what harm there is in permitting Nixon and Kissinger to conceal their formal capitulation with the rhetoric of 'peace with honour.' The answer should be obvious. Quite apart from any concern for historical accuracy; consider the likely consequences of success in Administration propaganda efforts. Naturally, the Nixon Administration seeks to convey the impression that its cool courage and unflinching commitment to 'peace with honour' compelled the 'North Vietnamese' to desist from their 'aggression.' If the public accepts their view, and the corollary that the GVN remains as the 'sole legitimate government of South Vietnam,' entitled to use the means described earlier to control its population, then there will be public support for new forms of American violence if the 'sole legitimate government' of South Vietnam begins to collapse, for whatever reason. Nixon and Kissinger may find themselves trapped by their own deceit. If, indeed, their iron will forced the enemy to capitulate, then surely it would be unprincipled to refrain from applying the rod once again if the 'legally constituted nation' whose freedom they have won is again 'subverted or invaded.' One might recall the words of another President, just twelve years ago: ' No matter what goes wrong or whose fault it really is, the argument will be that the Communists have stepped up their infiltration and we can't win unless we hit the North.'[55]

President Nixon warns 'that based on my actions over the past four years, that the North Vietnamese should not lightly disregard such expressions of concern, when they are made, with regard to a violation.'[56] He is referring to alleged North Vietnamese infiltration, and 'responsible' commentators underscore the seriousness of these Communist violations (see note 20). No such denunciations were heard when the United States and the GVN announced their intention to violate the Agreements they were about to sign, or when the Saigon regime, in accordance with its official pronouncements, then proceeded to impose its control over the population by a systematic programme of force and violence. By adopting the framework of government propaganda in the early stages of the United States intervention, the press contributed materially to the violence of subsequent years. Any state, democratic or totalitarian, must mobilize public support for dangerous, costly and vicious policies. By misrepresenting the American intervention as a defence of freedom, the mass media helped mobilize that public support, creating political pressures that would have made it difficult for United States policy makers to extricate themselves short of all-out war, even if they had so desired. It is astonishing that the simple lesson cannot be learned, and that the same process may now, once again, be unfolding.

Quite apart from the public statements of the United States government, the vast flow of military supplies to South Vietnam

Endgame: the Tactics of Peace in Vietnam 171

since the peace scare of October 1972 indicates a clear United States intention to remain in massive force. It is not very likely that the Nixon Administration is introducing vast quantities of military equipment in the expectation that they will be turned over to a government of national reconciliation that will include the National Liberation Front. Pentagon officials 'estimate that it will take ... up to two years ... to train pilots, engineers and electronic specialists needed by the augmented Air Force,' which is expected to have the capacity to provide air support at almost the level of United States air support, according to USAF officers.[57] Presumably, the United States command hopes that at least the 'elite' units – the Rangers, Marines and Air Force, which are largely commanded by Northern Catholics – will remain loyal to the regime and will serve as an effective force for 'controlling the population.' Whether the United States military forces operating from Thailand and the China Sea will be again called into action in case of need remains to be seen.

American officials in Saigon are reported to be 'secretly planning a major postwar presence of United States civilians in Vietnam, with many of them doing jobs formerly done by the military.' A spokesman for the United States military command refused to supply details, saying 'It's just not in the national interest to have these things known.' Spokesmen for companies contracting for this work also state that the Department of Defence has forbidden them to talk about it.[58] Five thousand 'civilians' arrived between October and February, and specialists are being sought with training in armament and electronic servicing, intelligence, and similar skills.[59] The AID programme will remain, perhaps serving as a cover for the CIA as it has in Laos since the 1962 agreements.[60] The CIA may well seek to employ its inter-Asian mercenary army alongside the quasi-mercenary army of the Saigon regime. No serious observer can feel any confidence that the United States will renounce the general policy of subversion and illegal use of force against local Communist 'rebellion' in Indochina and throughout East Asia, as laid down in secret immediately after the Geneva Agreements of 1954.[61]

One final point. Suppose that Western force actually is withdrawn from Indochina. There is little doubt that the struggle will quickly be joined elsewhere, at the second line of defence, where United States and Japanese investment and interest are expanding in this area of considerable economic and 'strategic' importance.

The struggle for national liberation and social change in the Far East and elsewhere will continue, and it will be resisted by imperial force. Apologists will speak of 'defence of the Four Freedoms.'[62] The facts will speak of something else. What will happen within the advanced industrial societies is far from clear, but there is little doubt that it will have a significant, possibly decisive impact on these inevitable conflicts.

Notes

INTRODUCTION

1. Gravel Edition of the Pentagon Papers, *The Defense Department History of United States Decisionmaking on Vietnam*, Beacon Press, Boston 1971, vol. II, p. 517. Since this edition is more generally accessible than the Government Edition (and is also properly paginated), I will refer to it, where possible, here and below.

2. The terms are common among 'pacification theorists.' See William A. Nighswonger, *Rural Pacification in Vietnam*, Praeger, New York, 1966.

3. Bernard Fall, *The Two Viet-Nams*, Praeger, New York, 1963; revised edition, 1964, p. 373. In later years, Fall was horrified at the savagery of the American war and questioned whether Vietnam would survive this attack. But he strongly supported United States aims in Vietnam, and at this time, objected only to the incompetence of American planners.

4. Roger Hilsman, *To Move a Nation*, 1964; Dell, New York, 1967, pp. 430, 432.

5. *Ibid.*, p. 463.

6. *Ibid.*, pp. 454, 456.

7. Fall, *op. cit.*, pp. 376, 378. Robert Sansom (captain, US Air Force; member of the National Security Council staff; specialist in rural insurgency) concludes that the Viet Cong 'correctly labeled the strategic hamlet as a "prison" that restricted peasant economic activities.' The GVN (which 'represented a movement of the elite' opposing the Vietcong, 'a movement of the masses') committed a 'blunder' in employing the strategic hamlet programme. *The Economics of Insurgency in the Mekong Delta of Vietnam*, Cambridge, MIT Press, 1970, pp. 238–9. For a careful study of the strategic hamlet programme, see Milton E. Osborne, *Strategic Hamlets in South Vietnam: a Survey and a Comparison*, Data Paper number 55, Southeast Asia Program, Department of Asian Studies, Cornell University, Ithaca, N.Y., April 1965.

8. Dennis J. Duncanson, *Government and Revolution in Vietnam*, Oxford, 1968, p. 321. Some United States government sources, he notes, estimated the 'migration' at about 300,000 people. It should not be supposed that Duncanson, a member of the British 'aid' mission, raises some objection to the strategic hamlet programme on other than technical grounds.

9. *Op. cit.*, pp. 437–8, 442.

10. *New York Times*, October 17, 1962. The figure excludes helicopter flights.

11. William R. Corson, *The Betrayal*, Norton, 1968, p. 48. In this book Corson goes on to explain how a population should be properly pacified, using the experience of the United States Marines as an example.

12. On motivations of regroupees, see J. J. Zasloff, *Political Motivation of the Vietcong*, RM-4703/2-ISA/ARPA, May 1968 (Rand Corporation study). Though extreme in its pro-government bias, this study nevertheless contains useful interviews, which indicate that regroupees volunteered with enthusiasm 'to help liberate their compatriots' (p. 72f.). On Diem's public renunciation of the Geneva Agreement, see Gravel Edition of the Pentagon Papers, I, 245.

13. *Ibid.*, II, chapter 2.

14. Eliot Marshall and Tom Geoghegan, 'Calculating the costs,' *The New Republic*, February 10, 1973.

15. Michael Harrington, chairman of the Socialist Party, *Village Voice*, July 2, 1970. Harrington does not go on to explain who, in his view, represents 'the value of democracy' in Vietnam.

16. Editorial, *New York Times*, May 7, 1972.

17. Norman A. Graebner, *Cold War Diplomacy, 1945–60*, Van Nostrand, 1962. Appropriately, given its content, the book is dedicated to George Kennan.

18. 'Corporations and American Foreign Relations,' *Annals* of the American Academy of Political and Social Science, *The Multinational Corporation*, September 1972.

19. I have discussed this matter at greater length in 'Scholarship and ideology: American historians as "experts in legitimation,"' *Social Scientist* (New Delhi, February 1973).

20. A. A. Berle, 'The formulation and implementation of American foreign policy,' in J. C. Vincent *et al.*, *America's Future in the Pacific*, Rutgers, 1947. On Berle's role, see G. William Domhoff, *The Higher Circles*, Random House, 1970.

21. The phrase is Graebner's, *op. cit.*, p. 9, referring to United States policy between the world wars. He adds that 'This nation's selfless search for order in world affairs [after World War II] could not sustain the gratitude of a troubled world' (p. 126).

22. *Washington Post*, April 25, 1972.

23. 'War with no end,' *New Society*, April 13, 1972.

24. Memorandum for the Secretary of Defense after a visit to South Vietnam in January 1961, *United States–Vietnam Relations, 1945–67*, Government Printing Office, 1971 [henceforth *DOD*], bk 2, IV.A.5, tab 4, p. 66. This is the government edition of the 'Pentagon Papers.'

24. *DOD*, bk 4, p. 2. Seaborn further warned of 'the greatest devastation' for North Vietnam if it persisted in the 'DRV-assisted pressures against South Vietnam.' United States planners were aware that 'Re-

groupees provided virtually all the infiltrators in the period 1959-64' (*DOD*, bk 2, IV.A.5, tab 3, p. 32), and that the insurgency was southern-rooted. Even Douglas Pike concedes that 'material aid by the DRV in the period before mid-1964 probably was minimal' (but its 'willingness potential was virtually unlimited,' and 'what is relevant is the potential'). *Viet Cong*, MIT Press, 1966, p. 325. On Canadian attitudes at the time of the Seaborn mission, see Chapter 2, note 52, below.

26. See references of Chapter 1, note 214.

27. For a striking example, see Chapter 1, section V. Also, note 202. When intelligence reports are available, we sometimes discover significant qualifications that disappear from the second-order record. Thus there is much ado about alleged DRV aggression in Laos from 1959, but when we investigate sources more closely, a different picture emerges. See my 'The Pentagon Papers as propaganda and as history,' in N. Chomsky and H. Zinn, eds, *Critical Essays on the Pentagon Papers*, Beacon Press, Boston, 1972. To cite another example, not mentioned there, we discover that what is called the NVA 335th Division,' the DRV command post allegedly set up in 1959 near the Laos border, 'had been formed from the "Lao volunteers" regrouped to the DRV in 1955' (*DOD*, bk 2, IV.A.5, tab 3, p. 62). For more information on this matter, see B. Fall, *Vietnam Witness*, Praeger 1966, pp. 249-50.

28. SNIE 63. 1-60; *DOD*, bk 2, tab IV.A.5, tab 4, p. 49.

29. Alexander Woodside's apt phrase. 'Ideology and integration in post-colonial Vietnamese nationalism,' *Pacific Affairs*, Winter 1971-2.

30. Daniel Southerland, 'Saigon land reform: still doubtful,' *Christian Science Monitor*, April 1, 1972. See also Jeffrey Race, *War Comes to Long An*, California, 1971, pp. 272-3. It is common to refer to the horrors of totalitarian collectivization under Communism, but while such critics properly condemn the killings in the early stages of land reform in the DRV, they rarely note the circumstances, or the fact that the land reform laid the basis for overcoming widespread starvation and injustice. For some discussion, see my *At War with Asia*, Fontana/Collins, 1970, pp. 218-20. I noted there that Hoang Van Chi's *From Colonialism to Communism*, Praeger, 1964, on which much of the discussion of the land reform is based, is an extremely dubious source with many errors and hopeless bias. Chi's documentation has recently been investigated by D. Gareth Porter, *The Myth of the Bloodbath*, Interim Report, no. 2, September 1972, International Relations of East Asia, Cornell University, Ithaca, New York. He demonstrates that it consists largely of fabrications and serious mistranslations. It is of some interest that none of these are noted by P. J. Honey, the British Vietnamese scholar who wrote the introduction to this book. Chi is the only cited source in existing estimates of those killed during the land reform. In an interview in the *Washington Post*, September 13, 1972, Chi concedes that his estimate was based on observations in one village of 200 people – surely one of the most amazing extrapolations on record, even if one were to accept the testimony of this totally-discredited

source. Colonel Nguyen Van Chau, director of the Psychological War Service of the South Vietnamese Armed Forces from 1956 to 1962, recently stated in an interview that Chi's accusations were 'wholly imaginary and without foundation' and that the alleged 'Communist bloodbath' in North Vietnam was '100% fabricated' by United States-financed Saigon intelligence services. Diana Johnstone, *St Louis Post-Dispatch*, September 24, 1972.

31. Phi Bang, 'Land: theory and practise,' *Far Eastern Economic Review*, April 23, 1970. Charles Mohr observes that 'one of the most imaginative and positive aspects [of the Saigon land reform] is that the plan did not attempt to overturn or disrupt the Vietcong's land redistribution.' *New York Times*, March 23, 1973.

32. See Chapter 1, The point is generally conceded; see, e.g., *At War with Asia*, Chapter 1, note 72.

33. William Beecher, 'Washington, discouraged, hints at wider bombings,' *New York Times*, May 3, 1972; Claude Julien, *Le Monde*, May 12, 1972; Joel Henri, 'Thirty minutes in Hanoi,' *New York Times*, May 11, 1972.

34. For an eyewitness account of a napalm attack on a French village, which left many dead, see Howard Zinn, *Vietnam: the Logic of Withdrawal*, Beacon, Boston, 1967, p. 51.

35. Corson, *op. cit.*, p. 71. He is referring to population removal near the DMZ in May 1967. He notes that none of the United States officials present 'batted an eye over the fact that out of the 13,000 [people moved] only about 100 were males between the ages of sixteen and forty-five.'

36. See Frances Fitzgerald, *Fire in the Lake*, Little-Brown, Boston, 1972, pp. 307, 342–3. It seems implausible that Giap expected regular forces to move far from base areas, given the overwhelming United States firepower advantage and total control of the air. In fact, the one province capital captured, Quang Tri, was apparently abandoned before combat.

37. Minor in context, though instructive. While the nation agonized over the Calley verdict, a new ground sweep in the area drove perhaps as many as 16,000 from their homes. A year later, the camp where the My Lai remnants were relocated was largely destroyed by ARVN air and artillery bombardment; the destruction was attributed to the Vietcong. Henry Kamm, 'New drive begins in area of Mylai,' *New York Times*, April 1, 1971; Martin Teitel, 'Again, the suffering of My Lai,' *New York Times*, June 7, 1972, and testimony before Subcommittee to Investigate Problems Connected with Refugees and Escapees, May 8, 1972, Govt. Printing Office, Washington, 1972. Teitel, who is director of the overseas refugee programme of the American Friends Service Committee, which has a hospital in the area, reports hospital estimates that 70 per cent of casualties result from allied firepower; all statistics, of course, relate only to areas under US–GVN control. United States spokesmen often attribute the bulk of casualties to

communist forces; they achieve this result by attributing all mine/ mortar casualties to NLF/NVA (Hearings, May 3, p. 66). However, the May Hearings reveal that the bulk of recorded casualties from mines are from US–ARVN mines. Teitel also described the far worse US–ARVN attacks on the Phu Quy area in the Batangan Peninsula, which has been subjected to some of the most prolonged United States terrorist attacks of the war, including naval, air and artillery bombardment, destruction of dikes, devastation by Rome ploughs, forced resettlement of the entire population, burning of villages, and – according to NLF sources – outright massacres. On the state of the area as of March 1973, see Chapter 2, below.

38. 'Ten get jail for raiding draft office' (sic), *New York Times*, June 10, 1970; Seymour Hersh, *Cover-up*, Random House, 1972; Hersh, 'The Army's Secret inquiry describes a 2nd massacre,' *New York Times*, June 5, 1972.

39. See Chapter 1, note 149.

40. 'Cohorts in immorality,' editorial, *Far Eastern Economic Review*, May 6, 1972. I select this example, among many, because the journal is one of the most independent and best-informed. On its objective approach, see my *For Reasons of State*, Fontana/Collins, 1973, Chapter 1, note 42.

41. Elsewhere, the editors explain that 'Nixon had demonstrated that he wanted to disengage from the war.' *Ibid.*, May 13, 1972. The demonstration failed to persuade the *Review*'s own correspondents, among others; see *For Reasons of State*, Chapter 2, note 2. But the editors were convinced, and by failing to agree, the DRV leaders become cohorts in immorality. On the United States disengagement and the likely reasons, see Chapter 2, below.

42. See T. D. Allman, 'Landscape without figures,' *Manchester Guardian Weekly*, January 1, 1972; *Far Eastern Economic Review*, January 8, 1972. Compare Allman's eyewitness description with the report by United States Air Force Secretary Robert Seamans who visited northern Laos at about the same time, but reported seeing 'no evidence of indiscriminate bombing.' George Wilson, *Washington Post–Boston Globe*, January 17, 1972. Cf. also the record of the Pentagon Papers with regard to the bombing of North and South Vietnam, discussed below in Chapter 1, sections I and VI.

43. For my views on the matter, see *At War with Asia*, Chapter 1. See also Michael Reich and David Finkelhor, 'Capitalism and the Military-Industrial Complex,' *Review of Radical Political Economics*, vol. 2, no. 4, 1970.

44. Editorial, *Far Eastern Economic Review*, June 24, 1972. The cited examples are rather curious (Albania will terminate its aggressive adventures? Israel can no longer rely on Communist support?).

45. This is not to imply that the risks of Armageddon have not been boldly faced. See my *Problems of Knowledge and Freedom*, Fontana/Collins 1972, pp. 80–2; Richard J. Walton, *Cold War and Counter-*

revolution, Penguin, 1972, pp. 84–93; Chapter 7. On Kissinger's remarkable views, see V. Brodine *et al.*, *Open Secret*, Harper and Row, 1972.

46. *The Essence of Security*, 1968, p. 109–10.

47. Anton Pannekoek, *Lenin as Philosopher*, 1938, p. 78–9. For more extensive discussion, see my *American Power and the New Mandarins*, Pantheon, New York, 1969, chapter 1; *Problems of Knowledge and Freedom*, Chapter 2.

THE BACKROOM BOYS

1. Gloria Emerson of the *New York Times*, 'Vietnam Diary,' *McCall's*, August 1971.

2. Philip Jones Griffiths, *Vietnam Inc.*

3. *The Pentagon Papers*, Senator Gravel Edition, vol IV, p. 48 [IV, 48] (his emphasis). References henceforth are to this edition, in the style indicated in brackets, except where otherwise noted. Other references are to Department of Defense, *United States–Vietnam Relations, 1945–67*, the government offset edition of the Pentagon Papers, censored but including valuable documents unavailable elsewhere, henceforth referred to as *DOD*. For a comparison of the various editions, see L. Rodberg, in *The Pentagon Papers*, Senator Gravel Edition, vol. 5, *Critical Essays*, eds Noam Chomsky and Howard Zinn.

4. II, 360. In November 1961, the president authorized 'execution of air-ground support,' and three helicopter companies were operating by February 1 with 22 helicopters each (II, 656–7). Air force units were also deployed for air-ground support, and the first C-123s were sent for defoliation missions. United States advisory teams were extended to battalion level. In one week of May, air force and United States helicopter units flew about 350 sorties: offensive, airlift, etc. (II, 656–8, 677). During 1962–1963, the United States 'provided helicopter companies for rapid tactical transport.' and 'tactical air and artillery support to assure ARVN firepower superiority over the insurgents.' This led to various complaints, such as 'that supporting air and artillery were an inducement to rely on indiscriminate firepower as a substitute for aggressiveness' (II, 455). For some of the effects on the population, see below, pp. 93–4.

For comparison, the French had about 10 operational helicopters at the time of Dien Bien Phu, and in the 56 days of the Dien Bien Phu battle, the French expended less bomb power than the United States did in a single day in 1966–67 (Bernard Fall, *Street Without Joy*, p. 242; *Last Reflections on a War*, p. 231). Fall adds: 'The French aircraft total in all of Indochina . . . was 112 fighters and 68 bombers. That is what the United States flies in a single mission.' Following a more classical imperial pattern, the French relied primarily on mercenaries rather than French nationals, and never sent conscripts to Vietnam. There were about 20,000 French nationals fighting in all Indochina in February 1949, about 51,000 (plus 6,000 advisers) in all Indochina as of April 1953.

(*DOD*, bk 8, p. 179; I, 400). Under 'Vietnamization,' the United States is reverting to the classic pattern, and an Asian mercenary army is being created involving nationals from many countries. See note 198 below for early stages. See also Fred Branfman, ed., *Voices from the Plain of Jars*, and Alfred W. McCoy, *et al.*, *The Politics of Heroin in Southeast Asia*.

5. George McT. Kahin and John W. Lewis, *The United States in Vietnam*, p. 186.

6. Bernard Fall, 'Vietnam Blitz,' *New Republic*, October 9, 1965.

7. 'Vietcong Motivation and Morale,' June–December 1965, reprinted in *Vietnam Perspectives*, May 1966, from Senate Armed Services and Appropriations Committee hearings, January–February 1966. Sections of the RAND study dealing with atrocities by the Korean mercenary forces in Vietnam (December 1966) were released by Alternative Features Service, PO Box 2250, Berkeley, California, June 9, 1972. Anthony Russo, who was working on the RAND studies in Saigon from February 1965 to September 1966, reports that the interviews revealed the National Liberation Front cadres to be dedicated idealists, intensely committed to freeing Vietnam from foreign control. But regardless of the content of the interviews, the project leader (Leon Gouré, probably the author of the memorandum cited above) would interpret them in such a way as to support his bias in favour of the use of American air power to weaken the NLF. Gouré's conclusion as of summer 1965 that refugee generation was hurting the NLF by depriving them of 'strategic support' soon became general United States military policy. Anthony Russo, 'Inside the RAND Corporation and Out: My Story,' *Ramparts*, April 1972.

8. According to the report, 'The interviews do not reveal any deep-seated resentment or hatred of the GVN or the Americans caused by air or artillery attacks on villages. [Deleted].' As Russo notes ('Inside the RAND Corporation'), there may well be a divergence between the content of interviews and the conclusions of the briefer. Nevertheless, the statement may be literally correct. That is, it may be true that refugees interviewed by agents of the military power that has blasted them out of their homes will say that they really didn't mind. I noticed the same, quite predictable phenomenon interviewing refugees from the Plain of Jars in Laos shortly after they had been removed to miserable camps near Vientiane. Quite a few said, at first, that they harboured no resentment against the Americans who had bombed their villages so intensively that they had to hide in tunnels deep in the forest to survive, farming only at night, if at all, because of the ever-present terror from the sky. The refugees, after all, are not imbeciles. See my *At War with Asia*, pp. 69, 241.

9. Cited by Richard Critchfield, *The Long Charade*, p. 173. Referring to the last quote, Critchfield states that 'obviously, Westmoreland was trying to balance common humanity against military necessity.' Later Critchfield blames the 'Hanoi Politburo' for the massive generation of refugees. 'This was exactly the effect [they] were trying to produce; it

was a skillful, calculated, logical exploitation of human suffering' (p. 177). Many other American observers have taken a similar position: it is the responsibility of Hanoi, a consequence of Communist viciousness, that the United States blasted the people of South Vietnam out of their homes.

10. Six years after its inception, the criminal programme of crop destruction was evaluated in a secret RAND report and found 'ineffective' against the Viet Cong. See Russo, the author of the report, 'Inside the RAND Corporation.' The programme was continued.

As was entirely predictable from the outset, crop destruction 'had its greatest effects on the enemy-controlled civilian populations' and 'created widespread misery and many refugees' (L. Craig Johnstone, Chief, Pacification Studies Group, Military Assistance Command, Vietnam, 1956–1970, 'Ecocide and the Geneva Protocol,' *Foreign Affairs*, vol. 49, no. 4 [1971]. Since 'neither the crop destruction program nor the defoliation program was anything but a liability to pacification,' both have been phased out. Besides, Rome ploughs are a more efficient tool of destruction. On this matter, see Arthur H. Westing, 'Leveling the Jungle,' *Environment*, November 1971.

There is only one casual and uninformative reference in the Pentagon study to the crop destruction and defoliation programmes. The military regarded it as a 'gimmick' from the start, at best an 'R&D effort' (II, 658). The victims, had they been asked, might have chosen different terms.

11. Colonel Charles Smith of the 196th Light Infantry Brigade, quoted by Griffiths, *Vietnam Inc.*, p. 67. J.-C. Pomonti of *Le Monde* reports that 'a series of urban ghettoes have sprung up' since 1965, containing 'at least half the population, whereas in 1960 the country was still 85% rural' ('The Other South Vietnam,' *Foreign Affairs*, vol. 50, no. 2 [1972].

12. Reference is to the massacre that took place in February 1968 after the communist capture of Hue. On this matter, see *For Reasons of State*, Chapter 1, p. 35.

13. Anthony Lake and Roger Morris, 'The Human Reality of Realpolitik,' *Foreign Policy*, vol. 1, no. 4 (1971).

14. *DOD*, bk 8, pp. 144–5. For further discussion of this important statement, see p. 49 below.

15. For biographical data, see Eqbal Ahmad, 'Revolutionary War and Counterinsurgency,' *Journal of International Affairs*, vol. 25, no. 1 (1971).

16. George K. Tanham and Dennis J. Duncanson, 'Some Dilemmas of Counterinsurgency,' *Foreign Affairs*, vol. 48, no. 1 (1969); an illuminating remark, with implications that should be carefully considered.

17. NSC 48/1, December 23, 1949; *DOD*, bk 8, p. 248. See pp. 55–7 below for extensive quotes.

18. See Anthony Russo's account of the 'naively carefree attitude' at RAND, 'Inside the Rand Corporation.'

19. Major-General George S. Beatty, chief of the United States military mission in Brazil, Hearings Before the [Church] Subcommittee on Western Hemisphere Affairs, U.S. Senate, May 1971, p. 86. Henceforth cited as Church Subcommittee Hearings.

20. III, 648; William Bundy, in a memorandum in which he asks, on November 24, 1964, whether the favoured escalatory option (option C) can be carried out in practice, 'in view of its requirement that we maintain a credible threat of major action while at the same time seeking to negotiate, even if quietly.' On the seriousness of the effort to negotiate, see VI, 5, 7.

21. I, 187. The 'letter of transmittal' (I, xvi) identifies Gelb as the author of the summary and analysis sections, including the one quoted above, p. 27 (II, 414–5).

22. Gabriel Kolko, 'The American Goals in Vietnam,' in Chomsky and Zinn, *Critical Essays*.

23. *Ibid*. Kolko notes that in this case, as in Indochina, it was the farther dominoes that were the really important ones. See Joyce and Gabriel Kolko, *The Limits of Power*, p. 340.

24. Sam Ervin, 'Executive Privilege: Secrecy in a Free Society,' *The Nation*, November 8, 1971.

25. Thomas Jefferson, in a letter of 1787, quoted by Hannah Arendt, *On Revolution*, p. 241.

26. On this matter, see Virginia Brodine and Mark Selden, 'The Kissinger–Nixon Doctrine,' in Brodine *et al.*, *Open Secret*.

27. Senator Stuart Symington, *Congressional Record*, August 3, 1971, p. S12931.

28. *Ibid.*, October 4, 1971, p. S15763. The Thai soldiers describe themselves as regular army troops serving in Laos for extra pay. It was reported that 12,000 would be 'available for combat' by March 1, 1972. See stories by Don Ronk and Tammy Arbuckle, reprinted in the *Congressional Record*, October 4, 1971, pp. S15768–9. 'Senior US sources' in Bangkok confirm these reports (see *Washington Post–Boston Globe*, January 22, 1972.

29. Hearings Before the Committee on Armed Services, US Senate, July 1971, pp. 4275–7.

30. *Congressional Record*, August 3, 1971, p. S12956.

31. *Ibid.*, October 4, 1971, p. S15773–4. It was left to Senator Hart to observe that 'all of the screaming about law and order in this country is talking about something minuscule if in fact it is established that one branch of the Government ignores the law of the lawmakers' (August 3, S12955).

32. Thomas Emerson, *Toward a General Theory of the First Amendment*, p. 20.

33. *United States Code*, vol. 18, sec. 793d,e. Classified information is continually leaked to correspondents for the particular purposes of the administration, and it is a common practice for ex-officials to release such information and documents in memoirs. An example relevant to

the present case is Lyndon Johnson's *The Vantage Point*, which contains, *inter alia*, classified material that appears in the Pentagon Papers, presented, arguably, for personal gain. A former president has no special rights in this regard. Similarly, pledges of secrecy are freely violated by the executive for its own purposes, as when Nixon chose to reveal secret negotiations on Indochina on January 25, 1972. The negotiations volumes of the Pentagon study are still suppressed by the government as supersensitive, but participants are leaking their private versions to the press (as did LBJ), with names and dates. See Benjamin Welles, *New York Times*, February 14, 1972.

34. Near v. Minnesota, 1931, cited by Justice Brennan, concurring in the decision against prior restraint in the case of the Pentagon Papers. See Gerald Gold *et al.*, eds, *The Pentagon Papers*, p. 656.

35. Anthony Austin, *The President's War*, pp. 313, 297-8. This is, however, hardly the most grotesque feature of the Tonkin Gulf story.

36. Emerson, *First Amendment*, introduction. For a review of the history of this matter, see Edward G. Hudon, *Freedom of Speech and Press in America*.

37. Cited in Gold *et al.*, *Pentagon Papers*, p. 467. The *Times* commentator (Fox Butterfield) states that 'neither General Westmoreland's requests nor President Johnson's approvals were made public.' In fact, as usual, the information had leaked to the press, and the request (though not the approval) was mentioned in a *Times* article from Saigon which the Pentagon historian states 'reflected thinking of many junior and mid-level officials in both the US Mission and the GVN' (II, 544). This is one of many examples which indicate that an observer with limitless time and energy, who was sufficiently realistic to treat government pronouncements with utter cynicism, might be able to follow events as they unfolded. Another example is the Hanson Baldwin report of the secret BARREL ROLL airstrikes in Laos in 1964, cited above, p. 35.

38. III, 217, 623; November 8, 1964. The Joint Chiefs commented, reassuringly, 'that the main risk is not to us but to the Chinese. "Possibly even the use of nuclear weapons at some point" is of course why we spend billions to have them.' Therefore they believed the risk of nuclear war to be low. They added that the loss of South Vietnam would be a disaster, worse even than the loss of Berlin (III, 628), rejecting the view of the NSC working group that 'the loss of South Vietnam' only '*could*' be as serious as the loss of Berlin.

39. Quoted, with some appropriate comment, by James Aronson, 'The Media and the Message,' in Chomsky and Zinn, *Critical Essays*. Taylor develops a similar view in his *Swords and Plowshares*, in discussing 'the new Cold War technique directed against the sources of our power,' more acute than ever 'because of the increasing strength and boldness of the international revolutionary movement and the mind-numbing power of press and television in their effect on the critical

judgment of the public.' To 'cope with [this threat], we need a new concept of national security broad enough to assure that defensive measures are taken against subversion in this form' (p. 413). Cited and discussed in 'The Mind of the Ruling Class,' *Monthly Review*, June 1972. For expression of similar concerns on the part of academic intellectuals, see *At War with Asia*, pp. 60–3. Complaints about media bias – that is, occasional departures from government propaganda – are now common among the military. See, for example, Colonel Wesley W. Yale (retired), 'On Ignorance of Armies,' *Army*, June 1972. He fears that 'editorial policy will probably not return to its World War II standards of responsibility by refusing to print material prejudicial to the national interest,' as defined by the army, quite properly, since 'the Army is the public.' This is a serious matter in an era when 'expropriation of US properties is damaging both psychologically and economically,' and when the population must be made to understand the 'painful truth that if you want economic influence and prosperity for yourself and your children you must not only be prepared to fight for it, but exhibit the will to do so'; 'a soft and affluent society must be made to see that all-out war is the most logical path to permanent peace.'

40. William Bundy, commenting on problems of lying, IV, 611.

41. On the contrary, 'false, fictitious or fraudulent statements or representations' by government officials in the area of their jurisdiction is a crime punishable by heavy fines or up to five years imprisonment (*United States Code*, vol. 18, sec. 1001). For discussion, see Peter Dale Scott, *The War Conspiracy*, a detailed examination of fraud and deception in the course of the Indochina war.

42. In December 1965, the 'intelligence community' estimated at almost fifty-fifty the probability that significant United States escalation would lead to the introduction of Chinese forces, always understood as the trigger for nuclear 'retaliation.' With the exception of State's INR, intelligence appeared to favour escalation, including strikes against North Vietnamese petroleum reserves (IV, 64–5). Senator Symington, long an advocate of more extensive use of airpower, has recently expressed the view that B-52 raids in northern Laos, far from the Ho Chi Minh Trail and conducted in secrecy, 'are dangerous to the security of the United States' and that 'any air activity around northern Laos has in it the incipient danger of starting a major war' (*Congressional Record*, August 3, 1971, pp. S12939, S12951).

43. Proudhon, cited in Daniel Guérin, ed., *Ni Dieu ni Maître*, p. 115.

44. My own views on this matter, relying on material prior to the Pentagon study, are presented in *For Reasons of State*, Chapter 1. See the references cited there. See also the important essays in Richard A. Falk, *Legal Order in a Violent World*, and in Falk, ed., *The International Law of Civil War*.

45. Noting that this doctrine, too, was devised to protect a tyrant from the right of resistance. See Gerald A. Sumida, 'The Right of Revolution,' in Charles A. Barker, ed., *Power and Law*, p. 133.

46. See Lawyers Committee on American Policy Toward Vietnam, *Vietnam and International Law*, pp. 27–8. On SEATO, see *For Reasons of State*, Chapter 6.

47. *Congressional Record*, June 6, 1967, S7733–4. Article 1, here also nonamendable, is the first article of the GVN Constitution of 1956. The DRV Constitution of 1960 states (article 1): 'The territory of Viet-Nam is a single, indivisible whole from North to South.' See Bernard Fall, *The Two Viet-Nams*, apps. 1, 2. The NLF has consistently put forward the official view that 'the southern zone' of Vietnam is to be 'an independent and sovereign state,' part of a neutral zone including Laos and Cambodia as well, with reunification to be a matter of slow evolution. Cf. the fourteen-point declaration of August 10, 1962, and other documents and official statements (George Chaffard, *Les Deux Guerres du Vietnam*, pp. 266, 255–6, Chapter 7 and 10, app.). The DRV has repeatedly indicated its acceptance of this position (*ibid.*, pp. 441–2).

48. Much later the documents commonly use the same terms. In April 1966: 'The overall objective is to cause NVN to cease supporting, directing, and controlling the insurgencies in South Vietnam and Laos' (IV, 81). Cf. also IV, 59, 562, etc.

49. Lyndon Johnson, September 28, 1964. Cited in Falk *et al.*, *Vietnam and International Law*, p. 35.

50. In March 1965, when combat marines were deployed, the Third Marine Expeditionary Force was renamed the 'Third Marine Amphibious Force,' to avoid offending Vietnamese sensibilities – for what Ambassador Sullivan referred to elsewhere as 'cosmetic purposes' (II, 282, 319; 355; III, 462).

51. I disregard certain other arguments that have been offered. For instance, Wilson C. McWilliams observes, with supreme irrelevance, that 'Washington did not *think* it was planning an aggressive war.' It was guilty only of inaccuracy, not crime. *New York Times Book Review*, September 26, 1971, review of Ralph Stavins, *et al.*, *Washington Plans an Aggressive War* – an accurate title for this study, which adds considerable supplementary information to the Pentagon Papers.

52. United Nations, Secretariat, *Annual Report of the Secretary-General, 16 June 1964 to 15 June 1965* (A/6001), p. 48, cited by William Bruce, 'The United States and the Law of Mankind,' in Barker, *Power and Law*, p. 100. Discussing the same matter, P. E. Corbett concludes that the various General Assembly resolutions 'appear to place intervention on behalf of an existing government on the same footing as aid to its rebel opposition,' noting, however, that this demands a radical change in the established practice of states. 'The Vietnam Struggle,' in Falk, *International Law of Civil War*, pp. 374, 402.

53. As reported by John Spencer, in *American Journal of International Law*, vol. 61, no. 3 (1967), cited by Nam-Yearl Chai, 'Law as a Barrier to Change,' in Barker, *Power and Law*, p. 114. Chai goes on to illustrate how 'the rules of law were used as legal barriers by Japan and Western powers to frustrate Korean aspirations for national independence' and

to explain why 'Koreans regarded law as an instrument of oppression.'

54. Edward Weisband and Thomas M. Franck, 'The Brezhnev–Johnson Two-World Doctrine,' *Trans-action*, October 1971. See also Franck and Weisband, *World Politics*, for an elaboration of these themes.

55. This section is largely excerpted from my article, 'The Pentagon Papers as Propaganda and as History,' in Chomsky and Zinn, *Critical Essays*, which contains extensive discussion and documentation on the matters mentioned briefly here, and on other related matters.

56. See my essay in Chomsky and Zinn, *Critical Essays*, for references and discussion. See particularly the important study by Jeffrey Race, *War Comes to Long An*. He points out that until 1959 the Communists had a near monopoly on violence. It was not until the Communists rescinded the prohibition against armed struggle in 1959 that 'the threat was equalized for both sides,' though in later years as well 'the government terrorized far more than did the revolutionary movement,' and by so doing, contributed to its growing strength. See also Chaffard, *Les Deux Guerres*, p. 233: in 1959 Hanoi responded to the appeal of the Viet Minh veterans of the South, permitting 'violence *only* in self-defense.'

57. *DOD*, bk 8, pp. 190–1. Characteristically, Acheson added that this appeared to be the only way to safeguard Vietnam from 'aggressive designs Commie Chi[na].'

58. *Ibid.*, pp. 145, 158. State Department policy statement of September 1948, cited above, p. 27.

59. IV, 488–9. He also points out (IV, 487) that in the Delta, with 40 per cent of the population, the Viet Cong effort is primarily indigenous and the North Vietnamese main-force units play almost no role (though United States combat forces were operating; see below, notes 133 and 147). Still, he is able to say that our objective is to permit the people of South Vietnam to determine their own future.

60. It might be added that the policy later called 'Vietnamization' was recommended in mid-1967 by System Analysis; IV, 459, 467. Cf. also IV, 558, option (4); 564.

61. See my articles in *Ramparts*, April and May 1972 (the latter in part incorporated in *For Reasons of State*, Chapter 2), and in the *New York Review of Books*, June 15, 1972; also Gabriel Kolko, 'The Nixon Administration's Strategy in Indochina 1972,' Paris World Assembly, February 1972. See section VI, 7 below.

62. Cf. Joseph Buttinger, *Vietnam: A Dragon Embattled*, vol. 2, p. 981: 'the National Liberation Front was truly the Vietminh reborn' there was a 'similarity, or better near identity, of the Vietminh and the National Liberation Front.' I noticed a similar usage of terminology in Laos, interviewing refugees from the Plain of Jars. They generally referred to the Pathet Lao as 'Issara,' the name of the independence movement that fought the Japanese and then the French. See Branfman, *Voices from the Plain of Jars*, p. 12. Though there is little doubt that the NLF incorporated much of the former southern Viet Minh, it repre-

sented itself as broader in base and not strictly socialist in character. Cf. Chaffard, *Les Deux Guerres*, p. 419. Chaffard and several other independent and highly qualified observers take this seriously, though sources close to the United States government generally do not.

63. Cited from AFP, in Nguyen Khac Vien, ed., *South Vietnam: Realities and Prospects*, p. 27.

64. For a detailed analysis, see Peter King, 'The Political Balance in Saigon,' *Pacific Affairs*, vol. 44, no. 3 (1971). See also Gareth Porter, 'The Diemist Restoration,' *Commonweal*, July 11, 1969. A further change in the character of the regime is its profound corruption, far beyond that of the Diem period, a direct consequence of the full-scale American invasion in the mid-1960s. On this matter, see *At War with Asia*, pp. 71–2, 195–6, 205, 257–8; Frances Fitzgerald, *Fire in the Lake*, pp. 311, 346–7; and McCoy, *et al.*, *Politics of Heroin*.

65. Cf. in particular Gabriel Kolko, *The Roots of American Foreign Policy*, and the discussion in Kolko and Kolko, *Limits of Power*; *At War with Asia*, chap. 1; Committee of Concerned Asian Scholars, *The Indochina Story*, pt 3; and other references cited earlier. See also the articles by Dower, Du Boff, and Kolko in Chomsky and Zinn, *Critical Essays*.

66. See Walt W. Rostow and Richard W. Hatch, *An American Policy in Asia*, p. 7. In Rostow's view, this 'ideological threat to our interest ... is as great as the military threat' posed by Communist China and the Soviet Union. It is essential, Rostow notes, 'to emphasize ... especially the close link between Japan's dangerous foreign trade problem and the requirements of growth in Southeast Asia' (p. 12), and to remove the 'illusory glamor' of trade with the Communist bloc, which 'represent[s] a powerful attraction' (though an unreal one), particularly to Japan (pp. 46–7). Furthermore, 'The relative performance of India and Communist China over the course of their respective First Five Year Plans may very well determine the outcome of the ideological struggle in Asia' (p. 37). 'India and Asia could be won to Communism without a Chinese Communist soldier crossing Chinese borders,' if 'the Communist bid to win Asia by demonstrating rapid industrialization' is more successful than development in 'Free Asian societies' (pp. 51–2). It is also necessary 'to learn to deal effectively with subversion and insurrection ... as now in South Vietnam' (p. 7). The book is interesting as the ideological expression of an influential planner of the 1960s, with its emphasis on our fundamental interest in preserving open societies with no 'concentrated power' in the state (pp. 4–5, 14; other forms of 'concentrated power' go unmentioned). For further discussion, see *American Power and the New Mandarins*, p. 332.

67. These fears were re-evaluated shortly, when it appeared that China was undergoing an economic crisis, but may well be voiced again in the future.

68. For some discussion, see Donald Zagoria, 'The Strategic Debate in Peking,' in Tang Tsou, ed., *China in Crisis*, vol. 2, pp. 249–50.

69. See, for example, Roger Hilsman's discussion of this speech in his *To Move a Nation*. For comments, see my *American Power and the New Mandarins*, Chapter 3, pp. 262–6.

70. For example, by Chester Cooper, 'The CIA and Decision-making,' *Foreign Affairs*, vol. 50, no. 2 (1972).

71. John Dower, 'The Superdomino in Postwar Asia: Japan in and out of the *Pentagon Papers*,' in Chomsky and Zinn, *Critical Essays*.

72. Compare Ho Chi Minh and Phibun Songkhram, the Japanese collaborator who had overthrown the government of Thailand in April 1948 after his poor showing in the elections, 'the first pro-Axis dictator to regain power after the war' (Frank C. Darling, *Thailand and the United States*, p. 65). Support from the United States was immediate, one of the measures taken 'to deter Communist aggression in Southeast Asia' (p. 67).

73. Cited in Chester Cooper, *The Lost Crusade*, p. 168. A bit 'melodramatic,' Cooper feels, but otherwise unexceptionable.

74. Robert W. Tucker, *The Radical Left and American Foreign Policy*, pp. 116–17.

75. On Japanese–Southeast Asian relations and their significance, see Jon Halliday and Gavan McCormack, *Japanese Imperialism*.

76. Cooper, *Lost Crusade*, pp. 410–11.

77. Stavins *et al.*, *Washington Plans an Aggressive War*, p. 20.

78. See *At War with Asia*, Chapter 1, for references. For general background, see Dower, 'The Superdomino in Postwar Asia.'

79. See C. Fred Bergsten, 'Crisis in U.S. Trade Policy,' *Foreign Affairs*, vol. 49, no. 4 (1971).

80. For data, see Yasuo Takeyama, 'Don't Take Japan for Granted,' *Foreign Policy*, vol. 1, no. 2 (1971–72).

81. Or, as Kindleberger puts it in his caricature, the theory that 'United States economic foreign policy is unrelievedly evil.' Review article on *The Age of Imperialism* by Harry Magdoff, *Public Policy*, summer 1971.

82. On the evolution of United States policy in the crucial 1945–1950 period, see John Dower, 'Occupied Japan and the American Lake,' in Edward Friedman and Mark Selden, eds, *America's Asia*. On the limits of American power in the real world, see Kolko and Kolko, *Limits of Power*.

83. Zbigniew Brzezinski, 'Japan's Global Engagement,' *Foreign Affairs*, vol. 50, no. 2 (1972); Takeyama, 'Don't Take Japan for Granted.' For comparison, American firms control about 40 per cent of the British computer industry (Raymond Vernon, *Sovereignty at Bay*, p. 240). Excluding table-top machines, IBM has about 70 per cent of Japan's computer market (Koji Nakamura, 'The Okinawa Payoff,' *Far Eastern Economic Review*, August 21, 1971).

84. On this and related matters, see Malcolm Caldwell, 'Oil and Imperialism in East Asia,' *Journal of Contemporary Asia*, vol. 1, no. 3 (1971).

85. Thus the director of USAID for Brazil finds it quite natural that 'we have spent $2 billion [since 1964] on a program one objective of which is the protection of a favorable investment climate for private business interests in this country,' while the total investment is about $1·7 billion. Senator Frank Church, in Church Subcommittee Hearings, pp. 165–6. On the other alleged objectives, see below, pp. 77.

86. This is argued, with reference to Vietnam, by Arthur Schlesinger, Jr, in testimony before the Senate Foreign Relations Committee, May 10, 1972; and commonly by others. Schlesinger considers the 'more sophisticated' economic argument that defeat in Vietnam would jeopardize American economic interests throughout the Third World, failing to notice that this is only part of the argument offered by those he hopes to refute. Rather, they have generally pointed out that United States policy in Indochina was closely related to its efforts to consolidate Japanese and Western European capitalism. Schlesinger also remarks that the Pentagon Papers seem to record 'no instances of business intervention in American Vietnam policy.' The relevance of this observation is not apparent, given the fact that the state executive is largely staffed by representatives of corporate interests, as has often been noted (see note 114). It is hardly necessary for business to 'intervene' in an enterprise that it largely controls. Schlesinger also urges that 'stupidity' should not be underestimated as a factor in shaping policy.

87. Derek Davies, 'The Region,' *Far Eastern Economic Review Yearbook*, 1971, p. 38; 1972, pp. 37–40. Although Davies refers to the domino theory as 'a flight of fantasy,' he unwittingly expresses a moderate version of it in such assessments as these. The economic and strategic significance of Southeast Asia is stressed by many observers. Few would go so far as Peter Lyon, who argues that if some enemy monopolized the region and exploited its resources fully (as Japan could not, in World War II), 'then plainly the world balance of power very probably would have swung already in favour of South-east Asia's new hegemon' (*War and Peace in South-east Asia*, p. 106). But, with qualifications, the point of view is not uncommon.

88. On the British precedent, see Michael Barratt Brown, *After Imperialism*; Eric Hobsbawm, *Industry and Empire*.

89. Leslie H. Gelb, 'Vietnam: The System Worked,' *Foreign Policy*, vol. 1, no. 3 (1971). See also his comments in 'On Schlesinger and Ellsberg: A Reply,' *New York Review of Books*, December 2, 1971, and in 'Lessons of the Pentagon Papers,' *Life*, September 17, 1971.

90. Daniel Ellsberg explores in detail the hypothesis that domestic factors, in particular the effect of anticommunism on electoral success, predominated in decision making. 'The Quagmire Myth and the Stalemate Machine,' *Public Policy*, spring 1971. See his *Papers on the War*, for an extended version. Emphasis on these factors is not inconsistent with the imperialist interpretation, if we inquire further into the origins of domestic anticommunism though an important question of emphasis remains (see note 102). Notice also that by 1965, questions of long-term

motive were of diminished importance. We were there. Period. See the remarks of John McNaughton (IV, 47).

91. Hannah Arendt, 'Lying in Politics: Reflections on the Pentagon Papers,' *New York Review of Books*, November 18, 1971.

92. Similarly, Leslie Gelb, discussing the origins of the insurgency, notes that no direct links had been established between Hanoi and the Southern insurgents in the 1956–1959 period. Still he tends, rather cautiously, towards the view that 'some form of DRV apparatus' may have 'originated and controlled the insurgency' in those years (though 'it can only be inferred' – the reader is invited to sample the evidence presented for the inference; I, 243).

93. Senate Concurrent Resolution 91 of June 25, 1954, found 'strong evidence of intervention by the international Communist movement in the State of Guatemala, whereby government institutions have been infiltrated by Communist agents, weapons of war have been secretly shipped into that country, and the pattern of Communist conquest has become manifest' (cited by Franck and Weisband, *World Politics*, p. 52).

94. It is sometimes argued that United States policy revealed its freedom from counterrevolutionary imperatives in Bolivia and Yugoslavia. In Bolivia, Eisenhower supported the most right-wing group that had any base of power – successfully, as it turned out, from the viewpoint of American economic interests. For a succint review, see Rebecca Scott, 'Economic Aid and Imperialism in Bolivia,' *Monthly Review*, May 1972. As for Tito, Acheson explained in connection with the possibility of a 'Titoist outcome' in Indochina that 'US attitude [could] take [account] such possibility only if every other possible avenue closed to preservation area from Kremlin control' (*DOD*, bk 8, p. 197; May 1949). Recall that Acheson had no evidence of Kremlin control in Indochina, nicely illustrating the point at issue. In general, United States policy towards Yugoslavia in the context of the cold war hardly serves as a counterexample to the thesis that it is guided by the principle of maintaining a 'stable' system of societies open to American economic penetration.

95. On this matter, see John Gittings, 'The Great Asian Conspiracy,' in Friedman and Selden, *America's Asia*. He shows how easily China replaced Russia as the master plotter in official and academic interpretation of Far Eastern affairs, when reliance on the alleged Russian role became too far-fetched. It now appears that the official demonology is being reconstructed once again, with the Soviet Union as the chief villain, surely a wise move by state propagandists. It would, for example, be difficult in the long run to gain taxpayer support for an immense military budget on the basis of the 'Chinese threat,' but it is considerably easier to whip up hysteria over the alleged Soviet menace, along the lines of the 'bomber gap' and 'missile gap' of earlier years. Precisely what we see today. The United States lead in deliverable warheads and strategic weapons technology (e.g. MIRV) notwith-

standing, the Alsop brothers and the like would have us believe that we are now virtually at the mercy of the Kremlin.

96. Peter Wiles, 'The Declining Self-confidence of the Super-powers,' *International Affairs*, vol. 47, no. 2 (1971).

97. William Pfaff, *Condemned to Freedom*, p. 80. A variant is the view expressed by Michael Howard: 'The suspicion, clumsiness, and brutality of the Russians; the inexperience and confusion of the Americans; the weariness, impotence and nostalgia of the British' – these were the major factors in preventing a post-war settlement. 'The Americans, bless them, still found it hard to believe that natural processes would not everywhere throw up regimes which would docilely accept their leadership' ('Realists and Romantics: On Maintaining an International Order,' *Encounter*, April 1972). This particular form of sentimentality finds little support in the historical record, which reveals fairly systematic policies designed to take over British positions of power and influence and to create a global capitalist order in which the United States, given its enormous advantages, would be likely to predominate. The United States did not believe that 'natural processes' would lead to subservient regimes in Southern Europe, France, East Asia, and the Caribbean, nor did it await such processes; rather, it acted directly and forcefully to undermine popular forces it opposed or to institute regimes of the sort it preferred. While not uniformly successful, these policies and their execution revealed no more inexperience or confusion than might be expected, given the unavoidable uncertainties of global planning. See Kolko and Kolko, *Limits of Power*.

98. On Italy, see Gabriel Kolko, *The Politics of War*. On Greece, see the references of note 192. On Korea, see Jon Halliday, 'The Korean Revolution,' *Socialist Revolution*, vol. 1, no. 6 (1970); also Soon Sung Cho, *Korea in World Politics, 1940–1950*, and Gregory Henderson, *Korea: The Politics of the Vortex*, Chapters 5–6. Though Cho and Henderson do not accept Halliday's interpretation of these events, what they describe is the destruction of indigenous Korean political social structures by force and terror and the imposition of a right-wing regime. Their explanation in terms of 'blunders,' 'ignorance and policy weakness,' and so on becomes much less persuasive if we consider United States Korean policy, not in isolation, as in common academic practice, but rather in its global context, where remarkable similarities appear to American intervention and its efforts elsewhere, as in Greece at exactly the same time.

Halliday's openly and clearly expressed sympathies for socialist revolution may be compared with the conservative bias implicit in – but, typically, never explicitly recognized – in Henderson and Cho. Consider such observations as these: Though under the People's Republic that the United States destroyed in South Korea there were occasional acts such as 'interventions, usually against landlords in landlord–tenant disputes,' nevertheless 'people were generally well-behaved' (Henderson, p. 119); '. . . the Americans in the South took steps to encourage democratization by establishing an effective Korean administration under the military government, and by stamping out what they felt were irresponsible leftist political movements' (Cho, p. 131), beginning with the outright suppression of the Communist party in late 1946.

In fact, the Korean Policy of the United States from 1945 presents suggestive analogies, in some interesting respects, to its policy in Vietnam, a matter that might be further explored.

99. Arthur M. Schlesinger, Jr., *A Thousand Days*, p. 769.

100. Tucker, *The Radical Left*, p. 112; *Nation or Empire?* p. 117.

101. This is admitted even by those who deny that 'Castro was unwillingly pushed into the Soviet camp by American blunders or malevolence' (Ernst Halperin, characterizing the position of Andrés Suárez, *Cuba: Castroism and Communism*, in the foreword). Thus Suárez points out that Cuba was attacked 'by airplanes based along the US coastline' at the time when the United States was using its influence to prevent the Cubans from buying jets in Great Britain (October 1959), and adds, 'I think this makes it sufficiently clear why, and for what, Soviet aid was sought' (p. 74). Though the matter is not relevant to refuting Tucker's contention, a good case can be made that American hostility was a factor of some importance in Castro's shift to the Soviet camp. See Maurice Zeitlin and Robert Scheer, *Cuba: Tragedy in Our Hemisphere*. For a general discussion of the background, see Gordon Connel-Smith, *The Inter-American System*. He draws the quite reasonable conclusion that 'the Cuban government's intention to implement a policy aimed at ending the privileged position hitherto enjoyed by the United States in the island's affairs' made the clash as inevitable as 'the growing links between Cuba and international communism' (p. 170); and this intention also lies behind the fact that 'the United States infinitely preferred Trujillo to Castro' (p. 169). Given the vagueness of his discussion, it is unclear whether Tucker would agree with this conclusion. If he would, then his objection to the 'radical critique' is of vanishing empirical content.

102. Tucker, *The Radical Left*, pp. 111–12. Emphasis mine. Tucker refers to a third consideration underlying Kennedy's observation on supporting a Trujillo as long as there is a risk of a Castro, namely, concern for domestic anticommunism. This overlooks the crucial question of the origins and function of this domestic anticommunism, in particular the role and purpose of state propaganda. On this matter see Richard M. Freeland, *The Truman Doctrine and the Origins of McCarthyism*, and several essays in David Horowitz, ed., *Corporations and the Cold War*.

103. On certain similarities, see *American Power and the New Mandarins*, Chapter 2; also Hilary Conroy, 'Japan's War in China: Historical Parallel to Vietnam?' *Pacific Affairs*, vol. 43, no. 2 (1970).

104. Supporting what might misleadingly be called a United States security interest. On the relation between Greece and American interests in the Middle East, see Kolko and Kolko, *Limits of Power*,

Chapter 8.

105. M. S. Modiano, 'Stans, in Athens, Hails the Regime,' *New York Times*, April 24, 1971. It may be recalled that the Truman Doctrine was, in the first instance, specifically directed to Greece and Turkey. Greece required United States assistance 'to become a self-supporting and self-respecting democracy' and 'the 'future of Turkey as an independent and economically sound state is clearly no less important to the freedom-loving peoples of the world than the future of Greece' (Harry S. Truman, March 12, 1947). A look at the state of freedom in Greece and Turkey twenty-five years later gives a certain insight into the 'policy of the United States,' as formulated by President Truman on that occasion: 'to support free peoples who are resisting attempted subjugation by armed minorities or by outside pressures.'

106. William Y. Elliot, ed., *The Political Economy of American Foreign Policy*, p. 42. For quotations from this interesting document, and some discussion, see my *At War with Asia*, pp. 5, 17, 35–8. See Brown, *After Imperialism*, for a historical discussion of this matter.

107. Raymond Vernon (*Sovereignty at Bay*) concludes that the multinational corporations are 'seen as posing a threat [in the host countries] for government leaders bent on control, for local businessmen who aspire to compete, and for intellectuals who are hoping to challenge the status quo' (pp. 249, 265). But he makes no mention of workers who are concerned, say, that management can break a strike by threatening to transfer operations to another country. Unions and others concerned with workers' interests take a different view. See, e.g., Hugh Scanlon, 'International Combines Versus the Unions,' *Bulletin of the Institute for Workers' Control*, vol. 1, no. 4 (1969); and several articles in the preceding special issue on the motor industry. These articles, incidentally, deal with concrete examples, not merely hypothetical concerns. See also John Gennard, *Multinational Corporations and British Labour*, again with several concrete examples. Vernon's failure to consider this matter cannot be attributed to his (likely) belief that the concern is irrational, since he does not seem overly impressed with the 'psychic needs' of the 'elite groups' he does consider.

It is, furthermore, disturbing to see how myths are perpetuated in such work. Consider Vernon's reference to the 'extraordinary concept of aid to less-developed countries' – a look at the facts would show that this concept is something less than extraordinary – or his speculation that nations will 'continue to emphasize such goals as the redistribution of personal income' (pp. 213, 257). Which nations will 'continue' to emphasize such goals? The United States?

108. Connel-Smith, *Inter-American System*, pp. 343–4.

109. Church Subcommittee Hearings, p. 165. See note 85 above.

110. *Ibid.*, p. 208. See, in this connection, 'The Hanna Industrial Complex, Part I,' *NACLA Newsletter*, vol. 2, no. 3 (May 1968). Hanna was one of the major beneficiaries of the 1964 coup.

111. *Washington Post*, December 6, 1971: some 'awkward points' for

visiting dictator Medici. Christopher Roper reports in the finance section of the *Manchester Guardian Weekly*, May 13, 1972: 'Wages have been deliberately held down, and statistical evidence shows that real wages of factory workers in São Paulo – the largest industrial centre in the southern hemisphere of the world – have been almost halved over the past 10 years. Family incomes have only kept pace by workers working longer hours and wives going out to work.' But, 'foreign capital has been given a warm welcome'; 'Volkswagen operates one of the largest integrated car manufacturing plants in the world; Ford is about to manufacture Pinto engines for Detroit in São Paulo [the ones Henry II decided not to make in Britain? cf. note 107]; and Nippon Steel from Japan is thinking about building one of the world's largest steel mills.' Notice that while United States policy is quite clearly determined, as stated, by 'the protection and expansion ... of our economic interests,' the rules of the international capitalist game, if more or less followed, lead to certain problems even for the strongest player.

112. Marcio Moreira Alves, 'Brazil: What Terror Is Like,' *The Nation*, March 15, 1971. Alves is a former member of Parliament, a leader of the Catholic left, now in exile in Paris. He cites figures indicating that the average wage for 70 per cent of workers has declined by almost 20 per cent since 1964, while production has increased by more than 20 per cent. He also describes the concentration of wealth, 'the hunger and misery that drive millions of landless peasants to the cities,' the destruction of peasant leagues by the army, the police and the private paramilitary forces of landlords, the banning in many places of the Catholic basic-education movement which promoted peasant organization, the destruction of schools for peasants established by foreign missionaries, 'the incredible violence that the state itself must use to keep the masses quiet while the privileged squander the nation's riches,' the torture and murder, the anti-Semitism of the military officers, and so on.

113. Church Subcommittee Hearings, p. 149.

114. On this matter, see Kolko, *Roots of American Foreign Policy*, Chapter 1; Richard Barnet, *The Economy of Death*, pt 2, and *Roots of War*, Chapter 3, and pt 2; G. William Domhoff, *The Higher Circle*, Chapter 5; David Horowitz, 'The Foundations,' *Ramparts*, April 1969, and 'The Making of America's China Policy,' *Ramparts*, October 1971. See also Scott, *War Conspiracy*, introduction and Chapter 8, on interconnections between the CIA and important business interests.

115. See pp. 59–60 above. This particular factor is explored by Seymour Melman in his *Pentagon Capitalism*.

116. See *At War with Asia*, Chapter 1, for some further discussion of the multiplicity of mutually supportive factors and the stable system they tend to produce.

117. For instance, Herbert Feis ridicules the view, which he attributes without specific reference to Gar Alperovitz, that 'the Soviet govern-

ment . . . was merely the hapless object of our vicious diplomacy.' The view that Alperovitz actually develops is that 'the Cold War cannot be understood simply as an American response to a Soviet challenge, but rather as the insidious interaction of mutual suspicions, blame for which must be shared by all' Cf. Alperovitz, *Cold War Essays*, pp. 135, 31; also Christopher Lasch's comments, in the introduction, on 'the general failure of orthodox historians to engage the revisionist argument.'

118. On the substance of the 'Nixon Doctrine,' see John Dower's essay in Brodine *et al.*, *Open Secret*.

119. McGeorge Bundy, February 7, 1965; III, 687–91. The reprisals against North Vietnam are for '*any* VC act of violence to persons or property,' as in the case of the Pleiku attack used as a pretext for initiating the bombing of the North, where there was not even a pretence that North Vietnamese were involved. This is quite in accord with NSC 5429/2, more than ten years before. Cf. p. 112 below.

120. April 6, 1964. The Security Council then proceeded to adopt a resolution condemning reprisals as 'incompatible with the purposes and principles of the United Nations.' For this and other references to the illegality of reprisal, see Falk *et al.*, *Vietnam and International Law*, pp. 53–4, 98–101.

121. In the North, at least. In the South, and under Nixon–Kissinger in Laos and Cambodia, the question arises in a different form. With memories of gas chambers, some may be reluctant (as I have been personally) to use such terms as 'genocide.' The question whether the term is technically appropriate, in the light of the United Nations Convention of 1948, is a different matter. It was considered by the Russell Tribunal well before the significant escalation of the technological war in 1968 and on the basis of a small fraction of the evidence now available. See John Duffett, ed., *Against the Crime of Silence*, pp. 612–43.

122. IV, 71–4. Discussing the plans to destroy North Vietnamese petroleum reserves, the analyst notes that 'neither in OSD nor the White House had anyone opposed these measures on other than prudential grounds – the risk of alienating allies or provoking Chinese or Russian intervention or uncertainty that results would justify either the risks or the costs' (IV, 74–5).

123. See Gabriel Kolko in Duffett, *Against the Crime of Silence*, p. 224.

124. See *Chronology of the Vietnam War*, bk 1, distributed by Association d'Amitié Franco-Vietnamienne, 5, rue Las Cases, 75-Paris (7).

125. Note that RT in 1965 amounted to 33,000 tons of bombs, of a total of about 530,000 dropped on North Vietnam by end 1968. See Rafael Littauer *et al.*, *The Air War in Indochina*, p. SS-14.

126. See *American Power and the New Mandarins*, p. 15; *For Reasons of State*, Ch. 1. See also Barry Weisberg, ed., *Ecocide in Indochina*, in particular the eyewitness report by Orville Schell and Barry Weisberg,

p. 24. Attacks on the 'dams and waterways in the crucial Red River Delta' were reported during the first monsoon season following the initiation of RT. ('The "Enemy": 20,000 Missions Later,' *Newsweek*, October 11, 1965). The planes struck in August, according to this report. On the logic of such attacks, see the staff study 'The Attack on the Irrigation Dams in North Korea,' *Air University Quarterly Review*, Winter 1953–54. Gloating over the USAF attack on dams which caused a flash flood that 'scooped clean 27 miles of valley below,' constituting 'one of the most significant air operations of the Korean War,' the study explains that the smashing of the dams means 'the destruction of their chief sustenance – rice': 'The Westerner can little conceive the awesome meaning which the loss of this staple food commodity has for the Asian – starvation and slow death . . . more feared than the deadliest plague. Hence the show of rage, the flare of violent tempers. . . .'

127. Bernard Fall, 'This Isn't Munich, It's Spain,' *Ramparts*, December 1965; reprinted in *Last Reflections*, pp. 232–3.

128. The hospital compound that replaced it was bombed on December 26, 1971. See the eyewitness report by Banning Garrett, who visited a few days later, *The Guardian* (New York), February 16, 1972; *New York Times*, February 10, 1972, contains a briefer report. The hospital was visited by George Wald on February 19; see his 'Our Bombs Fall on People,' *Washington Monthly*, May 1972. See also the report of Joel Henri of AFP, *New York Times*, May 9, 1972: 'In the bomb-scarred provinces of Thanhhoa and Namha, where no military target could be seen, this correspondent today visited a hospital and school struck by American bombs. . . . It was hard for the visitors to believe that the destruction [of the Thanh Hoa hospital], which was considerable, could have been the result of a mistake. The buildings, surrounded by rice fields, were also attacked last December, according to the North Vietnamese.' Henri is describing the raid of April 27, 1972. This final destruction of the hospital caused it to be evacuated to the mountains. Henri also visited a village where the primary school was bombed during morning classes, leaving 20 dead and 25 wounded: 'We looked for the military targets that might have justified the raid, but there was nothing – just mud and straw huts.'

129. C. O. Holmquist, 'Developments and Problems in Carrier-Based Attack Aircraft,' *Naval Review*, 1969, p. 214. Laser-controlled bombs and other innovations now give pinpoint accuracy, it is claimed. Therefore, the extensive destruction of civilian targets cannot be attributed to 'error.' Cf. Claude Julien, reporting from Hanoi on the 'remarkable precision of American bombings' of 'hospitals, dikes, villages,' *Le Monde*, May 20, 1972.

130. Stavins *et al.*, *Washington Plans an Aggressive War*, pp. 182–3. Stavins' analysis is also interesting with regard to the 'conspiracy' in the field against Washington. Pilots have complained that inter-service rivalries led to dangerous missions with high loss rate. See also Colonel James Donovan, *Militarism, U.S.A.*, pp. 180–1.

196 *The Backroom Boys*

131. IV, 408–9. Shortly after the Iron Triangle was 'destroyed' in Operation CEDAR FALLS, 'basically the same area' was invaded again in Operation JUNCTION CITY. The reader will find a brief description of the latter, but not the official map indicating the areas, including many villages, scheduled for destruction by preliminary air and artillery bombardment.

132. Griffiths, *Vietnam Inc.*, p. 89. Fall, *Last Reflections*, p. 248. See also Jonathan Schell, *The Village of Ben Suc*; *My American Power and the New Mandarins*, Chapter 3, n. 19, pp. 276–8.

133. B-52 raids in 1965 in the densely populated Mekong Delta were reported by Bernard Fall, 'Vietnam Blitz.' Takashi Oka reported B-52 raids in 'the populous delta' on December 4, 1965 (*Christian Science Monitor*; Melman, *In the Name of America* p. 248), noting the civilian casualties and the refugees fleeing to government-controlled areas 'because they could no longer bear the continuous bombings.' Fall also flew on bombing attacks on undefended villages, at about the same time ('This Isn't Munich, It's Spain'), as have many others. George Smith, a special forces sergeant captured by the NLF, reports B-52 raids (in Cambodia, he believes), along with constant and heavy bombing with napalm and high explosives in the free-fire zone where his camp was located, the latter from December 1964 (*P.O.W.: Two Years with the Vietcong*). Of course, the bombers were no more able to avoid villages than his POW camp. See also Russo, 'Inside the RAND Corporation,' on the effects of B-52 raids, as determined from refugee interviews. See also pp. 25–6 above.

134. Bernard Fall, 'Vietcong – the Unseen Enemy in Vietnam,' *New Society*, April 22, 1965, reprinted in Bernard Fall and Marcus G. Raskin, eds., *The Vietnam Reader*, p. 261.

135. T. D. Allman, 'The Blind Bombers,' *Far Eastern Economic Review*, January 29, 1972.

136. *New York Times*, letter, January 12, 1972.

137. Sidney Hook, 'Lord Russell and the War Crimes "Trial",' *New Leader*, October 24, 1966. The reader who suspects that Hook may have learned something since may turn to *The Humanist*, January 1971, where he describes the destruction in Vietnam as 'the unintended consequences of military action.'

138. Rather consistently. In the same (1966) article, Hook refers to the United States' Dominican intervention of 1965 as an 'error' traceable to 'mistaken appraisal of the involvement of foreign Communist regimes.'

139. McGeorge Bundy, 'End of Either/Or,' *Foreign Affairs*, vol. 45, no. 2 (1967). My reference is inexact, since Bundy seemed to regard anyone who disagreed on more than tactical matters as a wild man. Earlier, 'the McGeorge Bundy group' (which included McNaughton, Cooper, and Unger) drafted a memorandum (February 7, 1965; III, 309) which 'represents a highly personal Bundy assessment and point of view,' and which notes that 'none of the special solutions or criticisms

put forward with zeal by individual reformers in government or in the press is of major importance.' The Americans in Vietnam are the 'first team,' and though some of their tactical decisions may not have been perfect, clearly only a wild man in the wings would dare to question the first team in any more fundamental way.

140. A. J. Langguth, 'Vietnam – 1964: Exhilaration – 1968: Frustration – 1970: Hopelessness,' *New York Times Magazine*, October 4, 1970, p. 89. Five years earlier he wrote in the same place: 'I would say the war in South Vietnam changed irrevocably on Feb. 19, 1965 [when] America began using its immense air power [to] bomb South Vietnam' (Melman, *In the Name of America*, p. 174). The same source contains many other reports by American correspondents on the 'hundreds of air strikes every day against villages and other targets "suspected" of harboring the Viet Cong in cases where there is no ground engagement' (Raymond Coffey, p. 181), the pattern of forced refugee generation by bombs and shells. Recall the claims of General Tidwell, p. 86 above.

141. Reuters, *New York Times*, March 18, 1965; Melman, *In the Name of America*, p. 185.

142. Stanley Karnow, *New York Herald Tribune*, December 28, 1964; Melman, *In the Name of America*, pp. 184–5. Karnow blames the Viet Cong, whose presence led to the attack and who within a week were 'sanctimoniously denouncing "this monstrous crime".' Though convinced that the Viet Cong denunciation was 'sanctimonious,' Karnow does not address the more pertinent question: Was it correct?

It might incidentally be noted that ARVN reportedly used villagers, including children, specifically to draw enemy fire. See the August 1965 news report cited by Edward S. Herman, *Atrocities in Vietnam*, pp. 31–2. The United States has since refined this strategy. Local troops are used to establish contact with the enemy, then withdrawn (if possible) so that the area can be plastered with an air and artillery barrage (cf. Branfman, *Voices from the Plain of Jars*, p. 25). Sometimes, as in the Laos invasion of early 1971, the tactic partially backfires and the 'friendly' forces are decimated as well. A related device is the use of civilians to compel soldiers to fight, as when Montagnard families were denied evacuation from Kontum (spring 1972) or when the remnants of the Meo in Laos were denied the opportunity to move to unsettled areas to the west and kept in the path of the Pathet Lao–NVA advance towards Vientiane, according to well-informed observers.

143. Alain C. Enthoven and K. Wayne Smith, *How Much Is Enough?* pp. 305–6, reporting a Systems Analysis study. 'Unobserved strikes' are strikes against 'places where the enemy might be.' Civilians 'might be' there as well; or to be more realistic, they are the true enemy. The study concludes that the effects of such strikes on civilians in Viet Cong and friendly areas were often 'undesirable,' probably creating more Viet Cong than they 'eliminated.' Unobserved strikes constituted about 65 per cent of the tonnage of bombs and artillery rounds in 1966, and cost more than $2 billion. Despite the pretence of statistical evaluation, the

fact surely is that the United States has no information about the effects of this indiscriminate and blind attack on 'enemy' and 'friendly' areas.

On the rise in Viet Cong recruitment, generally attributed to unrestricted bombardment, see references in *American Power and the New Mandarins*, Chapter 3, n. 11, p. 276. Similar reports are common from Laos (see Fred Branfman, 'Presidential War in Laos,' in Adams and McCoy, *Laos*, p. 241) and Cambodia (see Richard Dudman, *Forty Days with the Enemy;* Boris Baczynskyj, 'Bombing Turns Cambodian Villagers into Refugees,' Dispatch News Service International, February 21, 1972, citing, for example, the case of a man who joined the Communists after an aerial attack left 50 dead in his native village).

144. Malcolm Browne, cited in *American Power and the New Mandarins*, p. 285, with further references from the same period (cf. pp. 335–6). More than half the total tonnage dropped on South Vietnam has been delivered by B-52s, much of it in settled areas. See Littauer *et al.*, *Air War*, pp. 4–8; also note 133, above. For details on bombing, see Jonathan Schell, *The Military Half*, and many other sources.

145. Cf. the comments by George Carver of the CIA (IV, 82) cited above, p. 77. Perhaps it is such comments as these that Chester Cooper had in mind when he observed that the Pentagon Papers make the CIA 'look good' ('The CIA and Decision-making,' p. 228).

146. Bernard Fall, 'Vietnam Blitz.' This, Fall suggests, is the reason why few weapons are found among the corpses. Note the early date of these comments. The author was very well informed, and no dove.

147. IV, 360. Cf. IV, 487, 548. The date of the 'first direct troop commitment to the Delta' is given as January 1967 (IV, 389). Jeffrey Race states that a battalion of the 25th Infantry Division arrived in Long An Province in September 1966, 'the first deployment of an American combat unit into the Mekong Delta,' though it was only in February 1967 that 'more aggressive tactics were adopted' *Long An*, pp. 216–17). NLF losses were high 'since the start of serious American combat operations in early 1967' (p. 270). The government 'violence program' involved heavy use of air and artillery attacks, which 'had a far more devastating impact on noncombatants than on combatants,' according to defectors. During 1968 artillery bombardment became so intense that 'large areas of the province looked (in words of one official) "like the face of the moon"' (pp. 236–7).

Race explains in detail how the NLF defeated the United States-backed GVN in this crucial delta province by 1965. Infiltration was 'negligible,' and the first PAVN (North Vietnamese) main-force battalions entered the province between December 1967 and February 1968, for missions against Saigon (p. 211). On press reports of PAVN troops in the delta, see *At War with Asia*, pp. 99–100.

148. January 9, 1967; Melman, *In the Name of America*, p. 98.

149. Cf. *ibid.*, p. 384; *At War with Asia*, pp. 93–101; Ellsberg, 'The Quagmire Myth.' Ellsberg notes that General Ewell, commanding the 9th Division in the delta, 'so completely freed his helicopter gunners

from restraints against firing on sampans in canals lined on both sides with housing that the Division reported body-count ratios of "friendly" to "enemy" dead unmatched in the history of the war.' Ewell was following the tactical principles laid down by the commanding general of the 1st Division, William DePuy, chief planner for Westmoreland, in the densely populated areas to the north. Kevin Buckley studied in detail one operation of Ewell's 9th Division in 1968, in the delta province of Kien Hoa. 'The death toll there,' he writes, 'made the My Lai massacre look trifling by comparison.' Official statistics cite nearly 11,000 killed, with 748 weapons found. An estimated 5,000 were noncombatant civilians ('at least'). The rest were combatants – that is, people defending their homes from the American aggressors. This operation was regarded as one of the most successful (and 'most representative') 'episodes in the history of pacification in Vietnam.' As General Abrams later stated, 'the performance of this division has been magnificent.' In this operation, 'the fabric of society long established by the NLF was destroyed' (*Newsweek*, June 19, 1972).

150. Naturally, this does not prevent the State Department (or the press) from referring to this as 'Hanoi's offensive' (IV, 581).

151. II, 517. Typically, the analyst does not notice the absurdity of this formulation, or what it implies as to who is 'the enemy.'

152. Littauer *et al.*, *Air War*, pp. 4–10. See Schell, *Military Half*.

153. *Boston Globe*, December 10, 1971; reprinted from the *Washington Post*.

154. General DePuy; cf. Ellsberg, 'The Quagmire Myth.'

155. Komer, 'Impact of Pacification on Insurgency in South Vietnam,' *Journal of International Affairs*, vol. 25, no. 1 (1971). Cf. *For Reasons of State*, Chapter 1.

156. Komer, 'Epilogue,' *ibid.*, no. 2; Eqbal Ahmad, 'Revolutionary War and Counter-insurgency,' *ibid.*, no. 1, pp. 44.

157. Komer, 'Pacification: A Look Back,' *Army*, June 1970, p. 23.

158. Allan Goodman, 'The Ending of the War as a Setting for the Future Development of South Vietnam,' *Asian Survey*, vol. 11, no. 4 (1971), p. 342 n.

159. UPI, *Le Monde*, November 5, 1971. Quotes are retranslated, since I have not come across this UPI report in the American press, apart from a reference by Richard Ward in *The Guardian*, November 17, 1971. For information on Operation Phoenix in 1968–9, see *At War with Asia*, pp. 301–2, and Herman, *Atrocities in Vietnam*, p. 47.

For more recent reports, see also Seymour Hersh, *Cover-up*; Race, *Long An*; Fitzgerald, *Fire in the Lake*. For a general review of the Phoenix programme, see Jon Cooper, 'Operation Phoenix,' Department of History, Dartmouth College.

The official figures cited in the UPI report are far more conservative than those cited in other sources. An official publication of the Saigon Ministry of Information gives the figure 40,994 killed in the Phoenix programme of a total of 81,039 convicted, killed, rallied. The period covered is August 1, 1968, given as the date of the launching of the Phoenix programme, through mid-1971 (*Vietnam 1967–71*, p. 52). Senator Kennedy refers to 'the estimated 48,000 civilians of the Vietcong infrastructure who have been killed by American-sponsored assassination teams' (*Problems of War Victims in Indochina*, Hearings before the [Kennedy] Subcommittee on Refugees and Escapees, US Senate, May 9, 1972, p. 9). The killing of 40,000 of the 'communist infrastructure' is reported by the Saigon Ministry of Information under the heading 'Programme Defending People Against Terrorism.'

160. Reported in Jon Cooper, 'Operation Phoenix.' The informant is Don Luce.

161. Tad Szulc, *New York Times*, April 7, 1971.

162. Frances Starner, 'I'll Do It My Way,' *Far Eastern Economic Review*, November 6, 1971.

163. Richard West, 'Vietnam: The Year of the Rat,' *New Statesman*, February 25, 1972. See also *For Reasons of State*, Chapter 1, note 71.

164. Former American participants report that US intelligence nets were also penetrated by right-wing Vietnamese groups who fed reports to fuel the 'bloodbath theory,' knowing that these would be transmitted to Washington and would leak to industrious reporters. To explain the absence of predicted uprisings and bloodbaths, the same right-wing agents point to the success of the Phoenix programme in weakening the NLF infrastructure. Thus while inciting bloodbath fears to gain United States support, these agents are also attempting to increase support for terror programmes which may well succeed in providing such sects as the VNQDD with a degree of political control under the American aegis. See the report by Jeffrey Stein, an agent handler in 1968–1969, 'Bloodbath over the Rainbow,' *The Phoenix* [Boston], May 10, 1972. As he notes, the bloodbath argument conveniently overlooks the absence of a bloodbath in areas under long NLF control – apart from the bloodbath caused by United States air and artillery.

165. See Jon Cooper, 'Operation Phoenix,' for details.

166. Pfaff, *Condemned to Freedom*, pp. 75–7, a close paraphrase (with no acknowledgment) of some remarkable passages in Townsend Hoopes's *Limits of Intervention*, on which I have commented elsewhere (*At War with Asia*, pp. 297–300). Since Hoopes mentions Pfaff in this earlier book, it is unclear who deserves the credit for these insights.

167. Pfaff adds at this point that 'it is not clear that [the Chinese Communists] understand the significance of the claim which Mao Tse-tung has made that China can "win" a nuclear war in which 300 million Chinese would die.' This 'claim' has been frequently attributed to Mao in anti-communist propaganda, but no source has been discovered. Chang Hsin-hai concludes that it is 'an outrageous and unmitigated falsehood, which everybody has accepted as gospel truth' (*America and China*, p. 227).

168. On the welfare of the Vietnamese under French rule, see Ngo Vinh Long, *Before the August Revolution*.

169. On the earlier period, see Truong Buu Lam, *Patterns of Vietnamese Response to Foreign Intervention*; Tam Vu and Nguyen Khac Vien, *A Century of National Struggle*; David G. Marr, *Vietnamese Anticolonialism*; Long, *August Revolution*.

170. Colin S. Gray, 'What RAND Hath Wrought,' *Foreign Policy*, vol. 1, no. 4 (1971).

171. 'The lucrative US presence . . . created a virtual gold mine of wealth which is directly or indirectly syphoned off and pocketed by the officials.' Compare the situation since. From 1966 through 1971, United States economic assistance to South Vietnam averaged over $600 million per year; the capital flow from South Vietnam is about one-third of this. The recent fiscal reforms (heralded as the 'autumn revolution' – fall 1971) raised the price of rice, sugar, milk powder, and pharmaceuticals while lowering prices for refrigerators and air conditioners. Rotten rice still sells at black-market prices. Phi Bang, 'South Vietnam: A Hand-to-Mouth Economy,' *Far Eastern Economic Review*, January 15, 1972. For more examples, see *Thoi-Bao Ga*, December 1971. On corruption, see references of note 64.

172. Cited in Philippe Devillers and Jean Lacouture, *End of a War*, pp. 322–3. The authors note that Chauvel's report described America's intentions 'with great clarity.' See *At War with Asia*, p. 33, for a longer excerpt.

173. For a discussion of the severe distortion of the crucial 1954–1960 period in the Pentagon history, see my essay in Chomsky and Zinn, *Critical Essays*, which also discusses covert activities that are reported in the Pentagon study, in particular the 34-A operations launched on February 1, 1964, and their bearing on the 1964 escalation of the war in Laos.

174. Bernard Fall, 'Viet-Nam – the Agonizing Reappraisal,' *Current History*, February 1965; reprinted in Fall and Raskin, *Vietnam Reader*, p. 339. See *American Power and the New Mandarins*, chap. 3, nn. 46, 47, for additional reports from the public record. A detailed account of these operations, which he dates from 1958, is given by Chaffard, *Les Deux Guerres*, pp. 366–75. See also Wilfred Burchett, 'The Receiving End,' in Chomsky and Zinn, *Critical Essays*, for reports from North Vietnam.

I have come across only one reference to Lansdale's missions in the Pentagon Papers *per se*, namely, *DOD*, bk 2, tab 1, IV.A.5, p. 11: 'Colonel Lansdale described a US-instigated black propaganda campaign of pamphlets and announcements, ostensibly Viet Minh in origin. . . .' This is from the material missing in the Gravel edition, I, 291.

175. For some amusing comments on the elections provision, see Dennis Duncanson, *Government and Revolution in Vietnam*, pp. 7–8. He regards it as a subsidiary detail, not a main feature, and claims that apart from the DRV, 'everybody else' took the agreements to be merely 'a deal to establish peace through territorial concessions.' On what

'everybody else' actually thought, there is an ample literature. See, e.g., S. R. SarDesai, *Indian Foreign Policy in Cambodia, Laos and Vietnam*, Chapter 4.

176. Quotes and comment from SarDesai, *Indian Foreign Policy*. See also Mieczyslaw Maneli (the strongly anticommunist former legal and political adviser to the Polish delegation of the ICC), *War of the Vanquished*, Chapter 2; Kahin and Lewis, *U.S. in Vietnam*; Marvin E. Gettleman, ed., *Vietnam: History, Documents and Opinions*, pt 5; and many other sources. Bernard Fall expresses the view of serious anticommunist sources when he states that 'South Viet-Nam refused to hold elections by July, 1956, since this would have meant handing over control of the South to Ho Chi Minh' (*Last Reflections*, p. 146). The problem was that Ho had created 'the *one* effective political organization the country has ever had' and that he was fighting for 'purely Vietnamese *national* objectives, and that fact is terribly important to this very day' (1967; *ibid.*, pp. 46, 87).

177. Gettleman, *Vietnam*, p. 172.

178. Cooper, *Lost Crusade*, p. 166.

179. Cf. Kahin and Lewis, *U.S. in Vietnam*. See also Kahin's comments on the history of American-promoted elections in *The New Republic*, February 12, 1972. Also Fall, 'Vietnam's 12 Elections,' in *Last Reflections*.

180. Thieu Son, in the Saigon newspaper *Dien Tin*, August 24, 1971; translated in part in *Thoi-Bao Ga*, October 1971.

181. May 1967; IV, 182. To realize this commitment, natives of South Vietnam who had infiltrated back 'should be expelled as a matter of principle,' or permitted to remain if they are 'prepared to accept peaceful political activity under the Constitution' (which prohibits communism). He does not add that they must be prepared to obey laws that make 'all plots and actions under the false name of peace and neutrality' a crime, punishable by one to five years imprisonment (May 17, 1965); see Fall, 'Vietnam's 12 Elections,' and Jon Cooper's study (note 159).

182. Robert Thompson, 'A Successful End to the War in Viet Nam,' *Pacific Community*, vol. 2, no. 3 (1971).

183. Roger Hilsman, 'Two American Counterstrategies to Guerrilla Warfare,' in Tang Tsou, *China in Crisis*, vol. 2, pp. 283, 291. Hilsman elaborates this concept of 'free choice' further in his book *To Move a Nation*.

184. Dean Rusk claimed in April 1963 that seven million Vietnamese – almost half the population – lived in strategic hamlets. Cited in Cooper, *Long Crusade*, p. 201.

185. See Austin, *President's War*; Scott, *War Conspiracy*, Chapter 3; Stavins *et al.*, *Washington Plans an Aggressive War*; Joseph C. Goulden, *Truth is the First Casualty*; E. G. Windchy, *Tonkin Gulf*. These studies raise serious doubts as to whether the August 4 incident in Tonkin Gulf, which led to the 'retaliatory' bombing, ever occurred. They make it

plain that whatever Washington may have chosen to believe, the evidence for the alleged attack was slight and contradictory, and that subsequent administration testimony demonstrated either astonishing ignorance or outright deception. Even if the attack did take place (with no damage to the American vessels), the retaliatory attack was indefensible, not only because of its scale but because of the extensive provocation: specifically, GVN naval attacks, with American vessels seeking to draw attention elsewhere. The Pentagon analyst concludes that the August 4 attack took place and was almost certainly deliberate (III, 186). His analysis, however, is superficial as compared with the studies cited. It generally follows the lines of McNamara's discredited Senate testimony.

186. Not surprisingly, Sir Robert Thompson regards the 1964 election in exactly the same light. 'Not until after the Tonkin Gulf incident in August, 1964, with its consequent Congress resolution and his own outstanding success against Senator Goldwater in the Presidential election at the end of the year was President Johnson in a position to take a major decision ... the only option left was escalation' (*No Exit from Vietnam*, p. 16).

187. Douglas Pike, *Vietcong*, p. 362.

188. After the decision to bomb the North, the White House informed Taylor in Saigon that a presidential announcement was under consideration which would state that the boming 'will be reported to the United Nations Security Council under the Provisions of Article 51 of the United Nations Charter' – that is, as a measure of collective self-defence – but the analyst states that this 'intention ... was dropped several days later.' There appears to be no other instance of any consideration of the legal obligations of the United States.

189. Recall the wording of the State Department White Paper of 1961, explaining how 'the authorities in South Viet-Nam refused to fall into this well-laid trap' – namely, the 1956 elections agreed upon at Geneva. Cited in Kahin and Lewis, *U.S. in Vietnam*, p. 58. Throughout, the United States executive and its local subsidiaries had to keep stepping lively to avoid such traps laid by the wily Communists.

190. See, e.g., Franz Schurmann *et al.*, *The Politics of Escalation in Vietnam*; Scott, *War Conspiracy*. Compare also Scott's discussion of the bombing of the Soviet ship *Turkestan* in Haiphong harbour, with the analyst's reference to 'an unfortunate case of bad aiming' (IV, 187) – possibly the case, though a serious analysis would hardly rest merely with repeating the government's excuses.

191. See Cooper, *Lost Crusade*, pp. 327–8. Also Draper, *Abuse of Power*, pp. 167–8; Chaffard, *Les Deux Guerres*, pp. 382–8, 393–4.

192. For example, Walt Rostow has claimed that the Indochinese Communists were 'enflamed' by Stalin after World War II and that Stalin was also responsible for the Greek rebellion. He cites no evidence. For some quotes, see my *American Power and the New Mandarins*, pp. 327–8, 360. For discussion of the facts with regard to Greece, see

Gabriel Kolko, *Politics of War*; Kolko and Kolko, *Limits of Power*; Richard Barnet, *Intervention and Revolution*. For some parallels between Greece and Vietnam, see Todd Gitlin, 'Counter-insurgency: Myth and Reality in Greece,' in David Horowitz, ed., *Containment and Revolution*; and L. S. Stavrianos, 'Greece's Other History,' *New York Review of Books*, June 17, 1971. The beliefs of Rostow and others with regard to Greece can perhaps be attributed to ignorance. With regard to Indochina, the assumption is unlikely. See also note 95. As part of the 'many good suggestions and wise counsel' given him by Truman, Lyndon Johnson cites Truman's experiences in facing 'problems of aggression' in Greece and Turkey (*Vantage Point*, p. 31). Comment is superfluous.

193. As compared with the 'democratically-elected Government of the Republic of Korea' (NSC memorandum, March 1949, *DOD*, bk 8, p. 269). For an example of the persistence of such astonishing illusions, see the secret memorandum to the president by George Ball, October 5, 1964, *Atlantic Monthly*, July 1972. Distinguishing the case of Korea from Vietnam, he writes: 'In 1950 the *Korean Government* under Syngman Rhee was stable. It had the general support of principal elements in the country. . . . The Korean people were still excited by their new-found freedom; they were fresh for the war.' On the facts, see the references of note 98. In *American Power and the New Mandarins*, I discussed many similar examples of historical fantasies at high levels of decision making (cf. Chapter 3, pp. 262–6, and Chapter 6, pp. 364–5, n. 29, on Hilsman's and Stevenson's 'proofs' of Chinese aggressiveness). Unfortunately, these absurdities must be taken seriously, given the vast resources of terror in the hands of those whose decisions are guided (or justified) by them.

194. Cited by Cooper, *Lost Crusade*, p. 171. See p. 71 above. Cooper wonders only why he didn't mention the North Vietnamese, 'who, even more than the Chinese Communists, were causing the mischief in Laos and Vietnam.' On events in Laos at the time, see notes 198–201, 215, 223.

195. This objective was assigned 20 per cent importance, as compared with 70 per cent importance to the objective: 'To avoid a humiliating U.S. defeat (to our reputation as a guarantor)'—(III, 349). The welfare of the Vietnamese was granted a 10 per cent share.

196. See also the curious conclusions of William Bundy in 1971, discussed in my *Problems of Knowledge and Freedom*, pp. 82–3.

197. On the character and significance of the May 1959 meeting in Hanoi, as discussed in the Pentagon Papers and by independent scholars see my essay in Chomsky and Zinn, *Critical Essays*.

198. See Gareth Porter, 'After Geneva: Subverting Laotian Neutrality,' in Adams and McCoy, *Laos*; Scott, *War Conspiracy*; C. A. Stevenson, *The End of Nowhere*. It is possible that there was North Vietnamese support for the Pathet Lao, as Arthur Dommen asserts, on evidence that hardly seems compelling. Thai pilots were sent to Laos for counterinsurgency missions in March 1964. The role of Thai rangers in

covert operations in Laos (Operation Hardnose) remains obscure (see III, 578, 610). Fred Branfman estimates that by 1970 the United States had brought in at least 10,000 Asians into Laos as mercenaries, in comparison with the perhaps 5,000 North Vietnamese engaged in combat ('Presidential War in Laos,' pp. 266, 278–9). Lansdale's report of July 1961 (II, 643–4) describes some of the early stages of these operations. The White Star Mobile Training Teams consisting of United States Special Forces personnel, introduced into Laos covertly in the last few weeks of the Eisenhower administration (Stevenson, *End of Nowhere*, p. 185) or perhaps in 1959 (Porter, 'After Geneva,' p. 183), 'had the purpose and effect of establishing U.S. control over foreign forces' (II, 464). Laos was serving as a model for Vietnam, in this and other instances. See the references cited for further evidence. On the contribution of the Pentagon history see Stevenson, *End of Nowhere*, postscript; Walter Haney, 'The Pentagon Papers and U.S. involvement in Laos,' in Chomsky and Zinn, *Critical Essays*; Jonathan Mirsky, 'High Drama on Foggy Bottom,' *Saturday Review*, January 1, 1972.

By 1964, United States involvement was extensive. Refugees report bombing from May 1964.

199. Hugh Toye, *Laos: Buffer State or Battleground*, p. 154. On the training of commandos abroad for covert operations in North Vietnam, see Chaffard, *Les Deux Guerres*, p. 368.

200. Jim Lucas of Scripps-Howard, cited in Stevenson, *End of Nowhere*, p. 89; Denis Warner, July 1961, cited in *At War with Asia*, p. 203.

201. The interpretation of events in Laos in this period is particularly distorted in the Pentagon Papers. See my essay in Chomsky and Zinn, *Critical Essays*.

202. On the scale and character of this infiltration, United States government estimates must be taken with a grain a salt. Chaffard reports that French intelligence gives far lower estimates (*Les Deux Guerres*, p. 359). This is a more neutral and probably more accurate source, given the long years of contact. The Pentagon analyst remarks that the judgments of a 'rise and change in the nature of infiltration' in August 1964 may have been influenced by the fact that this was expected in reaction to the 'Tonkin reprisals,' and that evidence of greatly increased infiltration was an explicit condition for 'systematic military action against DRV,' which top officials were beginning to regard as 'inevitable' (III, 192). A former DIA analyst reports that from 1964 to 1965 until 1967, 'the generals in Saigon worked to build up US troop strength' and therefore 'wanted every bit of evidence brought to the fore that could show that infiltration was increasing. DIA obliged' (also emphasizing the enemy's ability to recruit locally). Patrick McGarvey, cited by Graham T. Allison and Morton H. Halperin, 'Bureaucratic Politics,' *World Politics*, vol. 24, no. 3 (1972), p. 74. Cf. also Allen S. Whiting, 'Scholar and Policy-maker,' *ibid.*, p. 233, on the crucial role of

'insight and intuition' rather than '"hard" evidence clandestinely acquired' in intelligence estimates. The author, to mid-1966, was Director, Office of Research and Analysis of Far East, Bureau of Intelligence and Research, Department of State, from the evidence in the Pentagon Papers, the most successful of the intelligence agencies in analysis and evaluation.

203. The image of 'Indian fighting' was much on the minds of the American military. See *American Power and the New Mandarins*, Chapter 3, n. 42, for references. See also Michael Rogin, 'Liberal Society and the Indian Question,' *Politics and Society*, May 1971, for some interesting background.

204. II, 693; Bureau of Intelligence and Research, State Department, December 3, 1962.

205. Schlesinger, *Thousand Days*, p. 759.

206. See note 4. For some references from the public record, see *For Reasons of State*, Chapter 1.

207. Draper, *Abuse of Power*.

208. See my essay in Chomsky and Zinn, *Critical Essays*, for details on United States government beliefs with regard to PAVN units in the South, as revealed by the Pentagon history.

209. See pp. 113–14 above, and the references of note 198. In July 1967 it was discovered that Chinese Nationalists, 'disguised so as to appear to be South Vietnamese with Nung ancestry,' were being used on covert operations by the GVN, apparently the result of a secret agreement of 1966. The JCS disapproved, 'despite appeals from COMUSMACV.' MACV 'advised against US cooperation' in the occupation by the GVN of an island claimed by Communist and Nationalist China, with the intention of constructing an airfield (II, 402). Americans who have been engaged in clandestine operations in Indochina report the presence of CIA-trained Chinese Nationalists, but I have no way of verifying these reports. Many Chinese (up to 50,000) were reported in North Vietnam in construction and repair operations during the bombing of the north in 1965–8; these reports rarely note that the United States was bombing an internal Chinese railway, the only rail connection between south-western China and the rest of the country, which happened to pass near Hanoi. I noted no reference to this fact in the Pentagon study, but it is mentioned by George Ball (see note 192 above) as a possible reason why China might intervene.

210. See Hearings Before the [Symington] Subcommittee on United States Security Agreements and Commitments Abroad, U.S. Senate, 1969, pt 3: 'Kingdom of Thailand,' pp. 646–7, 753–4, 851–3 discussed in *For Reasons of State*, Chapter 5. The testimony here might be usefully contrasted with the remarks by Senator Gordon Allott, who claims that 'Red Chinese troops were [in 1962] roaming at will through a good portion of northern Thailand' and 'still are, except that now they are actually engaging in acts of war' (August 12, 1969, reprinted in *Congression Record*, August 3, 1971, p. S12948).

211. Cooper, *Lost Crusade*, pp. 264–5. See *For Reasons of State*, Chapter 1.

212. For a discussion of such evidence, see my chapter in Chomsky and Zinn, *Critical Essays*.

213. Jean-Claude Pomonti and Serge Thion, *Des courtisans aux partisans*, p. 209. Bernard Fall also questioned – in fact ridiculed – the 'American official view' ('Viet-Cong – The Unseen Enemy in Viet-Nam') as have other non-communist observers. Cf. Chaffard, *Les Deux Guerres*, for extensive discussion. Cf. also Richard West's report from Phu Quoc island, thirty miles west of the mainland and remote from infiltration but largely under NLF control (*Sketches from Vietnam*). Since United States intelligence sources are unavailable, it is impossible to evaluate them (see notes 164, 202). However, occasional comments raise questions as to how well they support the 'American official view' that Fall and others reject. Allan Goodman reports that 'Vietcong who defected in 1961–1962, in part, gave as their reason for changing sides the reluctance of Hanoi to authorize anything beyond political action among the population' ('Diplomatic and Strategic Outcomes of the Conflict,' in Walter Isard, ed., *Vietnam: Issues and Alternatives*). A survey of Viet Cong prisoners and defectors just prior to the American escalation of early 1965 found 'most native South Vietnamese guerrillas unaware of any North Vietnamese role in the war, except as a valued ally' (*New York Times*, June 7, 1965; cited in *American Power and the New Mandarins*, pp. 243, 282–3).

214. Cf. Race, *Long An*; Fitzgerald, *Fire in the Lake*, Chaffard, *Les Deux Guerres*; Robert Sansom, *The Economics of Insurgency in the Mekong Delta of Vietnam*. For some discussion of Race's valuable study in this context, see my essay in Chomsky and Zinn, *Critical Essays*. Also very useful is the documentation in Pike, *Viet Cong*.

215. In January 1962, Viet Cong forces were estimated at 16,500, as compared to 'South Vietnamese' forces of more than 175,000, with additional paramilitary forces of 110,000 (II, 656). The United States government assessment of the situation in Laos in the same year (1961) is not very different: 'By the spring the 1961 of NLHS [political arm of the Pathet Lao] appeared to be in a position to take over the entire country' (State Department *Background Notes*, March 1969), despite vast US efforts in support of the extreme right.

216. Note the analogy to the Nixon–Kissinger diplomacy today: China and the Soviet Union are to impose constraints on the DRV–PRG and influence them to call off the struggle against the United States-imposed regime in the South. It is natural that Kissinger, who fancies himself a geopolitician, should generalize the strategy of an earlier period to a global scale.

217. See note 47, and pp. 140–1 below.

218. Cooper, *Lost Crusade*, p. 256; cf. also pp. 313–14, 430. Cf. also the analysis of the situation of 1965 by Vann, discussed in *For Reasons of State*, Ch. 1, pp. 36–7. American officials in Saigon estimated in

1962 that half the population supported the NLF (Robert Scigliano, *South Vietnam: Nation Under Stress*, p. 145). A similar estimate is repeated even by Douglas Pike (*War, Peace and the Viet Cong*, p. 6). It is doubtful that George Washington could have claimed as much.

219. Cf. Jean Lacouture, *Vietnam: Between Two Truces*, p. 188.

220. For details, from an interesting document of December 1963, see my essay in Chomsky and Zinn, *Critical Essays*.

221. John T. McAlister, Jr, and Paul Mus, *The Vietnamese and their Revolution*, p. 160. For a particularly forceful statement, see Bernard Fall, cited in *For Reasons of State*, Ch. 1, p. 26. It should be recalled that Fall was bitterly anticommunist and strongly in support of United States aims in Vietnam, though appalled at the means by which they were being carried out, and concerned in the end that 'Viet-Nam as a cultural and historic entity ... is threatened with extinction' under the blows of the American war machine (*Last Reflections*, pp. 33–4).

222. Maneli, *War of the Vanquished*, pp. 214, 216. See note 176. The book is interesting for a number of revelations, in particular, in the support it gives to persistent rumours of a Diem–Nhu rapprochement with Hanoi that was under consideration in 1963, just prior to the coup that overthrew Diem. Cf. also Chaffard, *Les Deux Geurres*, Chapter 8. If this was indeed a factor in the coup, then the United States role was even more cynical than the record in the Pentagon Papers indicates. John P. Roche claims that the Kennedy administration had made a 'decision' that Diem and Nhu 'must not be permitted to make a private deal with Ho Chi Minh' and that Washington regarded the prospect of 'an American departure from the premises' (an expected consequence of a 'private deal,' that is, a political settlement) as 'unthinkable.' He also asserts that the Pentagon historians ignored evidence he had given them to this effect. 'The Pentagon Papers,' *Political Science Quarterly*, vol. 87, no. 2 1972). If he is correct, then the example stands as another case where the historians distorted the record in an effort to present United States actions in a less unfavourable light (to be sure, this is not Roche's point).

223. Chaffard, *Les Deux Guerres*, p. 288.

224. It is commonly asserted in American studies that the North Vietnamese are responsible for the breakdown of the Geneva Agreements of 1962, beginning with the refusal to withdraw the extensive military forces that the United States government claims they had deployed in Laos. Stevenson, in one of the more serious works, asserts that 'only forty of the estimated 10,000 North Vietnamese in Laos left through ICC checkpoints' (*End of Nowhere*, p. 179). His source is Arthur Dommen, *Conflict in Laos*, p. 240. Dommen's source is an unidentified spokesman of the British Foreign Office. As to Dommen's reliability see my essay in Chomsky and Zinn, *Critical Essays*. Evidently, on such evidence as this one can conclude virtually nothing, and it is irresponsible merely to cite these unsubstantiated claims by deeply committed commentators as proof that North Vietnam was responsible

for the breakdown of the Geneva Agreements. For further discussion, see *At War with Asia*, Chapter 4; Chaffard, *Les Deux Guerres*. Dommen concedes that CIA-supported Meo guerrillas, 'sitting astride the natural communication route between Vientiane and the NLHS base area in Sam Neua,' may have hampered communication sufficiently to have caused deterioration of the well-developed NLHS infrastructure (see above, notes 200, 215) in Vientiane Province (Dommen, p. 308); but he does not go on to point out that United States support for the guerrillas constituted a serious violation of the 1962 agreements from the outset and was a factor in the renewal of conflict.

225. This was, of course, the reason for the United States terror programme then intensified in the delta (cf. note 149), where, it will be recalled, few NVA troops were present.

226. King, 'Political Balance,' p. 405. He quotes (p. 417) the Saigon newspaper *Dien Tin*, March 30, 1971: in any place 'in which our magnificent allies the Americans are present, at that place Vietnamese lives weigh no more than those of earthworms or crickets,' a painfully accurate description.

227. Averell Harriman, 'Missed Opportunities: How We Got Where We Are,' *Washington Post*, May 9, 1972. Harriman also points out that when the negotiations began, North Vietnam withdrew 90 per cent of its troops from the northern two provinces, half of them over 200 miles into North Vietnam. 'The United States was then in a favorable bargaining position since it had over half a million men in South Vietnam,' not to speak of more than 50,000 Korean mercenaries. For references from the press at the time, see *At War with Asia*, pp. 43ff. From January to September 1969 there was a sharp decline in bombing of the infiltration routes in southern Laos, proably related to the same DRV withdrawal of military force in expectation of some results from the negotiations in Paris. The planes available were simply shifted to northern Laos. Cf. Hearings before the [Symington] Subcommittee on United States Security Agreements and Commitments Abroad, US Senate, October 1969, pt 2: 'Kingdom of Laos,' p. 464.

228. Roche, 'Pentagon Papers.'

229. Johnson, *Vantage Point*, p. 63.

230. On August 29, 1963, the French government announced its support for a policy in Vietnam based on 'independence vis-à-vis the outside, in peace and unity at home, and in concord with their neighbors.' Kennedy's comment, cited below, was a response to this statement (cf. Fall, *Two Viet-Nams*, p. 392; for Fall's reservations, see pp. 400ff.). On July 23, 1964, General de Gaulle recommended a conference aiming at establishing the neutrality of all Indochina. President Johnson responded, 'We do not believe in conferences called to ratify terror; so our policy is unchanged.' Cf. Chaffard, *Les Deux Guerres*, pp. 362ff.

231. Robert Shaplen, 'Letter from Vietnam,' *New Yorker*, June 24, 1972.

232. *Wall Street Journal*, June 16, 1972.

233. One of the highest interagency priorities recommended in April 1966; II, 582.

234. See, for example, Vietnam Veterans Against the War, eds., *Winter Soldier Investigation;* James S. Kunen, *Standard Operating Procedure*; D. Thorne and G. Butler, eds., *The New Soldier*; Citizen's Commission of Inquiry, *The Dellums Committee Hearings on War Crimes in Vietnam*.

235. Described, perhaps, as 'the familiar Communist-neutralist bray' (III, 621).

236. Robert Drinan, *Boston Globe*, February 7, 1972.

ENDGAME: THE TACTICS OF PEACE IN VIETNAM

*Much of this chapter appears in *Ramparts*, April 1973.

1. *The Pentagon Papers: The Defense Department History of United States Decisionmaking in Vietnam*, Gravel edition, vol. II, p. 22: Beacon Press, Boston, 1971. By the phrase 'South Vietnam' the author presumably refers to the GVN.

2. 'THIEU: an interview with Oriana Fallaci,' *The New Republic*, January 20, 1973.

3. *New York Times*, January 25, 1973.

4. *Congressional Record*, June 6, 1967, S7733.

5. *New York Times*, January 25, 1973.

6. Henry S. Hayward, *Christian Science Monitor*, January 23, 1973.

7. *New York Times*, January 23, 1973.

8. Peter Osnos and Thomas Lippman, *Washington Post*, January 23, 1973.

9. Reuters, January 24, 1973.

10. AP, October 31, 1972.

11. *New York Times*, November 23, 1972.

12. Laurence Stern, *Washington Post*, November 30, 1972.

13. *Vietnam 1967–71; Toward Peace and Prosperity*, Ministry of Information, Saigon, 1971, p. 52. Questioned about this by Senator Kennedy, Administration spokesman William Sullivan did not challenge the figure, but remarked that 'some could have been killed in taking part in military action.' He is aware, of course, of the distinction between military actions and 'neutralization' under the Phoenix programme. Hearing before the Subcommittee to Investigate Problems Connected with Refugees and Escapees, September 28, 1972; Government Printing Office, Washington, 1972, p. 22.

14. Michael Field, *The Prevailing Wind*, Methuen, London, 1965, p. 210.

15. *Far Eastern Economic Review*, February 26, 1973.

16. Fox Butterfield, *New York Times*, March 17, 1973. Allegedly, these villages were 'seized by the Communists in the early hours of the

cease-fire.' How they were seized is not described. This report also states that council elections will be held in villages, with Communists excluded, though hamlet chiefs will still apparently be appointed by the Province Chiefs, generally colonels responsible to the President.

17. *Christian Science Monitor*, February 8, 1973. It is unclear from his account whether the 'penetration' by Communist troops, apparently without combat in some cases at least, was before or after the cease-fire. Southerland is one of the few reporters now actually observing events in Vietnam.

18. Neil Davis, Reuters, *New York Times*, February 9, 1973.

19. *Christian Science Monitor*, March 16, 1973. 'We like the Americans very much,' one old woman said: 'We like them because they are leaving.'

20. AP, *New York Times*, March 16, 1973. The latter two reports gain a certain interest from the fact that they appear on the same day as the Nixon press conference in which the North Vietnamese were warned to refrain from 'infiltration.' Commenting, James Reston observes that 'Hanoi is obviously cheating on the truce agreement, and cheating big,' challenging American reliance on its 'good faith' (*New York Times*, March 18, 1973). No other violations of the agreements are noted.

21. *New Republic*, February 17, 1973. He also comments that 'the Vietcong considers [the PRG] to be a parallel administration,' failing to add that it is the Paris Agreements signed by the United States and the GVN that assign to the PRG a status exactly equivalent to that of the GVN.

22. David Hotham, commentary, in R. W. Lindholm, ed., *Vietnam: the First Five Years*, East Lansing, Michigan State University Press, 1959, p. 359.

23. Joseph Buttinger, 'Lösung für Vietnam,' *Neues Forum*, Vienna, August–September 1966; translated in E. S. Herman, *Atrocities in Vietnam: Myths and Realities*, Philadelphia, Pilgrim Press, 1970.

24. Memorandum for Secretary of Defense, after visit to Vietnam in January, 1961; United States Department of Defense, *United States–Vietnam Relations, 1945–67*, bk 2, tab. 4, pp. 66–77, Government Printing Office, Washington, 1971; the government edition of the Pentagon Papers.

25. *The Pentagon Papers*, Gravel edition, I, 259.

26. For a recent summary, see Holmes Brown and Don Luce, *Hostages of War*, Indochina Mobile Education Project, 1973. Occasional glimpses by United States correspondents give a fair indication of what has been happening in the prisons. Civilians imprisoned by the Thieu regime are described by *Time* (March 19, 1973) as 'shapes' rather than men – as 'grotesque sculptures of scarred flesh and gnarled limbs' (cf. *Nation*, March 26, 1973). Jacques Leslie of the *Los Angeles Times* reports a visit to the prison ward of the province hospital (March 8, 1973). Women patients were having 'violent seizures.' 'There is little doubt,' he writes, 'that the seizures are at least a psychological reaction

to being tortured with electricity at South Vietnamese police interrogation centers . . .' Prisoners gave elaborate descriptions of torture.

27. *Le Monde*, January 4, 1973. The two Frenchmen state explicitly that a November 9, 1972 story in the *New York Times* on the treatment of prisoners 'is false,' citing evidence. To my knowledge, the *New York Times* printed neither the AFP report of the Paris Press conference or any other report of statements of the two French prisoners, who are now (March 1973) touring the United States.

28. *New York Times*, January 27, 1973.

29. Brown and Luce, *op. cit.*

30. Kissinger's press conference appears in the *New York Times*, January 25, 1973, and with slight modifications, in the *State Department Bulletin*, February 12, 1973.

31. *New York Times*, December 17, 1972.

32. *New York Times*, October 27, 1972.

33. *Ibid.*

34. In a CBS TV interview of February 1, Kissinger described the American dilemma in December as he would like it to be perceived. The North Vietnamese were not serious, and 'the more difficult Hanoi was the more rigid Saigon grew.' The United States feared it 'would be caught between the two contending Vietnamese parties.' In order 'to bring home really to both Vietnamese parties that the continuation of the war had its price,' the United States bombed Hanoi and sent General Haig to Saigon; 'So we really moved in both directions simultaneously.' Putting aside the matter of the even-handedness of the United States response, as Kissinger describes it with his engaging cynicism, his account suffers from a few omissions: specifically, that Hanoi was publicly calling for signing of the October plan, which the United States then accepted in effect in the Paris Agreements after the failure of the Nixon–Kissinger terror bombings of late December. For lengthy excerpts from Kissinger's remarks, see 'the importance of calling a defeat a defeat,' *Monthly Review*, March 1973.

35. Cf. Douglas Pike, *Viet Cong*, Cambridge, MIT Press, 1966, pp. 363–5.

36. On United States estimates of support for the NLF in 1962, see references to Chapter 1, note 218. On support for Diem at that time, see, among other sources, the Pentagon Papers: 'By the time President Kennedy came to office in 1961, it was plain that support for the Saigon government among South Vietnam's peasants – 90% of the population – was weak and waning' (Gravel edition, I, 250–1). John Paul Vann, field operations coordinator of the US Operations Mission, was one of the many on the scene who recognized in 1965 that 'a popular political base for the Government of South Vietnam does not exist.' Cf. my *For Reasons of State*, Fontana/Collins 1973, Chapter 1, section III, for quotes from an important memorandum privately circulated by Vann at that time.

37. See Chapter 1, note 218.

38. *Op. cit.*, pp. 359f.; see also Chapter 1, notes 47, 223.

39. See Chapter 1, section VI, subsection 7.

40. Daniel Southerland, *Christian Science Monitor*, November 28, 1973.

41. See Chapter 1, note 149.

42. Telegram, December 24, 1954, Government edition of the Pentagon Papers (see note 24), bk 10, p. 854.

43. See William Whitworth, 'A reporter at large: interview with Eugene V. Rostow,' *New Yorker*, July 4, 1970.

44. See Chapter 1, section V.

45. UPI, *New York Times*, November 29, 1972.

46. Cited in Hernando J. Abaya, *The Untold Philippine Story*, Quezon City, Philippines, Malaya Books, Inc., 1967, p. 3.

47. Elizabeth Pond, *Christian Science Monitor*, November 10, 1972; Norman Thorpe, *Far Eastern Economic Review*, January 15, 1973.

48. Walt Rostow, op-ed column, *New York Times*, January 12, 1973.

49. Robert Shaplen, 'Letter from Vietnam,' *New Yorker*, January 13, 1973.

50. D. R. SarDesai, *Indian Foreign Policy in Cambodia, Laos, & Vietnam, 1947–1964*, Univ. of California Press, Berkeley–Los Angeles, 1968, p. 163.

51. For background on these matters, see my *At War with Asia*, Fontana/Collins 1970, Chapter 4, and references cited there; and also Charles A. Stevenson, *The End of Nowhere: American Policy toward Laos Since 1954*, Boston, Beacon Press, 1972; Walter Haney, 'The Pentagon Papers and US Involvement in Laos,' in *The Pentagon Papers*, Gravel edition, vol. 5; *Critical Essays*, edited by N. Chomsky and H. Zinn, Boston, Beacon Press, 1972.

52. SarDesai, *op. cit.*, pp. 140f. On Canada's role in Vietnam, see Claire Culhane, *Why is Canada in Vietnam?*, NC Press, Toronto, 1972. The still-unpublished negotiations volumes of the Pentagon Papers provide some further insights. Thus in *May 1964*, Prime Minister Lester Pearson, recipient of the 1957 Nobel Peace Prize, informed President Johnson that he had 'reservations' about the use of nuclear weapons but felt that 'punitive striking of targets by iron (non-nuclear) bombs would be 'a different thing.' See John Kincaid, 'The Pentagon Papers Trial,' *American Report*, February 12, 1973.

53. *Newsweek*, February 5, 1973.

54. *New York Times*, March 1, 1973.

55. John F. Kennedy, quoted in Roger Hilsman, *To Move a Nation*, Delta, 1967, p. 439.

56. *New York Times*, March 16, 1973.

57. *U.S. News and World Report*, November 27, 1972.

58. Fox Butterfield, *New York Times*, November 27, 1972.

59. P. de Beer, *Le Monde*, February 28, 1973. See also D. Aftergut and D. Roose, 'Civilianizing the war,' *American Report*, March 12, 1973. An extensive collection of press clippings relating to United

States plans in Indochina is available from the Indochina Resource Center, 1322 18th St. NW, Washington, D.C., 20036 (*The War is not Over*, 1973).

60. This was conceded by John Hannah, director of USAID, in an interview, June 7, 1970. For the text, see N. S. Adams and A. W. McCoy, eds, *Laos: War and Revolution*, Harper and Row, 1970, Chapter 24.

61. See Chapter 1, section VI, subsection 5.1.

62. See the comments of former British Foreign Secretary Lord George-Brown, *Saturday Review of the Society*, December 1972. In his considered view, the 'original aim of the exercise' in Indochina was to defend the Four Freedoms, which were 'threatened in Southeast Asia,' and the United States intervention, 'right and justified,' 'was in itself a great victory for the freedom to establish freedom.' 'As a Britisher,' he writes, 'I have always found it exceedingly difficult to understand the violence of the opposition to the war in the United States' – not very surprising, given the fantasy world that he apparently inhabits.

INDEX

Acheson, Dean, 28, 40, 45–6, 67, 69, 130
aggression: U.S. policy on, 124–35
Ahmad, Eqbal, 99
Allende, Salvador, 72
Alsop, Joseph, 14
Alsop, Stewart, 168
American Revolution, 124
Amnesty International, 156–7
Arbenz Guzmán, Jacobo, 72
Arendt, Hannah, 66
Army (journal), 109
Arnett, Peter, 95
Austin, Anthony, 35
Australia, 56; troops in Vietnam, 131
Ayub Khan, Mohammed, 53

Baldwin, Hanson, 35
Ball, George, 32, 137, 139
Bangkok Conference of Asian Jurists, 42
Bantangan Peninsula, 154
Bao Dai, 28, 46, 47
Ben Suc, 84
Berle, A. A., 12–13
Bien Hoa, 91, 130
Bien Hoa Province, 102
Bill of Rights, 37
Boer War, 63
bombing: B-52 raids, 25, 84–6, 92, 127, 160; of Cambodia, 9, 94, 161; of dikes and dams, 81–2, 83–4; Haiphong, 17, 35; of Hanoi, 122; of Laos, 35, 94, 128, 132, 156, 161; morale affected by, 25, 85, 90, 109–10; of North Vietnam, 17, 24, 26, 41, 80–4, 87–8, 92, 109, 120–2, 130, 160; of South Vietnam, 24–6, 84–99, 109–10, 111, 161, 165; of Viet Cong, 25, 85, 91–4; Viet Cong casualties, 85, 91, 94; as war crime, 86, 154
Bonesteel, Charles Hartwell, 109

Bosch, Juan, 72
Brazil, 72, 74; U.S. aid to, 76
Brown, Harold, 84
Brzezinski, Zbigniew, 62
Buddhists, 118, 120
Bundy, McGeorge, 54, 84, 88, 123, 126, 137
Bundy, William, 48, 51, 61, 68, 84–5, 90, 115, 116, 121–2, 123, 134, 138, 139
Bunker, Ellsworth, 101
Burma, 56
Byrnes, James F., 106

Cambodia, 51, 52, 66, 113; bombing of, 9, 94, 161; neutralization proposed, 138–9, 141, 144, 160; South Vietnamese forces in, 167; U.S. clandestine activities in, 30
Canada; views on ICC, 167
Carver, George, 77, 108, 125, 163
Castro, Fidel, 71, 72, 75
Central Intelligence Agency: *see* CIA
Chaffard, Georges, 141
Chauvel, Jean, 111
Chiang Kai-shek, 53, 54
Chi Hoa prison, 156
Chile, 72, 76
China, Nationalist, 113; military units in Vietnam and Laos, 104, 132
China, People's Republic of, 123; economic progress, 49; as enemy in U.S. policy, 57, 71, 112, 125–6, 134–5, 163; ideological expansion, 49, 53; India compared with, 53; influence in Vietnam, alleged, 28, 41, 51–2, 66–8, 74, 125–6; Japan influenced by, 61; national liberation movements, 52; Soviet aid to, 62; and unification of Vietnam, 51–2; U.S. trade with, 56

216 Index

Churchill, Winston, 105
CIA (Central Intelligence Agency), 81–4, 108, 125–6, 132, 171; analysis by (1964), 54; in Laos, 32, 117, 128, 132, 167; in pacification programme, 101, 104; report (1962), 93
CINCPAC, 84, 88–9, 133, 167; OPLAN, 49–79; Phase III, 134
Clifford Group, 83–4
cold-war system, 11, 20, 21, 65
Combined Campaign Plan (1967), 95, 101
communism: aims of, 22; international, alleged agents of, 52, 68, 70–1, 124–5, 132; in Southeast Asia, National Security Council statement, 111–12; U.S. opposition to, 71–80; Vietnam opposition to, 151
Communist countries, aid to North Vietnam, 41
Communists in Vietnam: alleged violation of cease-fire, 166; and coalition government, 138; and elections, 115–18, 143; distribution of land by, 17; unification of country, 51–2; U.S. aggression against, 114–35; U.S. regards as danger, 8, 26–8, 41, 50–3, 53–6, 60
COMUSMACV, 88, 90, 93, 97, 98, 100, 101
Connell-Smith, Gordon, 76
Con Son Island, 157
Cooper, Chester, 59, 115, 123, 133, 140
CORDS, 100–2
Corson, William, 9
Cuba: Bay of Pigs invasion, 72; missile crisis, 59
Czechoslovakia, Soviet invasion of, 69, 75, 131, 139

Da Nang, 88, 90, 91, 118; leaflet distribution in, 152
Defense Department, 16
de Gaulle, Charles, 144
democracy: U.S. capitalistic attitude towards, 75–7; in Vietnam, threat to, 22; U.S. version of, 117–20
developing countries, 75; national liberation in, 61

Diem, Ngo Dinh, *see* Ngo Dinh Diem
Dominican Republic, 69, 76
domino theory, 29, 49, 50, 53–5, 57–8, 60, 63, 126, 162, 163
Dower, John, 56
Draper, Theodore, 130, 131
Draper Committee, 129
Drinan, Robert, 146
DRV, *see* Vietnam, North
Dulles, John Foster, 106, 115, 162, 164
Dubrow, Ambassador, 117

economic determinism, 78
Economist, The, 155
Eisenhower, Dwight D., 108
Eisenhower administration, 56
elections in South Vietnam, 113–20, 143, 157
Ellsberg, Daniel, 33
Emerson, Thomas, 33–5
Ervin, Sam, 31
Espionage Act, 34
Ewell, Julian Johnson, 18, 161

Fall, Bernard, 8, 24, 82, 85, 114
Far Eastern Economic Review, 64
fascism, 74
Field, Michael, 153
First Amendment to Constitution, 33–6
Forrestal, Michael, 49, 94
France, 15, 18, 64
French in Indochina, 27, 45, 47–8, 50, 52, 54, 55, 67, 71, 74, 106, 124–5, 130, 136
Friedman, Alvin, 84
Fulbright, J. William, 32, 33

Gallagher, Philip, 106
Gelb, Leslie, 29, 65, 69
Geneva Agreements (1954), 30, 39, 158, 161, 168, 171; breakdown for Indochina, 166; renounced by Diem regime, 9, 155; U.S. rejection of, 15, 169; U.S. violation of, 41, 44, 111–16, 136
Geneva Agreements on Laos (1962), 141
Germany, West, 64
Gilpatric Task Force report, 125
Goldwater, Barry, 120

Index 217

Goodman, Allan, 102
Goulart, João, 76
Graebner, Norman, 11
Gravel, Mike, 193–4
Great Britain, 13, 14; automobile workers, 75; and Geneva Agreements (1954), 115; and Geneva Agreements (1962) on Laos, 141; Yemen raids on, 81
Greece: communism in, 13, 29, 68, 69, 124; fascism in, 74, 75; 'freedom' in, 164
Griffiths, Philip Jones, 23
Guatemala, 68, 69, 72, 76
GVN, see Vietnam, South

Haiphong, 35
hamlets, strategic, 8–10, 116–17
Hanoi: bombing of, 122; Communist Party meeting (1959), 127; U.S. consulate, 114
Hanoi government, see Vietnam, North
Harkins, General, 9
Harriman, Averell, 143
Hilsman, Roger, 8, 9, 116
Hoang Duc Nha, 152–3
Ho Chi Minh, 27, 46, 47, 48, 50, 51, 54, 55, 67, 163; as Chinese or Russian puppet, 20, 45, 47; in peace negotiations, 123
Holmquist, C. O., 82–3
Honolulu meeting (1965), 92, 130–1
Hook, Sidney, 87, 126–7
Hoopes, Townsend, 106
Hotham, David, 155
Hudson Institute, 106
Hue, 26, 118
Hungary, Soviet invasion of, 69

IBM Japan, 62–3
ICEX (Intelligence Coordination and Exploitation), 103
imperialism, U.S., 21, 63–6, 78–80
India, 54, 56; China compared with, 53
Indians, American, 129
Indonesia, 54, 55, 74, 129, 132, 163; oil, 56, 57
Institute for Defense Analysis, Jason division, 109
International Control Commission (in 1950s), 114–15, 166, 167; (in 1960s), 15
International relations: literature on, 12
Iron Triangle, 84

Japan, 112, 163; Communist influence in, 50, 54, 55–7, 61; fascism in, 74; industrial development, 62–5; in postwar development of Vietnam, 163; as U.S. ally, 62–3, 70, 77; U.S. policy on, 48–9, 55–9, 62–5, 113
Jefferson, Thomas, 31
Johnson, Alexis, 32–3
Johnson, Harold H., 89, 90
Johnson, Lyndon, B., 53, 89, 138; escalation of war, 36, 119, 121–2; *The Vantage Point*, 133, 144
Joint Chiefs of Staff, 43, 49–51, 56, 58, 88, 107, 109, 126–8, 130
Justice Department, 37

Karnow, Stanley, 154–5
Katzenback, Nicholas, 97
Kennedy, John F., 61, 114, 116; on Communist aggression, 125, 129–30; escalation of war, 15; foreign policy, 59; on Trujillo and Castro, 71; on Vietnam (1956 statement), 58
Kennedy administration, 28, 52
Khanh, Nguyen, see Nguyen Khanh
Khiem, see Tran Thien Khiem
Khrushchev, Nikita, 52
Kindleberger, Charles, 62
Kissinger, Henry, 19, 20, 21, 28, 32, 69, 149–52, 156–60, 164, 165, 168–70; on Vietnamese politics, 142–3
'Kissinger papers,' 13
Kolko, Gabriel, 29
Komer, Robert, 48; and pacification, 99–105; and refuge programmes, 97–8, 100
Kontum, 90
Korea, 54; CIA informers in, 164
Korean troops: in Vietnam, 131

land reform: in South Vietnam, 16, 17
Langguth, A. J., 90

218 Index

Lansdale, Edward G., 15, 114, 117, 155
Laos: bombing of, 51, 52, 55, 66, 108, 113, 134, 136, 139; bombing of, 35, 94, 128, 132, 156, 161; conference, plans for, 123; Geneva Agreements on (1962), 141; neutralization proposed, 138–9, 141, 144, 160; Thai troops in, 32–3; U.S. clandestine activities in, 30, 32–3, 117, 132; U.S. operations in, 20, 166–7; U.S. policy on, 16, 128–9
Lin Piao, 52
Lodge, Henry Cabot, 48, 110, 120, 138, 142, 144; and elections, 118
Long Kanh Province, 154

MACCORDS, 108
Malaya, 51, 57
Maneli, Mieczyslaw, 141
Mao Tse-tung, 52, 69
Marcos, President, 163–4
marines: at Da Nang, 90, 91; sent to Vietnam, 87–8
Marshall, George C., 29, 106
Marx, Karl: doctrine of, 12, 13
mass media: contribution to violence, 170; deceived by U.S. government, 159–60; on Paris Agreements, 168, 169
McAlister, John, 140
McCone, John A., 119, 137
McKinley, William, 164
McNamara, Robert, 25, 29, 52, 84, 88, 89, 92, 95, 96, 99, 105, 119, 125, 135, 137, 141, 144, 147, 165; on bombing, 82, 83, 85; and peace negotiations, 120–1; on social organization, 21; policy statement, 49; on training of Vietnamese, 108
McNaughton, John, 24, 43, 47, 51, 84, 87, 90, 91, 125, 136, 138, 142; on bombing, 81, 83
Mekong Delta, 18, 95, 104, 127
Mekong Valley, 32
Moffat, Abbot, 106
Monroe Doctrine, 13
Montagnards, 93
My Khe massacre, 18
My Lai massacre, 18, 102, 154

National Intelligence Estimate, 145
National Liberation Front, *see* NLF
national liberation movements: Communists and, 52, 59, 129 in developing countries, 61
National Planning Association, 75
National Security Council (NSC) 14, 41, 50, 55, 56–7, 61, 75, 101–3, 107, 125, 132, 139, 167; constructive programmes of, 16, 17; on Geneva Conference (NSC 5429/2), 111–14; NSAM 288 (1964), 60; report (1949), 55; staff study (1952), 57
Nehru, Jawaharlal, 114
Newsweek, 168, 169
New York Times, The, 114
Nghe An Province, 81
Ngo Dinh Diem, 16, 45, 47, 53, 60, 89, 106, 117, 136, 142; and elections, 9, 115, 118, 119; crimes of regime, 155; oppressiveness of regime, 16; removal of, 139
Ngo Dinh Nu, 116
Nguyen Cao Ky, 27, 118, 141–2
Nguyen Khanh, 36, 137
Nguyen Van Thieu, 27, 48, 150–2; opposition to Communists, 152
Nguyen Van Thieu regime, 152, 153, 161; commitment of U.S. to, 155
Nixon Richard M., 149, 151–2, 156, 159, 160, 164, 165, 168–70; Laos and Cambodia attacked, 94
Nixon administration, 21, 32, 94, 147, 161, 168, 169, 170, 171
NLF (National Liberation Front), 18, 99, 127, 132, 135–6, 138–41, 162, 171; casualties, 96; in land reform, 16, 17; North Vietnamese control of, alleged, 133, 169, in pacification programme, 104, 160–1; political position, 141; support of by peasants, 16; U.S. action against, 139
Nong Khang, 166
NSC, *see* National Security Council

Operation CEDAR FALLS, 84
Operation PHOENIX, 103
Operation ROLLING THUNDER, 81
Operation SPEEDY EXPRESS, 161, 165
Operation SUNRISE, 117

Operations Coordinating Board, plan (1959), 127

pacification programmes, 13, 18, 96, 99–105, 108–10, 155, 160, 161, 165
Pannekoek, Anton, 22
Paris Agreements, 149–50, 153, 155–8, 160, 161, 165, 166, 168–70; distribution of copies of by N. Vietnamese, 154–5; misrepresentation of by U.S., 158–60, 168, 169; Protocols on prisoners, 156; Protocols on the Cease Fire, 153; reasons for U.S. signature, 161–3; reconciliation of S. Vietnam parties, 153; U.S. violation of, 151, 155–6, 159, 160, 166, 170; Vietnam violation of, 153–5; White House reaction to, 149
Park Chung Hee, 164
Pathet Lao, 128, 167; North Vietnamese influence alleged, 133
peace negotiations: ceasefire, U.S. terms for, 142; and escalation of war, 120–3; breakdown of, 160; Kissinger and, 159; North Vietnamese position, 145; October 9-Point plan, 157–8, 159–60, 164–5; political settlement suggested, 138–45; rejection of by Kissinger, 159; *see also* Paris Agreements
Peers, William Raymond, 18
Pentagon Papers, 7, 9, 10, 22, 150, 161; analysis of, 23–147; historical record and, 44–8; long-term objectives, 48–60; military plans, 80–99, 137–45; political objectives, 135–45; release of, 31–7; war crimes, justification of, 37–43
Pfaff, William, 105–6
Pham Van Dong, 44
Philippines, 56, 164; invasion of, 164
Phnom Penh, 153
Phnom Penh government, *see* Cambodia
Phoenix programme, 19, 87, 103, 104, 151, 153, 162
Phong Saly province, 166
Phoumi Nosavan, 128
Phung Hoang programme, 103, 105, 142

Pike, Douglas, 120, 161
Plain of Jars, 20, 28
political prisoners: communist proposal for freeing, 151; deportation of, 156–7
Pond, Elizabeth, 164
Portugal, 74
Poulo Condor prison, 156
power, drive for, 73–4
President's Committee to Study the U.S. Military Assistance Programme (Draper Committee), 129
Proudhon, Pierre, 37

Race, Jeffrey, 162
RAND Corporation studies, 25, 92, 109–10
Ray, Dennis, 12
refugees: in South Vietnam, 19, 96–8, 100; prevention of return home, 152, 154
Revolutionary Development (RD), 101
Roche, John, 144
Rostow, Eugene, 163
Rostow, Walt, 49, 53, 69, 70, 166
Ruina, Jack, 109
Rumania, 62
Rusk, Dean, 20, 40, 52, 84, 119, 125, 137; on escalation of war, 36; on North Vietnamese troops in South, 130–1
Russell, Bertrand, 86
Russo, Anthony, 33

Saigon, 137; Viet Cong in area of, 95, 97
Saigon autocracy, 150; *see also* Vietnam, South
SALT agreements, 20
Sam Neua Province (Laos), 166
Sarit, 53
Schlesinger, Arthur, Jr., 14
Seaborn, Blair, 15
SEATO, 38–9, 129
Senate, investigation of CIA in Laos, 32–3
Senate Foreign Relations Committee, 40
Shaplen, Robert, 145, 166, 167
Sharp, Richard, 106
Sharp, U. S. G., 88
South Africa, 74

Southeast Asia: communism in, National Security Council statement, 111–12; Communist domination of, 50–1; U.S. allies in, 53; U.S. interests in, 7, 49, 57, 80–1; U.S. policy in, 58

Southerland, Daniel, 154

Souvanna Phouma, 128, 167

Soviet Union, 70, 107, 123, 163; aid to China, 62; aid to North Vietnam, 132; Czechoslovakia invaded, 69, 75, 131, 139; dominance of Asia, alleged threat of, 55–6; Hungary invaded, 69; influence in Vietnam, alleged, 28, 41, 67, 74, 132; intervention in Eastern Europe, 42; U.S. relations with, 59

Special Committee on Southeast Asia, 125

Stalin, Josef, 68, 166

Stans, Maurice, 74

State Department, 40, 56–7, 67, 111, intelligence report (1962), 93–4; policy statement (1948), 50; policy statement (1967), 47

Stavins, Ralph, 60, 84

Stevenson, Adlai, 69, 81, 124, 129; on Greece, 124

strategic hamlets, 8–10, 116–17

Sukarno, Achmed, 132

Sullivan, William, 49

Symington, Stuart, 33

Systems Analysis, 142, 145–6

Taiwan, *see* China, Nationalist

Taylor, Maxwell, 36–7, 107, 119, 130, 137–8; and bombing, 89–90, 92; and escalation of war, 121, 122; on North Vietnamese military action, 135

technical intelligentsia, 59, 109

Tet offensive (1968), 18, 26–7, 43, 47, 96–8, 126

Thailand, 51, 138, 171; communism as threat to, 50–2; military units in Laos, 32–3; military units in Vietnam, 104; North Vietnamese influence in, alleged, 133; U.S. activities in, 30, 113

Than Hoa, 82

Than Hoa Province, 81

Thant, U., 123

Thieu, Nguyen Van, *see* Nguyen Van Thieu

Thompson, Sir Robert, 8, 116–17

Tidwell, W. A., 86

Times, The, 155

Tin Song, 152

Tonkin Gulf, 35, 112, 119

Tran Thien Khiem, 27

Trujillo, Rafael, 71, 75

Truman administration, 56; doctrine, 164

Trung Lap, burning of, 154

Tucker, Robert W., 58, 71–2

Turkey, 29; 'freedom' in, 164

United Nations, 161

United Nations Charter, 38–42, 112, 113, 121, 129, 130

United Nations Security Council, 38, 124, 132

United States: and Geneva Agreements, 15, 169, capitalism, policy determined by, 75–9; communism, opposition to, 71–80; fear of peace plans, 161, 163; foreign policy of, 11; imperialism, 63–6, 77–80; influence of corporations on foreign policy, 11–12; intervention in other countries, 7–22, 42, 111–17, 155, 166–7, 168, 170–1; long-term objectives and global strategy, 48–80, 149–72, 157, 162, 165–6; mercenary forces of, 151, 171; 'modernization' policy in Vietnam, 162; past intervention in S. Vietnam, 149; post-war policies predicted, 171; reasons for signing Paris Agreements, 161–3; recognition of S. Vietnam government, 149–53, 158; training of personnel by, 150, 155; Vietnamese attitude towards, 47–8, 105–11; violation of Paris Agreements, 151, 155–6, 159, 160, 166, 170; withdrawal of forces, 161; in Vietnam war, *see* war crimes of U.S.

United States Military Assistance Advisory Group (USMAAG), 155; illegal entry into Laos, 166–7

United States Mission in Saigon, 160

USAID (Brazil), 76

Van Fleet, James A., 126
Viet Cong, 27, 28, 60, 66, 69; action of guerrillas, 155; as Chinese agents, 28; bombing of, 25–6, 85–6, 90–4; control of peasants by, 16; and elections, 116–17; North Vietnamese aid to, 60, 66, 127–8, 137; pacification programme against, 99–105, 109–10; strength of, 141–2; U.S. action against, 94–9, 127, 129–30, 136–8
Viet Minh, 27, 40, 44–5, 108, 127, 136; as agents of international communism, 15, 52, 68, 70, 124–5; in land reform, 16–17
Vietnam: coalition government possible, 138–9, 142–3, 161; nationalism, 27–8; neutralization opposed by U.S., 138–9, 141, 144–5; observance of demarcation line, 157–9, 168; territory defined, 39; unification of, 51–2, 141, 157–8, 163
Vietnam, North (Democratic Republic, DRV): aggression, alleged, 39–40, 44, 125–35; bombing of, *see* bombing; casualties in war, 96; Communist aid to, 41; economic development, 53–4; and elections, 115; and escalation of war, 120–3, military action as response to U.S. aggression, 41, 133–5; NLF allegedly controlled by, 132–3, 169; and peace negotiations, 120–3, 145; Russian –Chinese influence on, 165–6; Soviet aid to, 132; in Thailand, alleged influence, 133; U.S. propaganda in, 107; Viet Cong aided by, 60, 66, 127–8, 137
Vietnam, South (Republic, GVN): abandonment of by French, 150; armed forces trained by U.S., 94, 150; attitude towards, U.S., 47–8, 105–11; bombing of, *see* bombing; constitution structure of, 151; definition of, 39; desertions from army, 161; economic development, 53–4; elections, 113–20, 143, 157; failure of cease-fire, 153, 154, 156; governments peacetime rights, 149; intent to violate agreements, 153; isolation prison for Communists, 157; land reform, 16–17; National Assembly, 118; pacification proposals, 13, 18, 96, 99–105, 108–10, 155, 160, 161; 165; political settlement suggested, 138–45; proposals for by Communists, 151; Ranger units, 92–3; recognition of entity by Hanoi, 168; restoration of peace in, 149; self-determination for, 157, 158, 167, 168; sovereignty within, 157, 158, 160, 168; strategic hamlets, 8–10, 116–17; supply-flow into, 170–1; unlimited aid for, 149; U.S. interpretation of, 105–11, U.S. intervention in, 7–22, 39–41, 168; U.S. mercenary forces in, 151; U.S. 'modernization' policy in, 162; U.S. non-military aid to, 54; U.S. operations in, 17, 84–99; U.S. past intervention in, 149; U.S. recognition of government of, 149, 150, 152, 153, 158; training programmes, 108–10, 127; violence of government against civilians, 8, 45, 153, 155
Vietnam war: aggression, U.S. policy, 123–35; civilian casualties, 82–3, 95–6; escalation, 15, 16, 36, 41, 94–5, 119–22, 130–1, 135, 161, 163; peace, *see* peace negotiations; tactics of peace in, 149–72; U.S. expenses in, 63, 167; U.S. objectives, official policy, 45–8, 49–50, 60–1, 70–1, 113–14, 123–47; U.S. objectives, official policy, 45–8, 49–50, 60–1, 70–1, 113–14, 123–47; U.S. role summarized, 7–22; war crimes, *see* war crimes of U.S.
Vinh, 82

Walton, Frank, E., 157
war crimes of U.S., 99–105; bombing as crime, 9, 85–6, 156, 160, 161, 165; crimes against civilians, 18, 156, 157; justification of, 37–43
Warnke, Paul, 84

Index

Washington Post, 13
Westmoreland, William, 25, 36, 88, 91, 92, 97–9, 135; in pacification programme, 101, 103
Wheeler, Earle E., 88, 89, 119, 137, 142

White Paper, United States (1965), 132, 133
Wicker, Tom, 169
Woodrow Wilson Foundation, 75

Yemen, British raids on, 81

Chomsky
John Lyons

People speak of 'the Chomsky revolution'. By this they mean much more than the vast changes that Noam Chomsky has brought about in his own, highly specialised field – linguistics. Chomsky has made this once remote academic discipline a centre and a frontier in the thought of today. His search for the universal in language is a search for understanding of the human mind, and of the relationship of mind and body. It is this which crowds Chomsky's linguistics lectures with students of philosophy, psychology, biology, anthropology, and which requires anyone seeking to understand the revolution in thought of today to venture some distance into this somewhat forbidding field.

'His account is itself a minor modern masterpiece of compression and clarity.'
New Society

'... simply the best short introduction to his work in the English language.'
Times Educational Supplement

A Fontana Selection

Ideology in Social Science edited by Robin Blackburn

Stonehenge Decoded Gerald S. Hawkins

Romantic Image Frank Kermode

Memories, Dreams, Reflections C. G. Jung

The Dominant Man Humphry Knipe and George Maclay

Reformation Europe (1517–1559) G. R. Elton

Social Problems in Modern Britain
edited by Eric Butterworth and David Weir

The Screwtape Letters C. S. Lewis

My Early Life Winston Churchill

Voyage to Atlantis James W. Mavor

The First Four Georges J. H. Plumb

Natural History of Man in Britain
H. J. Fleure and M. Davies

Waiting on God Simone Weil

The Wandering Scholars Helen Waddell

Italian Painters of the Renaissance Bernhard Berenson

ENTR
ET

Du même auteur aux Éditions Michel Quintin

Alerte à l'ours,
 collection Grande Nature, 1998

Grande Nature

ENTRE CHIENS ET LOUPS

ANDRÉ VACHER

ÉDITIONS
MICHEL
QUINTIN

Données de catalogage avant publication (Canada)

Vacher, André, 1938-

　Entre chiens et loups

　(Grande nature)
　Pour les jeunes de 12 ans et plus.

　ISBN 2-89435-115-1

　1. Animaux - Moeurs et comportement - Territoires du Nord-Ouest - Ouvrages pour la jeunesse. 2. Animaux - Moeurs et comportement - Yukon - Ouvrages pour la jeunesse. 3. Animaux - Anecdotes - Ouvrages pour la jeunesse. I. Titre. II. Collection.

QL791.V32　　1999　　j591.5'09719　　C99-941238-8

Illustration : Jocelyne Bouchard
Infographie : Tecni-Chrome

La publication de cet ouvrage a été réalisée grâce au soutien financier de la SODEC, du PADIÉ et du Conseil des Arts du Canada.

Tous droits de traduction et d'adaptation réservés pour tous les pays. Toute reproduction d'un extrait quelconque de ce livre, par procédé mécanique ou électronique, y compris la microreproduction, est strictement interdite sans l'autorisation écrite de l'éditeur.

ISBN 2-89435-115-1
Dépôt légal - Bibliothèque nationale du Québec, 1999

© Copyright 1999
Éditions Michel Quintin
C.P. 340, Waterloo (Québec)
Canada　J0E 2N0
Tél. :　　(450) 539-3774
Téléc. :　(450) 539-4905
Courriel : mquintin@mquintin.com

1 2 3 4 5 6 7 8 9 0 A G M V 3 2 1 0 9

Imprimé au Canada

Tant que le cri du loup retentira dans les forêts du Nord, il restera une chance à l'homme de trouver le bonheur sur la terre.

Mot de l'auteur

Terre d'aventure, l'Ouest canadien est depuis des siècles le théâtre d'exploits merveilleux de la part des trappeurs et des coureurs des bois. Ces hommes rudes ont choisi la vie sauvage en forêt, avec son infinie liberté mais également ses exigences. Sous ces vastes horizons, on connaît la douceur des soirs d'été, mais plus encore l'emprise de la neige et du froid. En hiver, chaque geste est affaire de survie, pour les hommes comme pour les bêtes.
Si l'époque des pionniers est presque révolue, rien n'a cependant changé pour ceux qui préfèrent la paix profonde de la grande nature au confort sophistiqué de la ville et, de

nos jours encore, les histoires extraordinaires sont le lot quotidien de ces hommes hors du commun.

En voici quelques-unes de ces histoires, histoires d'hommes et de bêtes, indissociables sous ces latitudes. Elles auraient pu arriver il y a cent ans, mais elles sont récentes, récentes et authentiques car, par chance, il reste une immense partie de ce grand Canada où le temps s'arrête. Les épinettes y poussent toujours aussi lentement et les loups y hurlent toujours de la même façon.

Les deux amis

Sur le bord du lac Atlin, aux confins du Yukon et de la Colombie-Britannique, un homme habitait une cabane en rondins bâtie tout au bout du village. Coincé entre l'eau et la forêt, il avait déboisé une bande de terre juste assez large pour laisser passer le soleil du matin, car, en hiver, rien ne réchauffe mieux le coeur d'un trappeur qu'un rayon de soleil. Au couchant, il profitait à longueur d'année des somptueux flamboiements réfléchis par le lac, que sa surface fût d'eau ou de glace.

Cet homme avait six chiens qu'il utilisait pour chasser et trapper, et aussi quelquefois en été, lorsque au bout d'un voyage en canot il devait faire un long portage. Il emmenait alors les deux plus forts et leur installait des charges sur le dos, tandis que lui portait l'embarcation.

L'hiver, il ne s'écoulait pas trois jours sans qu'il parte pour une course en forêt, soit pour vérifier ses pièges, poser des collets à lièvre, ou bien relever un filet tendu sous la glace de quelque lac éloigné. Seuls ses chiens lui permettaient tous ces déplacements, aussi s'efforçait-il de les maintenir en bonne condition. Il les nourrissait avec les carcasses des animaux piégés, avec du poisson gelé ou, lorsque après les grosses tempêtes tout manquait, avec une pâtée faite d'un mélange en poudre dont il conservait toujours quelques sacs pour ces occasions-là.

Les six bêtes étaient magnifiques. Sans posséder l'élégance des huskies, elles avaient ce port noble du chien nordique qui doit au loup la force et l'endurance et à de nombreux croisements l'obéissance et l'attachement à son maître. Son seul défaut est d'être parfois terriblement querelleur. Même dans un attelage bien dressé, une bataille peut éclater n'importe quand sans que le conducteur en comprenne vraiment

Les deux amis

la raison. Il ne lui reste qu'à séparer les combattants au plus vite, en jouant du pied et du poing, en les tirant par la queue, en faisant tout pour leur éviter des blessures trop graves. Les oreilles déchirées, les lambeaux de peau arrachés, les pattes entaillées sont choses fréquentes qui se guérissent vite, mais il arrive quelquefois qu'un chien ne se relève plus, vidé de son sang par une morsure à la gorge.

Dans cet attelage-là, il y avait surtout un bagarreur, un chien nommé Reuf. Ni plus gros ni plus fort que les autres, il éprouvait constamment le besoin de se battre, même s'il ne sortait pas toujours vainqueur du combat. Il s'était successivement attaqué à tous ses compagnons d'équipage, et même à Buck, le chef, qui l'avait sérieusement corrigé. Seule la chienne Niska échappait à sa violence.

La principale victime de Reuf était Smoky, grand beau chien à la robe gris foncé, avec une bonne grosse tête carrée qu'éclairait le regard un peu nostalgique de deux yeux marrons. Smoky possédait toutes les qualités du chien de traîneau, la force, le courage et le calme. Il ne cherchait jamais querelle à personne mais, sans raison apparente, Reuf le haïssait. Il profitait de la moindre occasion, par exemple un moment d'inattention de son maître alors qu'il défaisait sa chaîne avant de l'atteler, pour bondir sur Smoky déjà harnaché. Ou alors, à l'arrêt, bien qu'il se trouvât toujours à bonne distance de lui dans l'équipage, il s'arrangeait pour bousculer ses compagnons afin de se placer à portée de crocs. Parfois, un ou deux autres se mettaient de la partie, et ce pauvre Smoky se voyait assailli de partout. Quelquefois, la nuit, Reuf réussissait à rompre son attache et, sans bruit, s'approchait de sa victime qu'il surprenait à moitié endormie et mordait cruellement.

Évidemment, le trappeur corrigeait Reuf chaque fois qu'il le voyait faire, mais les pires coups ne parvenaient à le mater. Dès que possible il recommençait, au point que l'homme, excédé par ces batailles, en arrivait à maudire de la même façon l'attaquant et l'attaqué. S'il reprochait à l'un son humeur belliqueuse, il en venait à blâmer l'autre pour sa passivité. Et comme tout l'attelage avait compris la situation, Smoky ne tarda pas à devenir le souffre-douleur qui, bien involontairement, se trouvait à l'origine de la plupart des batailles. La pauvre bête s'en ressentait profondément. À force de ne dormir que d'un oeil dans la crainte d'une attaque, Smoky se remettait mal de ses efforts dans le harnais. Il s'attendait sans cesse au pire et son travail perdait cette excellence à laquelle il avait habitué son maître.

Ce dernier en outre envisageait de s'en débarrasser. Il ne se laissait même plus attendrir par ses grands yeux tristes et, de plus en plus, le tenait pour responsable de la mauvaise ambiance qui régnait dans la meute.

— Mais défends-toi donc, tu es bien assez fort, lui cria-t-il un jour en laissant deux autres chiens pourtant moins puissants lui distribuer quelques méchants coups de dents.

À mesure que l'hiver avançait, l'homme se répétait que sans ce courage exemplaire dont Smoky faisait preuve sur la piste, il l'aurait depuis longtemps envoyé au paradis des chiens d'une balle bien placée, mais il avait encore besoin de lui. Six chiens n'étaient pas de trop dans la neige profonde. Néanmoins, la situation empirait chaque jour; aussi, après une nouvelle bataille sanglante, l'homme décida de se défaire de Smoky. Le chien boitait affreusement, mais il l'attela quand même, le plaça en queue, juste avant le traîneau, puis partit visiter un ami à l'autre extrémité du lac Atlin.

Une fois rendu, afin d'éviter un nouvel incident, il amarra solidement son traîneau à un arbre et libéra Smoky de son harnais pour l'attacher seul, à bonne distance des autres.

— Le voilà, mon problème, dit le trappeur à son ami Jack.

— C'est un bagarreur ?

— Que non ! Juste le contraire ! Il est tellement doux que même les plus faibles ne peuvent s'empêcher de lui sauter dessus...

— Pourtant il a l'air costaud, dit Jack.

— Bien sûr qu'il est costaud ! Et courageux, et obéissant, un vrai bon chien si ce n'était cette timidité ou je ne sais quoi qui pousse les autres à le tracasser sans arrêt.

— Et quelques coups bien appliqués ne les calment pas ?

— J'ai tout essayé, dit le trappeur, cette bête a mis la pagaille dans mon attelage.

Les deux amis

— C'est bien la première fois, dit Jack, que j'entends dire qu'un chien calme perturbe un attelage !

— C'est pourtant vrai. Tout a commencé avec Reuf, le brun là, taché de noir. Il s'est mis à le détester et les autres lui ont emboîté le pas.

— Et ton chef de meute laisse faire ?

— Au début il s'interposait, maintenant ça l'indiffère. Encore heureux qu'il ne s'y mette pas lui aussi !

— Il n'a pas assez d'autorité, dit Jack en connaisseur.

— Je n'en sais rien, depuis quelque temps je ne comprends plus rien aux chiens, mais je suis sûr d'une chose, c'est qu'il me faut six bêtes et que ça ne peut plus durer comme ça. Je suis venu te demander de me prêter un de tes chiens en échange de Smoky. Comme les tiens ne le connaissent pas, peut-être qu'ils l'accepteront mieux...

— Possible, dit Jack pensif, mais je ne pense pas que ce soit la solution.

— Ah ! et que proposes-tu ?

— J'ai huit chiens, c'est trop pour moi. J'en ai un, moi aussi, qui me donne du souci. C'est l'inverse de ton Smoky, un vrai batailleur. En le mettant avec les tiens, ça risque de faire diversion.

— Ou d'être pire encore... mais, au point où j'en suis, dit le trappeur, on peut toujours essayer. Va le chercher ton molosse, on va le présenter aux miens.

Jack disparut derrière sa cabane et revint en tenant par le collier un magnifique animal au pelage fauve, le nez griffé, les oreilles fendues, une masse de muscles qui se raidit et gronda en apercevant ces inconnus devant lui. Son oeil aussitôt s'alluma et il se passa la langue sur les babines, anticipant quelque échauffourée, mais Jack le souleva d'un coup sec, de sorte que ses pattes de devant ne touchant plus le sol il ne pouvait bondir.

— Il s'appelle Ayok, dit-il, il a trois ans.

— Belle bête, apprécia le trappeur.

— Commençons par ta chienne de tête, fit Jack.

Le trappeur, de la même façon, souleva Niska par son collier, et les deux hommes approchèrent leurs animaux respectifs en les tenant solidement d'une main, l'autre étant prête à cogner en cas de besoin. Le puissant Ayok souffla bruyamment mais ne découvrit même pas les crocs.

Les deux amis

— Normal, commenta Jack.

Au second chien, Ayok retroussa les babines en grognant du fond de la gorge mais, comme son vis-à-vis ne répliquait pas, il en resta là.

— Ça ira avec celui-là, dit Jack.

Il en fut de même avec le suivant.

Arrivé à Reuf, Ayok voulut s'élancer. Toute sa face n'était que plis hideux mettant à nu sa redoutable denture. Jack le retint à grand-peine, tandis que le maître de Reuf tirait lui aussi de toutes ses forces sur sa bête qui bavait de rage.

— Il faudra que l'un des deux cède, dit Jack.

Au chien suivant, mêmes grimaces, même haine subite.

Il ne restait plus que Smoky attaché en retrait.

— Oh! lui, dit le trappeur, ce n'est pas la peine que je le retienne, ton Ayok va tellement l'effrayer!

Jack s'approcha, prêt à contenir la fureur de son chien, le soulevant toujours par le collier mais, à la grande surprise des deux hommes, Smoky ne reculait pas ni ne manifestait de crainte comme l'avait prédit son maître, aussi ce dernier l'empoigna rapidement afin d'éviter tout assaut perfide.

Les deux bêtes se trouvaient face à face, à moins de cinquante centimètres.

Elles se dévisageaient calmement. Rien ne transparaissait sur leurs masques impassibles.

Les réactions précédentes avaient été si rapides que les deux hommes s'interrogeaient maintenant sur ce calme qui semblait s'éterniser.

Et puis, soudain, Ayok se mit à battre de la queue. Les deux coureurs des bois se regardèrent, interloqués; ils rapprochèrent un peu plus les chiens. Ayok émit un léger cri, comme en poussent les chiots qui veulent jouer. Jack le laissa avancer encore, jusqu'à ce que les truffes se rencontrent. Les deux bêtes reniflaient à petits coups saccadés. Leurs maîtres, tendus, s'apprêtaient à tirer rapidement au moindre faux geste, mais au contraire, sans plus rien comprendre, ils virent Ayok, le terrible Ayok, donner un coup de langue sur le museau de Smoky. L'autre répondit de la même façon, en agitant le fouet comme cela ne lui arrivait plus depuis bien longtemps.

— Je crois qu'ils s'entendront bien, dit Jack.

— Ça m'en a l'air.

Aucun des deux hommes ne portait attention à l'attelage qui observait la scène avec le plus vif intérêt. La meute entière, et Reuf en particulier, venait de comprendre que c'en était fini de tourmenter Smoky. Chez les chiens, l'amitié, la haine ou l'indifférence se décident en quelques secondes, à tout jamais. Dorénavant, Smoky pouvait compter sur un redoutable ami.

— Avec Ayok, dit Jack à son compagnon, je pense que ton problème va se régler tout seul.

— C'est bien possible, je saurai t'en reparler, dit-il en prenant congé.

Il avait attelé Ayok juste en avant du traîneau, là où il faut un chien puissant pour encaisser les à-coups et fournir l'effort qui permet d'éviter les obstacles. Devant lui trottait Smoky, enfin certain de ne pas se faire mordre les pattes.

Pour la nuit, le trappeur attachait chacun de ses chiens à un arbre, en prenant soin de les éloigner suffisamment l'un de l'autre afin que, même en bout de chaîne, ils ne puissent s'atteindre. Il leur coupait des branches d'épinette qui les isolaient de la neige et ainsi, en se réchauffant mieux, roulés en boule, le museau protégé par leur grosse queue touffue, ils refaisaient plus aisément leurs forces pour le lendemain.

Mais ce soir, en attachant Smoky à son arbre habituel, l'homme était perplexe. Il craignait une vengeance nocturne de Reuf qui, malgré les précautions, parvenait quelquefois à se libérer de sa chaîne. Même en sentant Ayok tout près, l'intrépide Reuf pouvait bien tenter un mauvais coup. Restait, bien sûr, la solution de mettre Ayok et Smoky au pied du même arbre. Malgré une indéniable fraternisation, cela semblait quand même prématuré. Leur rencontre était trop récente pour que le trappeur, encore sous la surprise, considère cette bonne entente comme définitive. C'est alors qu'il eut une idée.

— Je vais faire un test pendant le repas, dit-il pour lui seul. Je vais les placer côte à côte. S'ils arrivent à manger sans anicroche, ils dormiront de même.

Ainsi, il jeta un morceau de castor à chacun des chiens qui s'emparèrent prestement de leur dû et se mirent en frais de l'ingurgiter. La viande gelée, aussi dure que du roc, se détachait par petits morceaux sous la pression des mâchoires. Les os craquaient, réduits en miettes que les chiens avalaient sans distinction. Chaque animal s'acharnait sur sa ration, léchant à grands coups le peu de sang qui parvenait à fondre au contact de la salive. À peine si Ayok jetait un regard à Smoky près de lui, tout aussi indifférent.

« Voilà déjà un bon signe, pensa le trappeur, ils n'éprouvent pas de méfiance l'un envers l'autre. »

Mais, tandis qu'il les observait, il assista à une scène qui le laissa ébahi.

Smoky venait de terminer sa part et se nettoyait consciencieusement les babines, lorsqu'un morceau de la portion d'Ayok, projeté après un cassement d'os, vint rouler juste devant lui.

Ayok l'avait suivi du regard et Smoky le considérait maintenant.

Quelques secondes s'écoulèrent, les deux bêtes se fixèrent un instant, puis Smoky, calmement, avança la patte pour attraper le morceau. Ayok le regarda sans broncher et se remit à manger.

Le trappeur n'en croyait pas ses yeux. Il avait vu des chiens se battre à mort pour un geste identique. Il pensa tout à coup qu'il ignorait encore bien des aspects de la nature canine, malgré des années de course derrière un attelage. Néanmoins, ses dernières appréhensions au sujet des deux bêtes venaient de s'envoler, et le fait qu'elles pouvaient passer la nuit près du même arbre n'appelait plus maintenant la moindre restriction.

À partir de ce jour, tout changea rapidement dans la meute. Un nouvel ordre s'établit.

Dès la première occasion, Ayok et Reuf s'affrontèrent dans un terrible combat. Aucun autre chien ne vint s'en mêler, sachant qu'il s'agissait pour le nouveau venu de déterminer son rang exact dans la hiérarchie de l'attelage. Lorsque le trappeur réussit à les séparer, Ayok avait le dessus mais sa victoire ne semblait pas décisive, du moins aux yeux de Reuf qui l'attaqua de nouveau quelques jours plus tard.

La bataille fut aussi brève que violente et, avant que l'homme n'ait pu s'interposer, Ayok tenait à pleine gueule la gorge de Reuf.

Il lui suffisait de serrer pour le tuer, et rien, pas même les coups de son maître, n'aurait pu l'en empêcher. Mais il ne le fit pas car ce n'était pas son but. En tenant ainsi, au bout de ses crocs, la vie de Reuf, il venait de lui signifier sa supériorité; l'autre le savait et dorénavant accepterait la soumission.

Par ce geste, Ayok atteignit le haut de la hiérarchie, juste derrière le chef de meute, le gros Buck qu'aucun encore n'avait détrôné.

Ayok ne s'y risqua pas car il ne convoitait pas sa place. Peut-être aussi sentait-il que la force peu commune de Buck le maintiendrait là encore longtemps. Mais, si pareillement les autres chiens respectaient le rang d'Ayok, lui ne se gênait pas pour corriger ceux qui s'en prenaient à Smoky. En fait, peu l'attaquaient ouvertement maintenant qu'ils le savaient protégé. Néanmoins, deux ou trois, Reuf en tête, ne laissaient guère passer l'occasion de lui donner un coup de dent. Ayok, alors, rendait au centuple. Au point qu'en quelques semaines plus aucun n'osa même s'approcher de Smoky. Le rendement de l'attelage s'en trouva considérablement amélioré, une ambiance plus saine régnait dans la meute, et ce chien bagarreur qu'avait décrit Jack, s'avérait plutôt calme tant qu'on laissait Smoky en paix. À eux deux, d'ailleurs, ils faisaient un tandem d'une rare puissance dont le trappeur tirait parti en les plaçant en queue, s'évitant ainsi bien des efforts pour manoeuvrer le traîneau dans les passages difficiles.

Cela dura quelques hivers, jusqu'au jour où, progressant en bordure d'un ravin, le trappeur perdit le contrôle de son traîneau trop lourd qui dévala la pente en entraînant les chiens. Deux furent écrasés contre les rochers : Reuf et Smoky. Les autres en sortirent miraculeusement indemnes. Le trappeur connut les pires difficultés pour récupérer bêtes et matériel, mais plus encore pour arracher Ayok de l'endroit de l'accident. Le gros chien gémissait comme un chiot, s'agitait en gestes désordonnés, revenait sur Smoky qu'il léchait, qu'il poussait du museau, puis redressait la tête pour hurler au vent de lugubres complaintes.

À partir de ce jour, Ayok, le terrible Ayok, celui qui avait ramené l'ordre dans l'attelage, ne fut plus jamais le même. Une semaine après la catastrophe il refusait encore de manger. Il ne dormait pas non plus, tournant à longueur de nuit autour de l'arbre qu'il avait partagé avec Smoky. À tout moment il hurlait à la mort, avec une intensité qui terrorisait les autres chiens et même quelquefois leur maître lui-même. Ce dernier n'osait plus l'atteler, il le laissait près de la cabane et retrouvait intacte en revenant la nourriture donnée la veille. Un soir il lui présenta un gros morceau de caribou, frais et sanguinolent, mais le chien n'y toucha pas davantage.

Son extraordinaire résistance lui permit de conserver une certaine apparence pendant plusieurs semaines, mais au-delà il commença à dépérir. Le trappeur le voyait chaque matin plus affaibli, plus abattu.

L'homme n'arrivait pas à croire que la perte d'un ami puisse terrasser une bête aussi forte. Il ignorait que de tels sentiments existaient chez les chiens. Il espérait toujours qu'Ayok reprendrait le dessus. Mais non. Alors, décontenancé, il partit demander l'avis de Jack.

Mais lui non plus n'avait de conseils pour ces cas-là.

Lorsque le trappeur regagna sa cabane, Ayok était mort. Mort de son amitié pour Smoky.

Le meilleur choix

Deux hommes qui exploitaient des terrains de trappe voisins rivalisaient d'adresse dans la capture des animaux à fourrure. Leurs cabanes en rondins se dressaient à quelques kilomètres l'une de l'autre, le long de la rivière Mikkwa, au coeur de l'Athabasca[1]. Ils se rendaient visite assez souvent, l'été en canot, l'hiver, soit en traîneau à chiens, soit en motoneige. Et justement, depuis quelques années, ce choix entre les chiens et la motoneige devenait leur principal sujet de

---

[1] Dans le nord de l'Alberta.

conversation, avec toute la passion que peuvent engendrer, dans le Nord, des moyens de transport aussi vitaux.

Bob Grandfield avait, depuis trois ans déjà, remplacé son attelage par une motoneige, et Jim Harvey, lui, persistait à utiliser ses cinq chiens. Chacun avançait de bonnes raisons pour justifier son choix et, certes, les deux solutions présentaient autant d'avantages que d'inconvénients. Si la motoneige est plus rapide, par contre elle exige de l'essence, alors que les chiens peuvent, à l'occasion, rester plusieurs jours sans manger et courir quand même. Si les chiens sont moins forts, en retour ils savent déceler la mauvaise glace sur une rivière, tandis que la motoneige passera à travers. Ils peuvent aussi retrouver leur chemin si par mégarde le trappeur s'est égaré; dans un tel cas la motoneige devient tristement inutile. Sans parler des pannes pouvant survenir à mille lieues de la cabane, obligeant à de pénibles marches en raquettes si l'on n'est pas bon mécanicien. Bien sûr, les chiens se battent, se blessent, attrapent parfois des maladies, mais en revanche ils font des petits qu'il suffit de dresser. Ils ne coûtent que leur nourriture, alors qu'il faut débourser une fortune pour acheter l'engin mécanisé. Ni Bob Grandfield ni Jim Harvey ne parvenaient jamais à avoir le dernier mot, et chacun exploitait les avatars de l'autre pour essayer de le convaincre.

Cette année, les circonstances semblaient donner raison à Bob Grandfield : un hiver particulièrement rude amenait tempête sur tempête, le vent et la neige s'unissaient pour étouffer toute vie animale, forçant l'homme à se tenir dans sa cabane des journées entières, sans possibilité de chasser ou de poser des pièges.

— Alors, disait Bob la dernière fois que les deux trappeurs s'étaient vus, tu n'es pas encore las de passer ton temps à chasser pour nourrir tes chiens ! As-tu compté les jours que cela t'a coûtés depuis le début de la trappe ?

— C'est un hiver exceptionnel...

— Justement, les bêtes affamées sont moins méfiantes, et après les tempêtes il faut se hâter d'appâter les pièges, au lieu de courir après les caribous.

— Je n'ai guère le choix, mes chiens doivent manger...

— Tu conviens donc que ma motoneige est plus pratique. Je pars sitôt la tempête finie, et bien que les congères me donnent du mal, j'arrive quand même à mes pièges. Tiens, je ne suis pas meilleur trappeur que toi, mais j'ai certainement deux fois plus de peaux, et nous ne sommes qu'en janvier. À cette cadence, je l'aurai vite payée ma motoneige, et sans me fatiguer autant que toi!

De retour chez lui, Jim Harvey médita une fois encore sur cela. Bien sûr, il admettait secrètement les avantages de la motoneige, et même s'il jouait les sceptiques devant Bob Grandfield, il savait très bien que cette bruyante invention faciliterait grandement son travail. Le principal obstacle demeurait le prix, mais les marchands consentaient de gros crédits, et comme les fourrures se vendaient bien, en deux ou trois saisons tout serait remboursé... Pour l'essence, il suffisait de faire une bonne réserve en été. Oui, logiquement les risques semblaient minces, la motoneige s'imposait indiscutablement.

Seulement, Jim avait cinq chiens: Blackie, le meneur, Lissa, Smoky, Yuky et Nakos, cinq copains qui, dans ces immenses forêts, meublaient sa solitude d'une affection indéfectible. Le temps qu'il perdait pour leur procurer les énormes quantités de viande dévorées chaque semaine, Jim le regagnait dans le réconfort de leur présence. Il s'imaginait mal prenant en motoneige les pistes si souvent foulées par ses chiens. Il vivait depuis trop longtemps avec eux pour, subitement, reporter sa confiance sur une mécanique froide et impersonnelle. Malgré la tentation de s'épargner de la fatigue à un moment où l'âge commençait à peser, il ne pouvait se résoudre à franchir ce pas décisif. D'autre part, il entrevoyait aussi le jour où l'attelage serait trop lourd à entretenir. Alors que faire?

Un soir, il crut avoir trouvé un moyen terme : garder Blakie, son préféré, et vendre les autres. Il ne se priverait ainsi ni d'une présence amicale ni des bienfaits du progrès, mais il suffit qu'à la nuit tombante, ses cinq chiens se mettent à hurler à la lune pour qu'il regrette déjà cette musique sauvage qu'aucun moteur de motoneige ne remplacera jamais.

Cela le tracassait. Cette importante décision à prendre lui pesait comme une courbature. Toujours présente, obsédante, elle lui gâchait jusqu'au plaisir de voir courir ses bêtes en avant de son traîneau.

Comme un fait exprès, l'hiver s'acharnait sans vouloir faiblir. Il ne cessait de neiger et de venter. Le soleil n'apparaissait que les jours de très basse température, à une époque où habituellement la forêt commençait à se réchauffer. Jim peinait beaucoup pour faire régulièrement le tour de sa ligne de trappe. Chaque fois qu'il devenait urgent d'aller chercher du gibier pour les chiens, il devait délaisser les pièges et, immanquablement, trouvait à son retour quelques martres ou visons dévorés. Les caribous, qui d'ordinaire fournissaient une bonne réserve de nourriture à proximité, se tenaient plus au nord cette année. Les poursuivre serait inutile, cela prendrait du temps, demanderait plus aux chiens et finalement nuirait encore davantage à la trappe. Jim Harvey ne voyait pas son ballot de peaux grossir bien vite, et mieux que tout, cela traduisait ses difficultés.

Pendant ce temps, Bob Grandfield accumulait les fourrures. Il avait surtout des martres et des castors, mais aussi des visons, des renards, des pékans, et même deux loutres.

— J'ai rarement connu une aussi bonne saison, dit-il un jour qu'il venait montrer à Jim un renard exceptionnellement gros.

— Pour moi c'est juste le contraire, répondit son copain d'une voix dépitée.

— Ce n'est pas normal, tu es bon trappeur, tu pourrais avoir autant de fourrures que moi si tu te décidais à te moderniser. La preuve est faite, mon vieux, les chiens sont dépassés, c'est une motoneige qu'il te faut.

Ce soir-là, Jim réfléchit une autre fois à la question, envisagea à nouveau chaque détail, au point que son sommeil même s'en trouva fort compromis. Le matin, il se heurtait à la terrible évidence : oui, la preuve était bien faite, il devait se convertir à la motoneige. Pour celui qui vit en forêt, la trappe demeure le seul moyen de gagner l'argent permettant d'acheter canot, fusils, munitions, sucre, tabac, farine... produits essentiels sans lesquels la grande liberté du trappeur ne serait qu'illusion.

« En allant vendre mes quelques fourrures, je vendrai aussi mes chiens, pensa Jim Harvey, la mort dans l'âme, et je commanderai une motoneige pour l'hiver prochain. »

Jamais le printemps ne lui parut si long à venir que cette année-là. Il aurait volontiers donné sa maigre récolte de fourrures pour l'avancer de quelques jours, mais la neige et le froid ne désarmaient pas.

Un matin, alors qu'il faisait la tournée de ses pièges, il trouva un lynx retenu par une patte de derrière. L'animal venait sans doute de se faire prendre tout récemment, car il déployait de violents efforts pour se dégager. Ses yeux jaunes lançaient des éclairs, il feulait en retroussant les babines sur d'impressionnantes canines.

Jim s'avança avec un gourdin pour l'assommer. Il procédait toujours ainsi avec les animaux encore vivants, afin d'abréger leurs souffrances sans abîmer leur fourrure, mais celui-ci arracha soudain sa patte du piège et lui sauta au visage. Destiné à la martre, le piège était trop faible pour retenir la grosse patte d'un lynx. Les terribles griffes labourèrent le visage du trappeur qui se ramassa sur lui-même pour se protéger, mais l'animal rendu furieux le griffa férocement de nouveau et le mordit au cou.

Les chiens, attachés à proximité, en entendant les grognements du lynx se mirent à tirer comme des forcenés sur la corde. Chez eux, l'instinct de chasse n'est pas très développé, mais la perspective d'une bataille suscite toujours beaucoup d'excitation, quel que soit l'adversaire. En peu de temps le noeud céda et l'attelage emmené par Blackie se rua vers le lynx qui, en quelques bonds spectaculaires, eut tôt fait de s'éclipser, laissant les chiens dépités avec leur traîneau sur les talons. Indécis, stupéfaits, ils restèrent là un instant, à pousser de petits cris, à piétiner de nervosité dans l'attente de revoir ce gros chat qui venait de disparaître comme par enchantement. Mais le lynx ne se montra plus; alors, après avoir senti sa piste une ultime fois, les chiens se dirigèrent vers leur maître.

Une surprise les attendait. Jim ne s'était pas relevé. Il gisait inanimé dans la neige, la figure en sang, les mains déchirées, la nuque ouverte. Blackie le renifla longuement puis se mit à le lécher, à le pousser doucement du museau, sans que l'homme reprenne pour autant connaissance. Le brave chien se sentait désemparé, les autres gémissaient derrière lui tandis qu'il promenait de plus belle sa langue sur les blessures de son maître. Mais, malgré ses efforts, l'effet escompté ne se produisit pas. Jim ne bougeait pas plus qu'un billot de bois. Alors, au comble de l'angoisse, le gros Blackie rejeta la tête en arrière et lança dans le vent un terrible hurlement comme les loups ont coutume de le faire pour crier leurs malheurs à la lune. Puis il regarda à nouveau son maître inerte et, sans prévenir, bondit sur la piste en entraînant ses compagnons désorientés. Quelques sourds grognements les avertirent de ne pas contester sa décision.

Blackie suivit un moment les traces de l'aller, repassant ainsi près du piège précédent, puis de celui d'avant. Il avançait le plus vite qu'il pouvait et tout l'attelage lui emboîtait le pas sans faiblir, mais il arrivait que le traîneau, laissé à lui-même, se prenne dans une souche ou une branche, brisant d'un coup l'élan des chiens qui roulaient dans la neige sous le choc. Ils s'acharnaient alors pour neutraliser cette entrave, tirant de toutes les façons possibles jusqu'à ce que cède ou l'obstacle ou quelque partie du toboggan. D'autres fois, dans les pentes, le traîneau fou les rattrapait, cognait dans la croupe de Nakos et entraînait la meute entière dans une indescriptible mêlée. Les chiens ne se relevaient qu'au bas de la côte, reprenaient tant bien que mal la formation et repartaient en redoublant d'efforts pour rattraper le temps perdu.

Ils ne couraient que sur de brèves distances, lorsque la neige et le terrain le permettaient. La piste à peine marquée allait de piège en piège, aussi Blackie l'abandonna bientôt pour couper à travers une petite vallée empruntée quelquefois avec Jim pour rejoindre la rivière. Animé par une idée fixe, l'animal avançait sans hésitation, guidé tout à la fois par son instinct et sa mémoire.

Parvenu à la rivière, il imposa un rythme encore plus sévère à ses compagnons. À cause du faible courant, la glace épaisse recouvrait l'eau d'une rive à l'autre et de larges espaces à peine enneigés permettaient de courir très vite. Néanmoins, l'allure pouvait tomber subitement, soit à cause des congères où les chiens s'enfonçaient jusqu'au ventre, soit à cause de la glace que le vent mettait à nu, et sur laquelle les griffes même restaient sans prise. Chacun luttait de toutes ses forces, la langue pendante, le souffle court, happant la neige à pleine gueule pour se désaltérer. Bien que leur maître ne fût pas là pour les encourager, les bêtes obéissaient aveuglément à leur chef Blackie, se dépensant de la même façon, sans compter.

La course infernale durait depuis presque deux heures lorsque, enfin, les cinq chiens épuisés se laissèrent tomber devant la cabane de Bob Grandfield.

L'homme, occupé à préparer son repas, ne les avait pas vus arriver, aussi sursauta-t-il en entendant la grosse voix de Blackie l'appeler d'un ton impérieux. Puis, comme il ne se pressait pas assez pour ouvrir la porte, Blackie aboya une autre fois. Ce n'était pas dans ses habitudes, surtout de cette façon; Bob Grandfield abandonna ses chaudrons et se précipita dehors. En découvrant les cinq chiens pantelants et le traîneau vide, il comprit que Jim éprouvait des ennuis. En vitesse il enfila son parka, attrapa son bonnet, ses gants, et démarra sa motoneige puis, se ravisant, il revint prendre une carabine qu'il déposa dans le petit traîneau toujours attelé derrière. Il jeta un rapide coup d'oeil à celui de Jim, vide de pièges et d'outils, avec un montant cassé, la toile de côté déchirée... puis, sans hésiter, lança sa machine sur la piste des chiens, encore étendus devant sa porte, à bout de forces. La neige fraîchement tombée en conservait tous les détails, et le trappeur ne voyait rien d'autre que ces marques de pattes qu'il remontait aussi vite qu'il pouvait.

Tant qu'il resta sur la rivière, la surface plate et dégagée permit à la machine de fournir son maximum, mais, sitôt en forêt, la vitesse tomba d'un coup. Plus que les arbres, branchages, rochers ou autres accidents du terrain, l'absence de sentier freinait l'allure. La lourde motoneige avait besoin d'un chemin bien tassé, sinon elle s'enfonçait dans la neige au moindre obstacle. Par endroits, Bob devait même s'écarter de la piste, impraticable, pour faire un détour au-delà des arbres morts et des taillis. Il luttait contre d'innombrables difficultés dont la pire restait le trou que l'engin creusait avec ses propres chenillettes dès qu'une pente trop forte se présentait. Suant et soufflant, Bob s'escrimait ensuite pendant de longues minutes à le dégager, mais la nervosité, la peur de perdre un temps précieux ôtaient de l'efficacité à ses gestes. Il ne cessait d'envisager les multiples raisons ayant pu séparer son ami Jim de ses chiens, et l'appréhension de faire une mauvaise découverte ajoutait encore à sa fébrilité.

Il parvint bientôt au premier piège que Jim avait relevé. À partir de cet endroit, les traces des chiens devenaient plus nombreuses et il dut les examiner soigneusement pour ne pas se tromper de direction. La progression devenait très lente, tellement la forêt était encombrée mais, par contre, l'anxiété de Bob allait croissant car il sentait venir le terme de cette épouvantable chevauchée.

Et, soudain, il aperçut Jim étendu dans la neige. Il arrêta sa machine au plus près et se précipita.

— Mon pauvre vieux, soupira-t-il en le voyant si mal en point.

Jim ouvrit péniblement les yeux et son visage ensanglanté, boursouflé, méconnaissable, s'illumina brusquement de toute l'espérance du monde. Bob examina les blessures sur lesquelles le froid avait gelé le sang, terrible vision qui souleva le coeur, pourtant endurci, du coureur des bois.

— Quel animal a bien pu te mettre dans cet état-là ? dit-il sans vraiment poser la question.

Jim voulut répondre, mais sa figure lui faisait trop mal pour qu'il puisse seulement bouger les lèvres.

— Ne parle pas, dit Bob, essaye de te lever, je vais t'installer dans mon traîneau et te conduire chez moi.

Il le cala du mieux possible dans l'étroit toboggan et tendit une corde tout le long, d'un bord à l'autre, pour le retenir dans les passages délicats, puisque Jim se trouvait privé de l'usage de ses mains mutilées et terriblement douloureuses.

Le retour prit beaucoup de temps, car Bob dut faire de nombreux détours afin d'éviter les obstacles et chercher les meilleurs passages jusqu'à la rivière. Là, enfin, il put filer sans crainte de faire basculer le traîneau.

Lorsque, après cet interminable retour, ils parvinrent à la cabane de Bob Grandfield, les chiens de Jim étaient toujours là, couchés dans la neige. Le gros Blackie se leva lorsque la motoneige s'arrêta à sa hauteur et salua son maître d'un aboiement joyeux, mais celui-ci, trop durement secoué par le voyage, ne réagit pas.

Bob lava les blessures, les désinfecta, les pansa de son mieux. Néanmoins, durant quelques jours, Jim demeura fiévreux et affaibli. Les plaies de son visage se cicatrisaient très lentement, lui interdisant tout mouvement de la bouche, pour parler comme pour manger. Il ne s'alimentait que de bouillon de caribou qui, fort heureusement, contient assez de calories pour maintenir en vie l'homme le plus épuisé.

Dès qu'il put articuler quelques mots, il remercia Bob de l'avoir sauvé d'une mort certaine, mais la question le brûlait de savoir comment il l'avait découvert après l'attaque du lynx.

— Oh! ce n'est pas vraiment moi qui t'ai sauvé, répondit Bob, ce sont plutôt tes chiens...

— Mes chiens!

— Oui, mon vieux, tes chiens! Sans eux tu serais encore là-bas, raide comme bois! Après l'accident ils sont venus à toute allure me chercher.

— Te chercher!

— Comme je te le dis, ils sont arrivés à bout de forces avec le traîneau vide, et en deux coups de gueule Blackie m'a fait comprendre qu'il se passait quelque chose de grave. Après je n'ai eu qu'à remonter leur piste.

Jim resta un moment silencieux. Son visage abîmé ne pouvait traduire aucun sentiment, mais ses yeux bleus, miraculeusement préservés, révélaient à eux seuls une immense émotion.

— Et tu voudrais que je les vende pour acheter une motoneige après ça ! dit-il d'une drôle de voix.

Depuis, Jim Harvey a recommencé à trapper. À longueur d'hiver il parcourt en traîneau sa ligne de pièges, et peu lui importe s'il vend moins de fourrures que son ami Bob Grandfield, il sait plus que jamais qu'il peut compter sur ses cinq fidèles compagnons.

*Un repos
bien mérité*

Un Indien qui habitait près du Grand Lac de l'Ours[1] partait chaque semaine relever ses pièges le long de la rivière Kasisa[2]. Ce long périple lui demandait généralement deux jours, mais parfois aussi trois ou quatre, lorsque trop de neige fraîche ralentissait sa marche et l'obligeait à battre la piste en avant de ses chiens.

Ce matin-là, comme il achevait de préparer son traîneau et commençait à atteler ses bêtes, il hésita en arrivant à

---

[1] Dans les Territoires du Nord-Ouest.

[2] Entre le Grand Lac de l'Ours et le Grand Lac des Esclaves.

Yooka. La chienne attendait des petits et son comportement semblait annoncer la mise bas pour très bientôt. L'Indien l'examina soigneusement, car la tournée risquait d'être longue et pénible avec un attelage réduit, mais il préférait encore cela à la perspective de nouveaux problèmes. Il laissa donc Yooka au campement, la mettant exceptionnellement à l'abri, enfermée dans le porche de la cabane, avec pour nourriture un poisson gelé et une casserole d'eau. Il étendit dans un coin un vieux sac en guise de litière.

Dans le Nord, il faut un cas semblable ou une grave blessure pour qu'un chien de traîneau ne demeure pas à l'extérieur, dans son trou de neige par les pires températures, dos au vent, les pattes ramassées sous le museau et la queue par-dessus.

À son retour, trois jours plus tard, l'homme avait cinq chiens de plus, cinq petites boules goulues serrées contre le ventre de Yooka.

Il ne voulait pas les garder, son attelage de six bêtes lui suffisait, pourtant, il hésitait. Un de ses chiens encore jeune montrait des signes de faiblesse, ou de paresse, que les corrections ne parvenaient à réduire. Aussi l'Indien pensa qu'il serait bon de le remplacer l'hiver prochain. Il décida donc de garder un fils de Yooka.

Pour le choisir, pour être sûr de prendre le meilleur parmi ces cinq chiots identiques, il se fia à leur mère elle-même.

Après lui avoir retiré tous ses petits déposés à l'autre coin du réduit, il la laissa les reprendre et les rapporter sur la litière. Yooka n'en pouvait attraper qu'un à la fois, et le premier que son instinct lui fit délicatement saisir dans son énorme gueule était, sans aucun doute possible, le plus fort et le plus beau. L'Indien savait que la méthode ne trompait jamais, il l'avait vérifiée à plusieurs reprises, en prélevant ainsi deux ou trois chiots dans une portée. L'ordre de préférence établi par la mère se confirmait toujours quelques mois plus tard au moment du dressage.

L'homme prit à son tour le petit chien et le souleva par les pattes de derrière pour voir s'il avait déjà la force de se redresser : simple coutume chez des gens qui vivent avec les chiens depuis toujours. Oui, il le trouvait fort aussi; il le rendit à sa mère qui le lécha copieusement. Les autres furent immédiatement enfouis sous la neige, à bonne profondeur et assez loin du camp pour que Yooka ne les retrouve pas.

L'Indien ne chercha pas longtemps un nom à ce nouveau venu, il l'appela Waskoo, tout simplement parce que cela signifie pékan dans sa langue, et que le jour de sa naissance il en avait capturé deux. Peut-être même qu'il fallait voir là un bon présage?

Waskoo eut bientôt le poil assez fourni pour affronter le froid; un épais duvet laineux renforçait sa jeune fourrure crème tachetée de brun. S'il passait encore les nuits à l'abri avec sa mère, dans la journée il jouait avec elle autour de la cabane, se méfiant déjà des autres chiens qui n'auraient fait qu'une bouchée de son petit corps tendre et chaud. Au printemps, lors des ultimes courses sur une piste défoncée et humide, l'Indien l'emmenait quelquefois, le laissant courir en liberté à côté de l'attelage, le prenant dans le toboggan lorsque ses jeunes forces l'abandonnaient.

Son véritable entraînement débuta l'hiver suivant.

Bel animal de huit mois, gai et vigoureux, il était maintenant en âge de commencer à travailler. Déjà, dans l'été, son maître lui avait appris les ordres essentiels en le faisant tirer un billot en compagnie de Yooka. Waskoo considérait cela comme un jeu et se dépensait sans compter, mais, la première fois qu'il se retrouva harnaché au milieu de la meute, il sembla soudain avoir perdu toute envie de courir. Au moment du départ, il s'aplatit craintivement sur la neige et refusa de bouger. L'Indien, qui ne ménageait pas les coups en pareil cas, savait aussi que la méthode forte ne valait rien avec les jeunes chiens. Il lui parla calmement, le remit fermement sur ses pattes et, après plusieurs essais et néanmoins quelques tapes, réussit à le décider.

Waskoo ne recommença jamais. En quelques heures il réalisa que le temps des jeux venait de s'envoler, alors que débutait la dure carrière de chien de traîneau.

Comme tous ceux de sa race, il adorait courir et piétinait d'impatience lorsqu'il voyait son maître préparer les harnais, mais il dut vite apprendre à ne pas gaspiller toutes ses forces au départ, au risque de trouver l'étape terriblement longue ensuite, jusqu'au prochain arrêt. Et puis, maintenant qu'il tenait sa place dans l'attelage, il lui fallait aussi déterminer son rang dans la meute. Cela se décidait à coups de dents, et parfois le maître interrompait trop tôt le combat, avant que la victoire soit décisive, obligeant à tout recommencer à la première occasion. Il en résulta pour Waskoo des marques indélébiles au nez et aux oreilles, mais le jeune chien sut rapidement se faire craindre de certains tout en acceptant momentanément la supériorité des autres.

Il s'affirma en peu de temps comme un des éléments les plus prometteurs de l'attelage, au point que, l'hiver suivant, lorsque le chien de tête se brisa une patte et dut être abattu, l'Indien n'hésita pas à choisir Waskoo pour le remplacer. Quelques terribles batailles accompagnèrent sa promotion, mais une fois la nouvelle hiérarchie imposée par l'homme et le chien lui-même, toute la meute s'y soumit sans trop rechigner.

Il n'en subsistait pas moins les continuelles et inévitables difficultés que doit affronter tout chien de tête. Ainsi, une fois, l'attelage le força à partir sans le maître. L'Indien avait négligé d'attacher le traîneau et la meute poussa Waskoo à prendre le large. En pareille circonstance, aucun chien de tête ne serait assez fou pour résister : la volonté commune balayant d'un coup son autorité, il s'ensuivrait alors une bataille où, seul contre tous, il n'aurait pas la moindre chance de sauver sa vie. Waskoo céda donc, mais s'arrangea pour posséder quand même la bande de mutins.

Comme, malgré tout, c'était encore lui qui décidait du parcours, il trouva le moyen de conduire ses compagnons surexcités sur un cercle de plusieurs kilomètres, et de regagner le village par un entrecroisement de pistes. Puis, revenu au point de départ et ne voyant pas son maître, il pressentit que ce dernier courait sur leurs traces, alors il entraîna pour un second tour la meute apaisée qui commençait à s'essouffler dans ce train d'enfer. Waskoo avait vu juste. Au bout d'un moment ils rejoignirent l'Indien et s'arrêtèrent gentiment, comme six bons chiens qui rentraient de promenade. Mais l'homme ne voyait pas les choses ainsi, il les rossa à tour de rôle, sans chercher à comprendre d'où venait la faute. Waskoo reçut une correction comme les autres, et ce genre d'injustice ne le disposait guère à la sympathie pour son maître.

Cependant, malgré sa brutalité, l'Indien reconnaissait les qualités exceptionnelles de Waskoo et, au fil des voyages, il s'efforçait d'en faire un animal très sûr, aguerri à toutes les situations. Ainsi, Waskoo apprit bientôt à repérer la mauvaise glace sur une rivière, celle qu'un remous invisible ronge par en dessous et qui cède au passage. Il lui arriva de tomber ainsi dans l'eau glacée, échappant de peu à la noyade et au gel ensuite. Même en s'ébrouant aussitôt et en se roulant vigoureusement dans la neige pour chasser le restant d'humidité, il devient très difficile à un chien, par grand froid, de se réchauffer lorsque la piste ne permet pas de courir assez vite. Mais, rapidement, Waskoo sut éviter ce genre d'accident. De même, lorsqu'il vit un jour un de ses compagnons se faire prendre une patte dans un piège, il comprit qu'il valait mieux ne pas quitter les traces de raquettes lorsque le maître relevait ses trappes.

Un automne, comme il accompagnait l'Indien à la chasse dans le seul but de rapporter ensuite les quartiers de viande sur son dos, il montra d'étonnantes aptitudes à suivre une piste d'orignal et à le débusquer du plus profond d'un fourré. Cette qualité, assez rare chez un chien de traîneau, lui valut quelques égards supplémentaires, mais pas davantage d'amitié chez l'homme, qui le considérait toujours comme un instrument de travail, au même titre que son toboggan ou sa carabine.

C'est alors qu'un événement inattendu fit changer Waskoo de propriétaire. Il allait avoir quatre ans et respirait la force et l'assurance, marque incontestable du chef.

Quelques Indiens s'étaient réunis après la vente des fourrures pour se raconter leur hiver tout en buvant de la bière. La conversation roulait évidemment sur les chiens, et un certain Whapishee prétendait que son chien de tête était le plus fort de la région. Le maître de Waskoo vanta quelques-unes de ses prouesses, mais l'autre soutenait qu'aucun chien n'égalait le sien. Il le disait capable de tirer, seul, deux fûts de deux cents litres de mazout sur plus de vingt mètres. Un pari fut bientôt engagé et Waskoo se retrouva attelé devant deux barils d'huile, sur la même ligne que le champion de Whapishee. Un petit attroupement de curieux enthousiastes assistaient à l'épreuve. L'enjeu n'était rien de moins que les chiens eux-mêmes.

Au signal du départ, les bêtes arc-boutées, toutes griffes plantées dans la neige, décollèrent péniblement la charge qui commença à glisser. Chaque pas se traduisait par quelques centimètres seulement et, au bout d'un mètre, les deux concurrents se trouvaient encore à égalité. Leurs maîtres les encourageaient, mais les chiens ne semblaient pas entendre, concentrés sur l'effort, le corps tendu, la langue pendante. Puis, nettement, le chien de Whapishee commença à prendre un peu d'avance. Des cris fusèrent dans l'assistance. Le maître de Waskoo lui hurlait des ordres mais, n'ayant jamais tiré autre chose qu'un traîneau, l'animal ne connaissait pas les astuces de ce genre de défi. Malgré sa force et sa bonne volonté, il ne pouvait faire mieux. Le gros chien de Whapishee était maintenant cinquante centimètres en avant et il semblait certain que Waskoo ne pourrait plus le rattraper.

C'est alors que le drame se produisit.

La corde retenant les barils de Whapishee se dénoua, et son chien qui n'attendait qu'une occasion comme celle-là se rua sur Waskoo. Tout cela fut si rapide, qu'avant que les Indiens n'aient pu intervenir, une terrible bataille s'engageait. Déséquilibré, Waskoo roula sur la neige, mais, aussitôt revenu de sa surprise il se redressa nerveusement, prêt à défendre chèrement sa peau. Les hommes essayèrent de les séparer; en vain, car une subite et violente haine rendait les deux bêtes insensibles à leurs coups.

Dans un vacarme de cris et de grognements, les gueules dégoulinantes de bave happaient les chairs, tiraient, tordaient, déchiraient. Les combattants s'emmêlaient dans leurs cordes, manquaient leurs sauts, confondaient leurs corps dans une même masse rugissante, se repoussaient pour mieux se ruer... C'est ainsi que Waskoo, plus leste, en se dégageant d'un corps à corps, profita d'une seconde d'inattention de l'autre pour lui planter ses crocs dans la gorge. Les Indiens tapaient de toutes leurs forces afin de l'obliger à lâcher prise, mais c'était déjà trop tard. Les yeux du molosse terrassé s'embrouillaient, le sang coulait par jets sur sa poitrine. Il venait de succomber.

Waskoo se redressa en titubant, une oreille en lambeaux, la fourrure abîmée ; mais avant de pouvoir retrouver son calme, il recevait à nouveau une avalanche de coups de son maître furieux.

— Hé ! arrête, cria Whapishee, ne le bats pas trop fort, il est à moi à présent !

— À toi ?

— Oui, mon chien était largement en avance quand la corde s'est défaite, il aurait gagné.

— C'est vrai, approuvèrent les autres.

— Prends-le alors, dit l'Indien en s'en allant.

C'est ainsi que Waskoo devint le chien de tête de l'attelage de Whapishee. Il lui fallut quelques jours pour se remettre de ses blessures qui, par chance, se trouvaient toutes à portée de sa langue, de sorte qu'un léchage intensif en accéléra la cicatrisation. En voyant dans cet état le remplaçant de leur chef, les autres chiens comprirent que la bataille avait été effroyable. Connaissant la valeur du perdant, ils respectaient d'autant plus Waskoo, sans même s'être encore mesurés à ses crocs.

Quant au maître, il ressemblait assez au premier. Il appréciait les qualités du chien mais, s'il admirait sa force, il ne lui pardonnait pas pour autant d'avoir tué son prédécesseur, surtout devant un groupe d'Indiens à qui il voulait prouver sa supériorité. À cause de cette humiliation, il ne supportait de Waskoo la moindre incartade et le punissait exagérément. Presque trois hivers passèrent ainsi, où Waskoo conduisit ses nouveaux compagnons sur la ligne de trappe de Whapishee. En automne il participait à la chasse à l'orignal et parcourait de longues distances, le dos écrasé par d'énormes quartiers de viande à ramener au canot ou parfois au campement. Les courses en avant de la meute lui plaisaient davantage, malgré la longueur des étapes, car il savait que le soir un repas l'attendait, ce qui n'était pas toujours le cas en été.

Et puis, un jour de fin d'hiver, un inconnu se présenta à la cabane de Whapishee. Il s'agissait d'un trappeur blanc à la recherche d'un chien de tête pour remplacer le sien malencontreusement tué d'un coup de carabine. Aucune autre bête de son attelage ne faisait l'affaire, et l'homme se trouvait très ennuyé. Devant la somme offerte, l'Indien hésita; il avait lui aussi besoin de Waskoo et proposa une chienne qui répondait bien aux ordres, mais l'homme voulait un chien sûr, parfaitement dressé. Finalement, le Blanc coupa court à la discussion en rajoutant cinquante dollars sur la table et le marché fut conclu.

Le nouveau maître de Waskoo s'appelait Charlie Mackay. Il avait bâti sa cabane sur les bords de la rivière Nakina[1] et exploitait un terrain de trappe à proximité. Il vivait là depuis deux ans, après avoir longtemps sillonné cet immense pays entre le lac de l'Ours et l'océan Pacifique, se faisant tantôt prospecteur, tantôt trappeur ou bûcheron, selon son humeur et les possibilités de l'endroit. Il aimait avant tout la liberté que procurait cette vie sans artifices dans la grande nature, même s'il fallait parfois travailler dur pour obtenir la pitance quotidienne. Dans son isolement, Charlie Mackay appréciait grandement la compagnie de ses chiens. Certes, pour s'en faire obéir il devait se montrer sévère quelquefois, mais il s'efforçait toujours de

---

[1] Autre rivière des environs du Grand Lac de l'Ours.

rester juste et modéré dans ses punitions. Son attelage était bien dressé, très discipliné, et Waskoo n'eut pas trop de difficultés à s'en faire admettre.

Sa méfiance envers les hommes tomba un peu avec ce maître qui savait se montrer généreux, et Waskoo, ahuri, découvrit qu'un conducteur de traîneau pouvait s'approcher d'un chien pour le caresser et pas uniquement pour le battre. Les premières fois, il appréhendait quelque traîtrise, mais bien vite il ne dédaigna pas de se faire tapoter les flancs et gratter la tête.

Cet hiver-là, Waskoo apprit à connaître de nouvelles pistes le long de la rivière Nakina. Sa mémoire les enregistra si bien qu'un jour de tempête où son maître désorienté ne savait plus quelle direction prendre dans ces nuages de neige poudreuse, Waskoo, tout seul, sut retrouver la cabane malgré le vent qui efface les traces et confond les paysages. À mesure qu'il parcourait les forêts avec Charlie Mackay, Waskoo sentait naître un sentiment inconnu, quelque chose d'imprécis, totalement différent de la crainte ou de la soumission qui jusqu'alors avaient été son lot. Le chien ressentait de la confiance et même de l'attachement pour cet homme qui le traitait différemment. Il s'en trouvait stimulé, et la fatigue ne semblait plus l'atteindre, même lorsque, au bout d'une longue course, la mauvaise neige collait au traîneau trop chargé.

Hélas ! ce bonheur tout neuf devait connaître une brutale interruption.

Un matin, Charlie Mackay partit à la recherche d'un orignal dont il avait relevé les pistes quelques jours auparavant. Comme il n'avait pas grand chemin à parcourir, il préféra aller seul, en raquettes, se proposant de revenir chercher les chiens au moment de transporter la viande. Bien qu'il dût marcher un peu plus que prévu, il retrouva néanmoins son gibier et, la chasse faite, il regagna son campement pour prendre le traîneau.

Mais, à sa grande surprise, Waskoo n'était plus là.

Sa chaîne s'allongeait près de l'arbre avec, à l'extrémité, le mousqueton tout déformé, tordu au point de ne pouvoir se refermer. Charlie l'examina attentivement, fort étonné que malgré sa force, le chien ait pu venir à bout de cette pièce métallique.

Il se dit que peut-être un animal sauvage avait voulu s'approcher de la cabane, et qu'en bondissant pour le chasser Waskoo avait rompu l'attache... mais cela semblait peu vraisemblable, tout comme l'hypothèse de la fugue.

Il rechercha les traces alentour et, bien que le vent ait bouleversé la neige, il découvrit bientôt des empreintes de raquettes qui n'étaient pas les siennes. La preuve s'inscrivait donc là, irréfutable : on lui avait volé Waskoo. Et qui, sinon son ancien propriétaire ? Ou le précédent qui l'avait sottement perdu ?

« Comment retracer le voleur ? se dit Mackay. L'Indien qui m'a vendu le chien se trouvait dans un camp de chasse à ce moment-là ; il s'est déplacé depuis et je ne sais pas où il habite vraiment... Impossible de visiter toutes les cabanes d'Indiens de la région, et puis ils ne me diront rien de toute façon. »

Charlie Mackay trouva difficilement le sommeil cette nuit-là. Il pensait à Waskoo. Il tenait à ce chien, le meilleur qui ait jamais conduit sa meute. Il regrettait l'ami qu'il commençait à devenir. Il se refusait à croire qu'il ne le reverrait plus mais, connaissant les Indiens, il savait aussi que l'espoir restait mince s'ils avaient décidé de reprendre Waskoo.

Les jours suivants il trappa intensément. Le temps radouci permettait de sortir plus souvent, mais ces voyages en forêt n'étaient pas de tout repos. La confusion régnait à nouveau dans l'attelage. Le chien placé en tête exécutait mal les ordres, impressionné par les autres auxquels il ne parvenait pas à s'imposer. Il s'ensuivait une tension continuelle distrayant chacun sur son harnais. Le travail du trappeur s'en ressentait grandement. Durant trois semaines il essaya par tous les moyens de ramener l'ordre chez ses bêtes. Sans succès. Aussi décida-t-il de se mettre à la recherche d'Indiens trappant dans la contrée pour se procurer un autre chien de tête.

La veille de son départ, il fit la tournée de ses pièges pour récupérer les prises et renouveler les appâts. Bien que parti très tôt le matin, il ne put vérifier toute sa ligne de trappe et, en rentrant, il espérait qu'aucun prédateur ne viendrait lui dérober ses captures d'ici à son retour. Il trouvait bien embêtant d'avoir à entreprendre ce voyage dont il n'était pas certain de revenir avec un chien capable de régler les problèmes de sa meute. À mesure qu'il se rapprochait de chez lui, il essayait de se convaincre que cette bête-là existait et qu'il la trouverait, qu'il la ramènerait coûte que coûte. Il en était là de ses réflexions lorsqu'il déboucha dans la petite clairière en avant de sa cabane où, aussitôt son regard fut attiré par un chien roulé en boule sur le pas de sa porte. Charlie se précipita.

C'était Waskoo, maigre, sale, un bout de corde effilochée autour du cou.

L'animal leva des yeux suppliants, et l'homme remarqua sur sa tête un peu de sang coagulé. À ses pattes, des boulettes de glace écartaient les coussinets en entaillant les chairs, preuve de la longue distance parcourue sur des neiges malaisées pour revenir jusqu'ici. En l'examinant mieux, Charlie découvrit, ça et là, des traces de coups attestant sans l'ombre d'un doute la difficulté de sa capture comme les moyens déployés ensuite pour le dissuader de s'échapper. Waskoo avait cependant réussi et se trouvait à présent, épuisé mais heureux, auprès du seul homme à qui il faisait confiance, ce Charlie Mackay qui délaissait tout l'attelage pour s'occuper au plus vite de nettoyer ses blessures.

Waskoo eut la permission de dormir dans la cabane bien chauffée et, grâce à d'énormes quantités de viande, en quelques jours il se retrouva sur pied, débordant d'énergie pour reprendre le commandement de l'attelage. La discipline revint aussitôt dans la meute et la saison se termina sans que Waskoo ne manque un seul jour de prouver, par quelque façon bien à lui, sa reconnaissance à son maître.

À la vente des fourrures au printemps, Charlie Mackay s'attarda parmi les nombreux Indiens venus d'un peu partout dans la région, mais il ne revit pas celui qu'il soupçonnait d'avoir volé son chien.

D'autres hivers passèrent, qui scellèrent davantage l'amitié de l'homme et de la bête. De nouveaux éléments remplacèrent les plus vieux dans l'attelage, et Waskoo en demeurait le chef qui depuis longtemps n'ignorait plus rien de la piste et de ses dangers. À peine si, avec le temps, ses forces commençaient à s'user.

Charlie aussi ressentait la fatigue à présent et, par un mois de janvier particulièrement froid, il tomba malade. Tout d'abord il crut à un simple refroidissement survenu après avoir transpiré en cassant du bois, mais une fièvre insidieuse lui brûla bientôt le front, lui coupant tout appétit, le privant de ses énergies, le forçant à garder le lit. Il n'avait bien sûr aucun médicament, car depuis toujours il ignorait la maladie, et cette situation le laissait désemparé, lui si robuste, rompu à tant de misères. Et puis il commença à tousser, de longues quintes qui lui arrachaient la poitrine, le laissant pantelant, épuisé au point qu'il déployait un effort surhumain pour nourrir ses chiens et rentrer du bois pour le poêle. Certains jours, même cette nécessité semblait trop écrasante, impossible à satisfaire. Alors, la mort dans l'âme, il laissait les chiens, Waskoo en tête, hurler derrière la cabane. Charlie Mackay voulait garder confiance, mais le mal rongeait aussi son moral.

Il commençait à s'abandonner au désespoir lorsqu'un matin, en entendant soudain aboyer, il comprit qu'un visiteur arrivait. C'était le missionnaire du district, un petit homme barbu qui, malgré son âge avancé, effectuait encore de longs périples en traîneau pour rejoindre les campements indiens. Il ne manquait jamais de faire un détour par la cabane de Charlie pour discuter un moment avec lui, mais là, il n'en était guère question. Le missionnaire jugea aussitôt de l'état du malade. Sans perdre un instant il l'installa dans son traîneau, l'enveloppa de toutes les couvertures disponibles et le ramena à la mission. Néanmoins, la maladie trop avancée exigeait un traitement d'urgence que le père ne pouvait donner lui-même, aussi demanda-t-il par radio que l'on vienne d'urgence chercher Charlie. Le lendemain, un petit avion le conduisait dans un hôpital d'Edmonton.

Le missionnaire avait recueilli Waskoo et la meute; avec ses chiens à lui, cela faisait onze bêtes à nourrir, beaucoup trop pour un homme qui n'a plus l'âge de chasser à longueur d'hiver. Mais la solidarité fait partie de la vie du Nord, tout comme la neige ou le vent, et les Indiens vivant à proximité de la mission apportaient régulièrement des carcasses d'animaux dépouillés. Le père parvenait ainsi, tant bien que mal, à satisfaire les onze appétits. Pour ses visites, il utilisait à tour de rôle chacun des attelages afin que tous les chiens puissent courir, car il n'est pire frustration pour un chien de traîneau que de voir partir ses compagnons alors qu'il reste enchaîné à son poteau.

Quelques mois passèrent ainsi, puis une lettre de Charlie Mackay parvint au missionnaire. Elle disait que c'en était fini du Nord pour lui, qu'une terrible maladie lui avait mangé les poumons, que plus jamais il n'aurait assez de souffle pour conduire un traîneau.

— Vendez mes chiens, ajoutait-il, mais si je peux vous demander un autre service, gardez Waskoo avec vous, peut-être qu'un jour je viendrai le reprendre.

C'est ce que fit le missionnaire, il vendit les chiens de Charlie et les siens aussi, car après quarante hivers dans le Nord, il constatait tristement que chaque sortie en traîneau l'épuisait tant que le moindre incident pouvait devenir tragique. Il ne garda que Waskoo, âgé maintenant de douze ans, trop vieux lui aussi pour tenir tête aux jeunes fous d'un attelage.

À partir de ce jour, ils s'installèrent tous deux dans une espèce de quiétude baignée de nostalgie. Ils pouvaient rester des heures immobiles, le regard accroché à l'horizon, sans rien regarder, sans rien voir d'autre que leurs souvenirs. Puis, un soir, sans raison apparente, Waskoo hurla longuement de tristes, de lugubres plaintes qui n'en finissaient pas de s'étrangler dans sa gorge. Aucun chien des environs n'y répondit, comme si la détresse de Waskoo ne les concernait pas.

Quelques jours après, le missionnaire apprenait que Charlie Mackay venait de mourir. Il prit la grosse tête du chien dans ses mains et, en fixant ses yeux tristes, il lui dit :

— T'en fais pas, mon vieux Waskoo, même si c'est fini de courir la forêt, on peut encore vivre quelques belles années ensemble.

Le numéro huit de Whitehorse

Dans les régions nordiques du Yukon ou de l'Alaska, le chien a très longtemps joué un rôle essentiel. Lui seul permettait le transport des marchandises, du courrier, les longs périples de chasse ou de trappe, et bien des hommes se valorisaient grâce à leurs chiens. Les histoires les plus formidables couraient au sujet de ces attelages sillonnant le pays à longueur d'hiver. Aussi, dès le début du siècle, on organisa des courses de traîneau pour dégager la vérité de toutes ces fabulations. La coutume s'en répandit rapidement pour devenir, dans ces endroits isolés, l'événement de l'année au gros de la froidure, le moment privilégié de la grande fête du chien.

De nos jours, malgré les moyens modernes, malgré les motoneiges, bien des coureurs des bois utilisent encore des chiens et, de Nome à Fairbanks, de Dawson City à Atlin, on dispute toujours des courses. Certaines sont très longues, telle la célèbre Iditarod qui, d'Anchorage à Nome, exige trois semaines terriblement éprouvantes pour venir à bout des 1700 kilomètres de cette piste infernale. Cependant, la plupart des autres se déroulent sur des parcours beaucoup plus modestes.

À Whitehorse, au Yukon, elles constituent l'attraction principale du fameux Sourdough, ce carnaval d'hiver qui tire son nom des premiers chercheurs d'or. Là, pendant une semaine le chien est à l'honneur, comme jadis. Malamute ou husky, samoyède ou grand eskimo, labrador ou simple petit chien indien, qu'il ait les yeux couleur de banquise ou les oreilles tombantes, qu'il ressemble à un loup ou à un ours, il suscite l'admiration des milliers de gens venus le voir courir. Il vole la vedette à son maître, même si celui-ci compte parmi les meilleurs mushers[1] du pays.

Ces hommes rudes parcourent les bois de novembre à mai pour relever leurs pièges et, malgré cela, ils s'entraînent encore en vue des courses. Ils connaissent parfaitement les moyens et le caractère de chacune de leurs bêtes mais, le matin de l'épreuve, ils doivent toujours compter avec l'humeur de la journée. Un bon chien peut très bien ne pas avoir envie de faire vingt kilomètres comme un forcené, un autre qui aura mal dormi sera nerveux et querelleur, un troisième débordera d'énergie qu'il faudra utiliser au mieux en lui choisissant la place adéquate dans l'attelage. À part le chien de tête que ses qualités exceptionnelles placent toujours en avant, les autres peuvent être permutés en fonction de mille détails dont un seul suffit à ruiner des mois d'entraînement et d'espoir.

Bob Njootka avait un chien nommé Nuluk en tête de son attelage, et tous les autres chiens le craignaient depuis le terrible combat qui l'avait imposé comme leur chef. Voilà deux ans déjà que Bob se

---
[1] Conducteurs de traîneau à chiens.

fiait à Nuluk pour mener son traîneau en forêt, et une complicité comme il en connut peu s'était établie entre lui et l'animal.

Pour la première fois, Bob avait décidé de participer au Sourdough de Whitehorse. Il gagnait régulièrement des courses dans son village indien de Old Crow mais, pour les plus grandes compétitions, il appréhendait de quitter sa forêt pour des villes qu'il appréciait peu. Cette fois, ses amis l'avaient tant pressé qu'il avait fini par accepter, ne visant pas moins que la victoire pour compenser ce grand dérangement.

Escorté de quelques supporters, il partit avec ses douze chiens dans un petit camion. Sur le toit, il avait placé deux traîneaux. Il arriva plus d'une semaine en avance pour permettre à ses bêtes et à lui-même de s'acclimater à cette ambiance tellement différente de celle qu'ils connaissaient à Old Crow. Il employa tout ce temps à reconnaître le parcours, à s'entraîner sans relâche. À peine si, le soir, il allait vider un verre ou deux dans les bars surchauffés où les conversations ne roulaient que sur un seul sujet: la course.

Les paris clandestins allaient bon train mais, comme Bob Njootka restait inconnu de la plupart, son nom apparaissait rarement. On le savait Indien et à ce titre, pourtant, certains le prenaient en considération, car à Whitehorse comme dans toutes les courses du pays, existait une rivalité amicale entre les mushers blancs et indiens. Si l'on connaissait toujours les Blancs, on redoutait constamment une surprise de la part des Indiens nouveaux venus.

Le matin du grand jour, Bob se sentait confiant. Lorsqu'il arriva dans l'enclos réservé aux préparatifs, d'autres coureurs s'y trouvaient déjà, qui tendaient leur interminable chaîne le long de laquelle, à intervalles réguliers, seraient attachés les chiens en attendant de prendre les harnais. La plupart des concurrents possédaient des huskies, ces grands chiens minces aux yeux clairs, ou bien des malamutes, plus puissants. Ceux de Bob ressemblaient plutôt à des coyotes, avec dans le regard un peu de crainte et de tristesse. L'Indien les répartit sur la chaîne pour qu'ils puissent se dégourdir les pattes. Le froid sec leur arrachait de la gueule des nuages de vapeur qui se déposaient en givre sur leurs moustaches.

Les départs se faisaient de trois en trois minutes et, lors du tirage au sort, Bob obtint le numéro huit. C'est-à-dire que sur les vingt concurrents, il se trouvait à peu près au milieu. Cela lui convenait, il n'aimait guère partir dans les premiers, préférant toujours sentir devant lui quelques attelages qui stimuleraient ses chiens.

Il attendit le dernier moment pour atteler ses bêtes, car la nervosité les gagnait alors et risquait de leur faire prendre un mauvais départ. Il organisa soigneusement son attelage : Ayok derrière Niska que la crainte aiguillonnerait, Yooka qui paressait quelquefois, juste en avant du traîneau pour qu'elle se sente surveillée, Komy et Otak, qui s'étaient battus la veille, le plus éloignés possible... Puis, lorsque tout sembla parfait et qu'aucune lanière ne se torsadait plus, qu'aucune boucle ne restait ouverte, il plaça Nuluk devant ses onze compagnons qui piétinaient en poussant des cris d'impatience. Le chien de tête n'en conservait pas moins son calme, le masque grave, conscient de ses responsabilités.

Il était tout juste treize heures, ce 23 février, lorsque Bob Njootka se rendit à la ligne de départ. Cinq solides gaillards l'aidaient à maintenir son attelage, au comble de l'excitation. Une foule immense se pressait derrière les barrières. Pour ne pas déranger les chiens, seuls quelques juges pouvaient se tenir le long du parcours; aussi le public se concentrait-il au départ et à l'arrivée, situés à cinquante mètres de distance, après une boucle de vingt kilomètres.

Le haut-parleur annonça:
— Numéro huit, Bob Njootka de Old Crow!

Quelques cris d'encouragement fusèrent, puis, au *go!* du chronométreur, les hommes lâchèrent les chiens qui se ruèrent littéralement sur la piste. Bob, debout sur les patins, se cramponna de toutes ses forces pour ne pas être renversé. Ce train d'enfer tomba cependant quelques centaines de mètres plus loin, où une allure plus normale s'installa; l'Indien, alors, se mit à courir aussi, en se tenant aux montants du traîneau. On n'entendait que le halètement des chiens et le glissement des patins, merveilleuse musique qui rythmait les efforts. Bob laissait Nuluk déterminer la cadence, il encourageait sans cesse ses bêtes mais ne les forçait pas, sachant qu'il aurait suffisamment à le faire d'ici à l'arrivée.

La piste était bien tassée, tant à travers bois qu'en terrain découvert. Quelques dures montées en augmentaient les difficultés, et ces ralentissements brusques éprouvaient terriblement chiens et conducteur. Bob poussait alors le traîneau et, sitôt au sommet, se remettait à courir ou à « pomper » : un pied sur un patin, de l'autre il donnait de puissantes impulsions. À cet effet, sa mère avait cousu sous ses mocassins une semelle en peau de phoque qui accroche mieux la neige à rebrousse-poil. Jamais l'Indien ne se laissait traîner, il travaillait autant que ses bêtes.

Il venait de déboucher dans une longue ligne droite lorsqu'il aperçut un traîneau en avant. Nuluk le vit au même instant et accéléra pour le rattraper. En peu de temps ils se trouvèrent derrière et Bob cria pour demander le passage. C'était le numéro sept. Le conducteur se retourna, stoppa son attelage et le retint comme le règlement l'exigeait. Bob le doubla sans problème en le remerciant de la main. Peu après il rattrapait le numéro six qui semblait avoir quelques difficultés avec son chien de tête.

Au quart du parcours, cela le stimulait. Ses chiens maintenaient une excellente allure sans avoir l'air de se fatiguer, et lui-même se sentait très en forme. Par moments il distinguait, à travers les arbres, un autre attelage assez loin en avant, mais il n'incitait pas Nuluk à se hâter de le rejoindre, considérant qu'il y parviendrait de toute façon, sans gaspillage de forces. En effet, l'écart diminuait tranquillement, jusqu'à ce que Bob arrive assez près pour identifier le numéro cinq. Il se souvint alors de la moue dédaigneuse de l'homme, lorsqu'il l'avait vu descendre ses chiens du camion ce matin, ses chiens indiens à face de coyote, beaucoup plus petits que ses magnifiques huskies.

Lorsqu'il arriva à portée de voix, Bob demanda la piste. Le numéro cinq, un grand rouquin d'Edmonton, se retourna et, surpris de voir l'Indien sur ses talons, fit comme s'il n'existait pas. Il conserva la même place sans modifier son allure.

Bob cria encore, mais l'homme ne se dérangea pas davantage. Nuluk tournait la tête vers son maître, inquiet lui aussi de ne pouvoir passer. Une pente raide se présentait, qui allait mettre les chiens au pas. Bob se dit qu'il faudrait doubler coûte que coûte, au risque de perdre un temps précieux. Il courait le long de son traîneau en cherchant un moyen de venir à bout de cet entêté qui perturbait sa course. Au pied de la côte, commençait un grand virage aboutissant pratiquement au sommet et, soudain, l'Indien remarqua des traces de raquettes qui semblaient couper tout droit.

— *Gee*[1]! *Gee* Nuluk! hurla-t-il aussitôt, tandis que l'attelage quittait la piste sans hésitation.

La neige portait moins bien, les chiens s'enfonçaient jusqu'à la mi-patte, mais Bob maintenant les forçait tant qu'il pouvait. Il devait absolument déboucher en avant du numéro cinq, surtout pas en même temps, car il s'ensuivrait une bataille générale des chiens. Non, il fallait qu'il soit le premier en haut.

---

[1] À droite!

En voyant la manoeuvre, le numéro cinq poussa aussi ses bêtes, confiant cependant de détenir l'avantage du terrain, malgré une plus grande distance à parcourir. À cause des arbres, il ne distinguait pas très bien son adversaire, mais restait persuadé que cette forte pente sans chemin tracé, encombrée d'obstacles, aurait raison de ses petits chiens. Et Bob le crut aussi un instant: la neige profonde, les arbustes, gênaient constamment sa progression. Il ne cessait d'encourager ses bêtes qui s'acharnaient, tandis qu'il repoussait les branches en travers du traîneau.

Cette ascension n'en finissait plus. Bob désespérait de réussir. Le sommet n'était pourtant qu'à une dizaine de mètres, mais il voyait sur sa gauche le numéro cinq qui se rapprochait. À grands cris l'Indien demanda encore un effort à ses bêtes, et Nuluk s'engagea enfin sur la piste. Le numéro cinq était tout près. Derrière Nuluk, Pakos passa aussi, puis Otak, Niska, Ayok... et enfin Yooka. Le numéro cinq était là maintenant, avec ses grands huskies... Bob lança un cri sec comme un coup de fouet, et l'attelage arracha le traîneau du fossé, si fort qu'il buta contre le chien de tête du grand rouquin. Un instant immobilisé, l'homme jurait, fou de rage, mais les vaillants petits coyotes prenaient déjà de la distance. D'eux-mêmes, lorsqu'ils sentirent l'écart suffisant, ils ralentirent pour récupérer. Bob aussi en avait besoin. Tout comme ses bêtes il poussait devant lui le nuage de son haleine blanchie par le froid.

L'Indien était maintenant certain de se trouver en bonne position : trois concurrents doublés avant la mi-parcours en donnaient le meilleur indice. Ne trouvant pas ses chiens trop marqués par ce rude effort pour gravir la pente, il décida de forcer un peu l'allure. C'est alors qu'il s'aperçut que Pakos, qui venait juste derrière Nuluk, boitillait. Et Nuluk le devinait aussi, car il s'était plusieurs fois retourné, sentant qu'il tirait mal. Pour en juger vraiment, l'Indien augmenta encore la cadence et là, aucun doute possible, l'animal ne pouvait supporter le train. Bob connaissait le courage de ses bêtes, et surtout de Pakos, qui, juste derrière le chien de tête, savait lui aussi stimuler l'attelage. Alors l'Indien n'hésita pas. Il se trouvait trop loin encore de l'arrivée pour conserver Pakos, il profita de son avance sur le numéro cinq pour stopper. Prestement il détacha l'animal et le déposa dans le traîneau. Le règlement imposait de revenir avec le même nombre de bêtes qu'au départ, sur pied ou couchées. Pakos se roula en boule et se mit à lécher sa patte douloureuse en gémissant. Sans doute se l'était-il tordue sur quelque branche en coupant le grand virage. Moins d'une minute suffit pour le changement, et déjà la piste défilait à nouveau, à bonne vitesse, sous les patins.

Les chiens avaient tous compris qu'il leur faudrait fournir un effort supplémentaire, et comme entre eux ils ne sont guère enclins à la pitié, on entendait parfois un grognement de protestation contre Pakos qui se laissait traîner. L'Indien y allait aussitôt d'un grand cri pour étouffer ces jalousies.

Peu après le poteau de la mi-course, Bob doubla un autre concurrent, un Indien de Carmacks qui lui cria bonne chance. Les contrôleurs installés sur le parcours signalaient par radio la position des traîneaux, et maintenant que les vingt attelages avaient pris le départ, on pouvait établir un classement provisoire. Les haut-parleurs annoncèrent à la foule massée à l'arrivée que le numéro huit, Bob Njootka, de Old Crow, se trouvait en tête avec un chien dans son traîneau. Il lui restait neuf kilomètres à parcourir, pourrait-il maintenir son avance ? Les parieurs analysèrent longuement le moindre renseignement et pesèrent chaque détail avant de remettre leurs mises.

Mais Bob, lui, ne savait pas vraiment qu'il menait la course. Certes, au nombre de concurrents doublés il s'en doutait, mais il pouvait toujours se trouver parmi les derniers partis un attelage plus rapide qui, sans jamais le rattraper, ferait quand même un meilleur temps. Le souci de l'Indien était de conserver la même allure malgré la blessure de Pakos. Le handicap tenait autant de son absence aux harnais que du poids supplémentaire qu'il imposait aux autres. Bob courait tant qu'il pouvait pour ne pas augmenter cette charge. Il laissait Nuluk régler la cadence, se contentant de lui crier des encouragements.

Et soudain, alors que la piste serpentait à travers bois, tout l'équipage accéléra brusquement, excité par de féroces aboiements venus d'en avant. Ses ordres restant sans effet, l'Indien dut mettre le frein pour arrêter ses bêtes, à peu de distance d'une épouvantable mêlée regroupant deux attelages dont les chiens se ruaient comme des fauves, mordant, griffant, bavant de rage. Les conducteurs essayaient vainement de les séparer, frappant du pied et du poing, empoignant un cou ou une queue, cherchant à s'y retrouver dans ce fouillis de harnais, de crocs et de poils. Bob savait que ses petits coyotes rêvaient de se joindre à la bagarre, aussi fit-il un long détour en tenant Nuluk par le collier. Puis, de nouveau sur la piste, il reprit la course.

Il avait reconnu le numéro deux, un homme de la Police montée avec un superbe équipage que beaucoup donnaient favori. La course était finie pour lui et l'Indien commença sérieusement à penser à la victoire.

Il se mit à forcer ses chiens. La fatigue leur alourdissait doucement les pattes, mais les circonstances exigeaient ce nouvel effort. Lui de même, trop essoufflé pour courir constamment, se contentait de pomper afin de récupérer sans trop briser le train.

Le givre accumulé sur ses joues, dans ses sourcils, sur le bord de son bonnet le rendait méconnaissable. Malgré le froid intense, il sentait son dos humide de sueur. Pakos, lové dans le traîneau, levait vers lui des yeux attristés, mais Bob ne le voyait pas, il regardait la piste et la ligne mouvante de ses onze coyotes. Dans un passage à découvert, il aperçut un équipage en avant, sans pouvoir distinguer le numéro de son musher. Plus que les cris, cette apparition encouragea les chiens, mais l'inconnu, ayant aussi remarqué ses poursuivants, ne semblait guère disposé à se laisser rattraper. En fait, Bob le perdit de vue un long moment puis, au hasard d'une série de tournants, le retrouva à la même distance et put voir qu'il s'agissait du numéro trois. Un calcul rapide lui révéla que cet homme était parti quinze minutes avant lui et ne possédait plus maintenant qu'une avance d'environ trois cents mètres. Décidément, pour Bob Njootka, la victoire prenait forme.

Il ne restait que quelques kilomètres à parcourir, et le numéro trois devint son objectif. Il se jura de le dépasser avant l'arrivée. Il exigea plus encore de ses chiens, et lui-même, négligeant sa fatigue, courait le plus souvent en arrière du traîneau : un effort colossal pour grignoter quelques dizaines de mètres. Le numéro trois se retournait sans cesse, faisant lui aussi le maximum contre les petits coyotes qui se rapprochaient irrésistiblement.

Au panneau annonçant l'arrivée à un kilomètre, Bob n'était plus qu'à trente mètres derrière le numéro trois. Il hurlait à ses chiens d'aller plus vite, mais Nuluk, Ayok, Niska, Komy, Otak et les autres couraient déjà au bout de leurs moyens. Bob le savait mais il criait quand même, pour les aider et s'aider aussi, tandis que l'écart diminuait doucement.

Dans le dernier coude avant la ligne droite de l'arrivée, Nuluk talonnait littéralement l'homme au dossard numéro trois.

À partir de là, la piste s'élargissait pour permettre à deux attelages de courir de front. En prenant mieux son virage, Bob se porta immédiatement à la hauteur de l'autre attelage. Les deux chiens de tête luttèrent un instant côte à côte, puis Nuluk se détacha, et Otak, et Ayok... La foule hurlait. Les petits chiens indiens étaient en train de surclasser les fiers malamutes et les nobles huskies.

Plus que cinquante mètres.

Le traîneau de Bob arrivait maintenant au niveau de l'autre chien de tête. L'Indien avait onze chiens d'avance.

Il pompait avec ses ultimes énergies. Il n'entendait plus rien que le sang qui lui cognait aux tempes. Il ne voyait que cette banderole au bout, là-bas. D'un regard rapide, il comprit qu'il avait encore arraché quelques mètres au numéro trois, quelques mètres... La banderole se rapprochait à toute allure. À présent, elle était là, là... Une immense acclamation montait de la foule.

Et soudain ce fut le vide. Un grand trou noir dans lequel bascula Bob.

Des gens se précipitèrent. On releva l'Indien qui avait roulé dans la neige sitôt la ligne franchie. Il semblait inconscient. On lui tapota le visage, on desserra son parka. Rien n'y fit.

Bob Njootka venait de succomber à un trop grand effort. Il avait magnifiquement gagné et ne le saurait jamais.

C'est depuis ce jour qu'il n'y a plus de numéro huit dans les courses de chiens de Whitehorse.

Le vieil homme et le loup

Trois jours durant, la tempête avait paralysé le Yukon. L'immense forêt qui recouvre le pays courbait l'échine sous les attaques d'un vent si violent qu'il brisait les sapins secs comme du menu bois. La neige folle fuyait en tourbillons, dressant partout des écrans opaques où même le renard ne retrouvait plus son chemin. Toutes les bêtes s'étaient réfugiées dans leur tanière ou sous les branches basses des épinettes, au plus profond des futaies.

Maintenant que le calme revenait, et que le silence étouffait tous ces craquements, ces grondements, ces sifflements, le petit peuple des bois, poussé par la faim, s'efforçait de trouver pitance. Les orignaux, de la neige jusqu'au ventre, se dressaient désespérément pour atteindre les rameaux de tremble ou de peuplier, les rongeurs fouissaient de la patte et du nez, à la recherche de quelque graine ou cône de pin. Les carnassiers se remettaient en chasse.

Les hommes aussi, que la tourmente avait pareillement réduits à l'inactivité. C'est ainsi que deux jeunes Indiens réussirent à blesser un orignal qui leur échappa en profitant de la surface gelée d'un ruisseau. Il s'enfonça dans les taillis où toute poursuite en raquettes devenait impossible.

Non loin de là, un grand loup gris et sa famille cheminaient à la queue leu leu, en quête de gibier. Le chef marchait devant, suivi de trois jeunes et de la louve. Chacun posait instinctivement les pattes dans les traces de celui qui le précédait, de sorte que la piste semblait ne provenir que d'un seul animal. Le meneur s'arrêtait régulièrement, brièvement, pour écouter, pour sentir, mais, là, il s'attardait à questionner le vent. Des effluves d'animal blessé lui parvenaient comme une promesse de nourriture. Il força l'allure malgré la neige qui cédait parfois sous son pas. La bande affamée progressait sans autre bruit qu'un discret halètement qui faisait de petits nuages blancs dans l'air glacial et laissait à chacun de grosses moustaches de givre.

Bientôt les loups croisèrent la piste de l'orignal. Ils s'arrêtèrent un peu pour la flairer, puis reprirent la traque, sans pour autant se mettre à courir, conscients que rien n'épuise comme une course dans la neige lorsqu'il importe de ménager ses moyens. Ils allaient le long des traces de leur gibier, et la vue de ces énormes empreintes tachées de sang les soutenait dans leur effort. Ils auraient pu marcher longtemps, très longtemps comme cela, mais soudain le chef s'arrêta.

Il venait d'apercevoir l'orignal couché près d'un sapin.

Le grand loup gris connaissait le danger d'attaquer ainsi un animal aux forces colossales qu'une blessure n'entame pas si facilement. Il redoutait les sabots effilés tout autant que la ramure aux longues pointes. Mais les jeunes avaient faim et contrôlaient moins bien leurs instincts.

Le loup gris dut montrer les crocs pour les ramener à la raison. Pendant ce temps l'orignal s'était levé, prêt à se battre. Sur son échine, le poil dressé faisait comme une crinière.

Le chef des loups tenta une première approche pour juger de sa vigueur. L'orignal se cabra, ses sabots démesurés battirent l'air, mais l'effort amena un filet de sang sur son poitrail et il s'effondra dans la neige. Les loups se tenaient quand même à distance. Leur chef s'avança pour provoquer une autre réaction de l'animal, qui l'affaiblirait davantage. Cette fois l'orignal se redressa et baissa la tête pour l'encorner. Les loups l'encerclèrent en tentant de le mordre aux pattes, mais il restait prompt à lancer des coups de sabot. La neige profonde gênait leurs mouvements et ils roulaient sur eux-mêmes en grognant de douleur. Sans vraiment avoir été mordu, l'orignal s'écroula à nouveau.

C'est alors que la louve provoqua l'assaut.

Elle lui sauta sur la croupe et, tandis qu'il tournait la tête dans sa direction, le grand loup gris en profita pour se jeter à sa gorge, juste où la grosse veine du cou fait une boursouflure sous le poil. Il mordit de toutes ses forces pour contenir les coups violents que l'animal donnait avec sa tête. Il faillit bien lâcher prise, mais le blessé avait perdu trop de sang avec les balles des Indiens pour résister à une morsure aussi décisive. Ses mouvements se firent plus mous, sa ramure si dangereuse sembla soudain trop lourde à porter, sa tête inerte retomba sur le côté. Le géant des forêts canadiennes venait de succomber. Les cinq loups pouvaient maintenant assouvir leur faim.

La bataille n'avait pas duré très longtemps mais, bien qu'elle demeurât discrète, l'air cristallin du Nord en avait dispersé les rumeurs parvenues jusqu'aux deux Indiens qui avaient retrouvé les traces de leur gibier.

Les loups, trop occupés à manger, ne les entendirent pas approcher, silencieux sur leurs raquettes. Ils ne les sentirent pas non plus; l'odeur de la bête abattue supplantait toutes les autres. Dissimulés derrière les arbres, les chasseurs purent venir assez près et, soudain, un coup de feu claqua, puis un autre et d'autres encore. Les jeunes loups inexpérimentés n'eurent pas le temps de comprendre qu'ils tombaient morts sur l'orignal. La louve tenta un bond, mais une balle brisa son élan et la laissa sans vie.

Le grand loup gris s'enfuyait lorsqu'il fut atteint à l'épaule. Un trait de feu qui l'envoya rouler dans la neige. Il se releva cependant assez vite pour éviter deux autres balles qui firent voler une touffe de poils. Une terrible douleur l'engourdissait, pourtant il courut tant bien que mal vers la sécurité d'un fourré. Le sang coulait le long de sa patte mais il ne s'arrêta pas, voulant s'éloigner le plus possible des chasseurs. Il parvint à couvrir une bonne distance avant de s'écrouler, épuisé. Au prix d'un dernier effort, il se traîna dans un creux de rocher puis lécha longuement sa blessure, empêchant avec sa langue de s'écouler le peu de vie qui lui restait.

Les Indiens songèrent un instant à le poursuivre, tant que ses marques s'imprimaient bien dans la neige, mais ils préférèrent se mettre au dépeçage de l'orignal avant que le froid n'en durcisse les chairs et rende la besogne très difficile. Et puis, ils s'estimaient comblés ce matin : beaucoup de viande et quatre peaux de loups, c'est plus qu'ils n'en espéraient.

Le grand loup gris resta longtemps dans son abri. Le moindre mouvement lui arrachait des gémissements et, même lorsqu'il demeurait immobile, roulé en boule pour lutter contre le froid, une douleur sourde lui donnait comme des coups dans l'épaule. Sa plaie semblait refermée, cependant il savait qu'un rien pouvait la rouvrir, aussi il attendait que commençât la cicatrisation. Mais la faim le tenaillait. Il n'avait pu arracher que quelques bouchées avant le déchaînement meurtrier des Indiens, et il ressentait impérativement le besoin de refaire ses forces pour survivre à cette blessure.

Mais comment chasser avec une épaule brisée ?

Comment poursuivre une proie ?

Comment bondir, après l'affût ?

À moins de découvrir une carcasse abandonnée, ou quelque animal mort dans un piège... Le froid pénétrait sa fourrure, il commença à grelotter et cela le força, malgré la douleur, à se remettre en marche.

Sur le territoire qu'il avait coutume de parcourir, il connaissait l'emplacement d'une ligne de trappe, pour en avoir maintes fois évité les pièges. C'est par là qu'il choisit d'aller.

Mais ses énergies répondaient mal à ses désirs.

Il avançait péniblement sur trois pattes, s'arrêtant souvent pour reprendre haleine, pour lécher son sang qui coulait à nouveau. Il restait debout, de peur de ne pouvoir se relever, et mordait la neige à pleine gueule pour apaiser son estomac et calmer sa fièvre. Son corps entier lui faisait mal. Lorsqu'il trébuchait et tombait, il mettait de longues minutes ensuite avant de retrouver son aplomb. Toute la journée il lutta ainsi et, lui qui appréciait tant la nuit pour chasser, la redoutait à présent, à mesure que la noirceur gagnait. Un gros corbeau vint se poser sur un arbre proche et le considéra de son oeil aigu avant de pousser un croassement qui le fit frissonner. Il avait pu s'installer contre un arbre abattu et, de là, découvrait une clairière cernée d'épinettes. La pleine lune jetait sa lumière blafarde en découpant des ombres mystérieuses.

Il aurait voulu hurler à cette lune de le secourir, elle qui avait si souvent favorisé ses chasses, mais il n'en trouva point la force. Et puis, qui répondrait à son cri, maintenant que sa femelle et ses petits étaient morts ? Il se sentit plus faible encore et ne sut jamais s'il s'endormit ou perdit connaissance.

Des bruits de pas le réveillèrent. Plus que le craquement sourd des raquettes sur la neige, c'est la conscience d'une présence humaine qui le mit en alerte. Il ouvrit les yeux mais, bien qu'il fît grand jour, sa vue embrouillée ne lui révéla qu'un vague contraste entre la neige éblouissante et le vert des sapins. Il savait pourtant qu'un homme se tenait tout près. Il rassembla ses maigres forces pour montrer les crocs, prêt à livrer une ultime bataille.

Prestement l'homme avait épaulé. Le loup s'alignait déjà dans la mire, mais le chasseur retint son doigt sur la détente. Il l'observait mieux. Il détaillait cette tache de sang à l'épaule. Le grand loup gris se dressa mais, trop faible pour faire un pas, retomba sur le flanc. Alors l'homme abaissa son arme et resta là, immobile, comme fasciné. Il fixait ce loup mourant, pendant que dans sa tête d'autres images se formaient.

Il se revoyait lui aussi allongé dans la neige, épuisé, affamé, vidé de son sang à cause d'une terrible coupure au genou, faite avec sa propre hache. Il avait perdu tout espoir. Seul dans l'immense forêt il attendait la « mort blanche », celle qui vient doucement quand on s'endort dans la neige par des températures polaires. C'est alors que, dans la nuit, tandis qu'il ne savait plus s'il dormait ou s'il était déjà mort, il entendit hurler des loups. D'abord ils lui semblèrent loin, mais bien vite il comprit que non, les cris partaient de là, derrière les sapins. Tremblant de peur, il trouva juste assez d'énergie pour prendre sa carabine.

— Ils ne m'auront pas si facilement, murmura-t-il pour se donner du courage.

Puis il attendit.

Chaque seconde s'étirait interminablement. Dans sa poitrine son coeur cognait très fort, et vite. Très vite. Glacé d'effroi, le blessé en oubliait la douleur qui le clouait là.

Mais les bêtes n'approchaient pas.

Aux bruits qui lui parvenaient, l'homme comprit enfin qu'elles s'intéressaient à autre chose. Les grognements, craquements d'os, révélaient sans aucun doute que la bande se repaissait d'une proie forcée et abattue tout à côté. L'homme qui n'avait pas mangé depuis deux jours envisagea soudain le moyen de reprendre vigueur, et peut-être de sortir de ce mauvais pas. Il tira dans les arbres un coup de carabine qui retentit comme le tonnerre dans la nuit. Surpris, les loups s'enfuirent, effrayés, en abandonnant leur gibier.

Stimulé par l'espoir, le blessé rassembla ses dernières forces pour ramper jusque-là. La neige multipliait les difficultés, l'effort surhumain qu'il faisait s'accompagnait d'un flot de plaintes et, malgré le froid, la sueur baignait son front. À bout, il allait abandonner quand il aperçut la carcasse qu'un rayon de lune découpait sur la neige. Il serra plus fort les dents et continua. Lorsque enfin il toucha au but, il s'agrippa à l'orignal pour se hisser dessus et, pire qu'un loup, mordit à pleines dents dans la chair rouge, buvant le sang comme du lait. Il demeura quelques jours près de cette manne, et fut bientôt assez fort pour regagner sa cabane et soigner son genou.

L'homme qui aujourd'hui regardait ce loup blessé se reconnaissait dans l'animal. Les ans avaient blanchi ses cheveux et, s'il ne savait plus guère à combien d'hivers remontait la tragédie, le vieux trappeur s'en souvenait jusque dans les moindres détails. Jamais il n'oublierait qu'il devait la vie à des loups. Oui, à des loups. Alors il fouilla dans son sac et en extirpa un lièvre encore chaud, tout juste retiré d'un collet. Il le lança au grand loup gris.

— Tiens, dit-il, si ça peut t'aider à t'en sortir, c'est de bon coeur. C'est Noël ce soir, et lorsque les tiens m'ont sauvé, c'était Noël aussi. J'espère que tu auras autant de chance.

Et il poursuivit son chemin en boitant sur ses raquettes.

Jos et Pax

Depuis plusieurs années, un homme vivait seul avec son chien, aux confins des fleuves Athabasca et Mackenzie[1]. Les Indiens chipewyans qui habitaient la région délaissaient de plus en plus la forêt pour aller s'établir dans des villages et travailler sur les chantiers de forage. Avec les sables bitumineux, le pétrole et les mines, certains allaient même jusqu'à Yellowknife, sur le Grand Lac des Esclaves.

Quelques-uns cependant trappaient encore, et ceux-là, Jos les connaissait tous.

---

[1] Le Mackenzie prend sa source dans le Grand Lac des Esclaves (Territoires du Nord-Ouest).

Il les rencontrait quelquefois, car leurs territoires de trappe avoisinaient le sien. Les Indiens aimaient bien le vieux Jos, ils appréciaient ses qualités de coureur des bois et, à ce titre, le considéraient un peu comme un des leurs, lui qui avait toujours préféré la forêt à la ville. Certains faisaient régulièrement un détour par sa cabane pour venir bourrer leur pipe de son tabac, et aussi pour admirer Pax, son gros chien tout en muscles, d'une force impressionnante.

On n'aurait su dire qui, du chien ou du tabac, plaisait le plus aux Indiens.

Le tabac était un savant mélange de virginie et de hollande que Jos payait au prix fort chaque printemps, lorsque le marchand venait collecter les fourrures. Il le conservait dans un grand sac, en y mêlant des feuilles de rhubarbe sauvage pour le garder bien frais, car depuis toujours il adorait fumer la pipe, et plus encore depuis qu'il habitait les solitudes du Nord.

Quant au chien, il ne ressemblait à aucun autre dans la région. Les Indiens utilisaient de petits chiens pareils à des coyotes, capables de tirer longtemps les traîneaux sans réclamer beaucoup de nourriture. Pax, lui, faisait peut-être le double de leur poids. Né du croisement d'un labrador et d'un puissant chien eskimo, il possédait la force, l'intelligence et la douceur. Jos l'avait recueilli tout petit, d'un voyageur qui ne savait qu'en faire depuis que sa mère était morte. Ainsi l'animal fut élevé dans l'affection et les bons soins, bien que la nourriture manquât quelquefois sur la table du trappeur. Mais le peu qu'il avait, Jos le partageait avec Pax.

La supériorité du chiot s'affirma rapidement. Déjà, à quelques mois, il pouvait tirer seul un petit toboggan. Jos lui enseigna les commandements de base qu'il retint avec une étonnante facilité. Il aurait fait un excellent chien de tête dans un attelage, mais le trappeur commençait à vieillir et ne se sentait plus le courage de chasser pour nourrir cinq ou six chiens. En hiver, Pax lui suffisait pour tirer le traîneau avec les pièges, les appâts et les animaux capturés. En été, il pouvait porter un sac sur son dos, ce qui allégeait d'autant celui de son maître. Ainsi, en quelques années, s'établit entre Jos et Pax une complicité, une amitié qui dépassait de beaucoup ce qu'un homme, même au fond des bois, attend ordinairement de son chien.

Tout autant que ces qualités exceptionnelles, c'est cela qui intriguait les Indiens, eux qui battaient facilement leurs chiens et ne les toléraient qu'en fonction des services qu'ils pouvaient rendre.

L'intelligence et la ruse de Pax étaient d'un précieux secours à son maître. Que ce soit pour débusquer le gibier, pour signaler la présence du redoutable grizzly, pour repérer, l'hiver, la mauvaise glace sur les lacs, ou même pour attraper les saumons qui montaient frayer en bancs serrés, le chien faisait merveille, et Jos gardait pour lui d'incroyables histoires, de peur qu'on ne le prenne pour un menteur.

Un jour d'été, au retour d'un long périple, lui et son chien descendaient une rivière en canot. Jos se tenait à l'arrière avec sa pagaie et le chien était assis tout à l'avant. Au centre, dans la partie large, s'entassaient le matériel pour camper et un plein sac de belles truites prises au filet dans un lac éloigné. Jos se proposait de les fumer une fois rendu à sa cabane, afin de les conserver jusqu'à l'hiver. Ils voyageaient sur une rivière capricieuse, mais l'homme en connaissait les traîtrises pour les avoir maintes fois affrontées. Lorsque apparurent les eaux blanches annonçant les premiers rapides, il cria à Pax de se coucher. Le chien obéit et s'aplatit au fond, bien qu'il n'aimât guère se trouver ainsi, sans possibilité de voir venir le danger, mais le canot y gagnait beaucoup en stabilité.

La vitesse augmentait rapidement, les berges se resserraient et de gros rochers noirs faisaient des *V* à la surface. Jos s'engagea résolument en plein milieu, tantôt creusant l'eau avec sa pagaie pour changer de direction, tantôt se servant de la palette comme d'un gouvernail. Les méandres étroits longeaient par endroits des falaises contre lesquelles l'eau tourbillonnait, noire et inquiétante. Le canot dévalait, mais Jos pagayait pour augmenter encore sa vitesse, car une série de rouleaux arrivait, qu'il devait passer très vite pour vaincre le contre-courant en arrière. Il crut un instant qu'il n'y parviendrait pas. Pax s'écrasait sur le ventre, apeuré malgré la confiance qu'il portait à son maître. Puis vint une petite chute; le canot sembla décoller avant de retomber lourdement. Deux gerbes d'eau giflèrent Jos au passage.

« Je ne la pensais pas si haute, celle-là, se dit-il. On ne peut jamais connaître une rivière, il suffit d'une averse pour la rendre différente. »

Il lui semblait qu'il luttait depuis des heures contre cette rivière en furie.

Maintenant, voilà qu'un coude à angle droit se présentait, un mur de pierre qui repoussait l'eau avec violence. Jos connaissait le danger d'être drossé[1] là, aussi s'efforçait-il de se tenir à distance, mais ses bras fatigués répondaient mal, il heurta la falaise et ne se rétablit qu'à grand-peine. Néanmoins il était passé. Il ne restait plus maintenant qu'un très fort courant. Déjà la rivière s'élargissait et, quelques tournants plus loin, l'eau sauvage redeviendrait docile; Jos l'apercevait, calme et sombre, là-bas.

Mais soudain, alors qu'il ne s'y attendait plus, un choc à l'avant du canot, un craquement et l'embarcation chavirait, déséquilibrée par un tronc d'épinette fiché au fond et invisible à la surface. Jos et Pax furent happés par ces eaux encore trop violentes pour leur laisser quelque initiative.

---

[1] Entraîné vers la rive.

Incapables de nager, ils roulèrent comme des paquets en tentant de leur mieux d'éviter les écueils affleurant çà et là. En un dernier accès de folie, la rivière se brisait sur une barrière rocheuse avant de s'assagir définitivement. Pax réussit à passer. Il se retrouva dans le calme, hébété, meurtri, mais son instinct lui commanda aussitôt de nager et bientôt il abordait à la berge de sable. En prenant pied, il s'ébroua, étira ses muscles endoloris, lécha une coupure au ventre et regarda si son maître arrivait. Il le vit en effet, mais pas comme il s'y attendait : le vieux Jos dérivait, inerte au beau milieu de la rivière.

Pax n'hésita pas une seconde, il s'élança à son secours en nageant de toutes ses forces. Dès qu'il l'eut atteint, il prit dans sa gueule le col de sa chemise et tira vers le bord. Tant que l'eau resta profonde, il n'éprouva pas trop de peine, mais bien vite cette masse sans réaction devint très lourde et difficile à manoeuvrer, à mesure qu'il gagnait la berge. Sitôt qu'il toucha le fond, le chien s'arc-bouta pour une meilleure prise, mais le sable se dérobait sous ses pattes, ou bien le tissu craquait, ce qui l'obligea à de terribles efforts pour parvenir à sortir son maître jusqu'à mi-corps.

Cependant, Jos ne reprenait toujours pas connaissance, et cela décontenançait beaucoup Pax. Fébrile, il tournait autour de lui en gémissant, il lui léchait le visage, les mains; parfois, il poussait un aboiement impératif pour l'arracher à cet inquiétant sommeil, puis il aperçut du sang collé dans ses cheveux. Sa tête avait sans doute cogné contre un rocher et le choc l'avait assommé.

Le chien passa délicatement sa langue sur la blessure, et cela dut aviver la douleur, car le vieux Jos commença à revenir à lui. Il ouvrit lentement les yeux; son regard ahuri découvrit la grosse tête de Pax penchée sur son visage. Le chien se mit à frétiller de la queue et lança de petits cris de joie et d'encouragement. Alors, tranquillement, à mesure qu'il reprenait vie, le trappeur comprit ce qui venait de se passer.

— Ah! mon brave Pax, fit-il en serrant l'animal contre lui, je te dois une fière chandelle!

Il se redressa en s'appuyant sur le dos du chien et pensa soudain au canot.

— Le canot! Le canot! L'as-tu vu?

Oui, il l'avait vu. Il n'était pas loin, juste un peu en amont, coincé par des rochers. Le chien aboya et marcha dans cette direction.

— Attends, dit l'homme, attends quelques instants que je me remette mieux, il n'ira pas plus loin maintenant.

Tout en parlant, il scrutait la rivière pour voir si quelque partie du chargement ne se trouvait pas retenue le long des berges. Puis il ôta ses habits et alluma un feu pour les faire sécher. En coureur des bois avisé, il conservait toujours dans sa poche une petite boîte étanche qui contenait des allumettes.

La tête lui faisait très mal; il déchira un morceau de sa chemise pour se faire une compresse. Les rapides rugissaient là-bas, et ce bruit infernal rendait sa douleur terriblement lancinante. Encore sous le choc, il essayait péniblement de rassembler ses esprits. Lui qui avait connu tant d'aventures en forêt croyait à peine à celle-là.

— Ah! ça oui, dit-il en tapotant le dos de son chien, sans toi, mon vieux, je serais bel et bien mort cette fois.

Il resta étendu jusqu'à ce que ses habits soient secs et ses forces revenues, puis il marcha le long du torrent jusqu'à la hauteur du canot. Une mauvaise surprise l'attendait encore : l'embarcation en équilibre sur les rochers n'était pas seulement trouée, mais carrément défoncée sur un côté. L'équipement se trouvait encore à l'intérieur, car Jos prenait toujours la précaution de tout arrimer lorsqu'il voyageait sur une rivière turbulente. Le canot n'était qu'à cinq ou six mètres du bord, mais la profondeur et le fort courant interdisaient de se mettre à l'eau pour l'atteindre sans danger. La corde qui sert à l'amarrer avait heureusement passé par-dessus bord et s'allongeait bien droite à la surface. Jos chercha un bâton assez long pour l'attraper mais n'en trouva pas, il ne poussait que des arbustes rachitiques par ici.

Une fois encore, seul Pax pouvait sauver la situation.

Son maître n'eut pas à lui expliquer longtemps : le chien sauta dans le courant un peu en amont et se laissa emporter vers le canot. De ses pattes il amortit le choc contre les rochers, puis glissa le long d'eux pour pénétrer dans le remous en arrière, où flottait la corde. Il la saisit dans sa gueule et tenta de regagner la berge. Cela demandait un gros effort car, la corde n'étant pas très longue, le chien devrait absolument vaincre le courant sans se laisser trop déporter. Sa tête et ses épaules seulement émergeaient. Il nageait de toutes ses forces, progressant lentement contre ces eaux brutales qui le repoussaient. Son maître, impuissant à l'aider, ne pouvait que l'encourager de la voix. Pax luttait avec acharnement. À présent, il arrivait tout près du but, un mètre au plus. Jos se pencha pour agripper la corde, mais la rivière sauvage eut raison des énergies de son chien. Épuisé, vaincu, l'animal lâcha prise et dériva jusqu'au banc de cailloux en contrebas. De là, il grimpa péniblement sur la berge où il s'effondra, la langue pendante, les flancs secoués par une respiration saccadée.

Jos s'était approché et lui caressait la tête :

— Repose-toi, mon vieux, tu vas l'avoir la deuxième fois. Il faut la prendre tout au bout, la corde, sinon tu n'as pas assez de longueur pour atteindre le bord. Tu as compris ? Tout au bout. Tout au bout.

Le chien le fixait, et Jos, qui connaissait bien son regard, savait que son fidèle compagnon mettrait ses paroles à profit. Ils restèrent quelques instants sans bouger puis, lorsque son souffle redevint régulier, Pax se leva, s'ébroua, s'étira et trottina jusqu'en amont du canot. Il se piqua sur le bord et envisagea l'eau. Non qu'il hésitât; il semblait plutôt calculer son coup.

Et il sauta.

Comme la première fois, il se laissa entraîner dans le remous, heurta l'amarre avec son nez mais ne la prit pas, glissant encore un peu. Puis, brutalement il saisit la corde dans sa gueule, à dix centimètres à peine du bout. Et il entreprit le plus difficile, cette traversée de six mètres à peine, multipliés par la violence d'un courant que, malgré sa force exceptionnelle, il n'était pas certain de pouvoir surmonter. Le vieux Jos lui prodiguait ses encouragements et le chien, lentement, très lentement, approchait de la berge. Il mettait toute sa vigueur dans cette bataille contre l'eau qui parfois le submergeait en entier.

Moins d'un mètre à présent.

Jos, à plat ventre, tendait désespérément les bras vers son chien qui nageait comme un enragé sans même avancer tant la rivière était puissante. Jos se pencha encore un peu. Il ne manquait plus que l'espace d'une main.

— Allez, Pax, un dernier effort, le dernier. Allez! Allez!

Le chien déploya ses ultimes énergies et réussit à franchir la minuscule distance. Jos toucha la corde, l'empoigna. Alors Pax desserra les crocs et s'abandonna au courant. Il s'échoua brutalement sur les cailloux quelques secondes plus tard et, chancelant, regagna la rive où il se laissa choir, exténué.

Jos fixa solidement la corde à une pierre et alla s'asseoir près de Pax en attendant qu'il se remette car il avait encore besoin de lui.

Certes, en tirant fort sur l'amarre, le trappeur aurait pu, seul, libérer le canot des rochers, mais il craignait qu'il se remplisse d'eau et ne devienne alors beaucoup trop lourd pour lui. Lorsque Pax se releva pour étirer ses muscles, Jos comprit qu'il avait récupéré et il se dirigea vers l'embarcation, le chien sur ses talons. Il lui mit l'extrémité de la corde dans la gueule et la serra lui-même solidement des deux mains.

— On y va, Pax, on tire! Oh! hisse!

Le canot glissa un peu, oscilla puis bascula, sitôt happé par le courant.

— Allez, Pax ! Allez ! Allez ! criait Jos.

Tous deux arc-boutés, ils s'efforçaient de haler l'embarcation avant qu'elle ne coule, car elle se remplissait très vite. Et même sur une aussi courte distance, leurs efforts conjugués vinrent difficilement à bout du courant. Lorsque, enfin, l'épave fut sur la berge, Jos l'examina en détail.

— Beaux dégâts, fit-il en retirant des lattes brisées. Un trou ça s'arrange, mais tout un côté défoncé, c'est autre chose...

Fabriqué par les Indiens, le canot se composait de fines pièces de cèdre courbes recouvertes d'écorce de bouleau. L'absence de ces matériaux interdisait de le réparer sur place.

Jos récupéra son sac de poissons et ses affaires qu'il déballa pour les faire sécher.

— On va passer la nuit ici, mon gros, dit-il à son chien, demain on envisagera.

Il ne se trouvait pas à plus de vingt kilomètres de sa cabane, mais le seul chemin était la rivière, car le terrain marécageux et accidenté ne se prêtait pas toujours à la marche. Il organisa tranquillement son bivouac avant de réfléchir à la situation.

Le lendemain, à la pointe du jour, il levait le camp. Il installa le sac de poissons sur le dos de Pax, prit lui-même son propre sac, et ils se mirent en route, laissant là le canot inutilisable. Ils s'efforçaient de suivre tant bien que mal le cours d'eau, faisant parfois de longs détours pour éviter certains passages infranchissables. Mais cela restait encore la meilleure voie, car ailleurs un inextricable fouillis d'arbustes, de ronces, d'épinettes rendait toute progression lente et pénible, en plus de favoriser les erreurs d'orientation. Ce n'est qu'après deux longues journées, à la nuit tombante, qu'ils arrivèrent chez eux.

Jos fit cuire deux poissons qu'il partagea avec Pax et, malgré la fatigue, il s'attarda à fumer sa pipe. Ce soir, dans le confort rustique de sa cabane en rondins, il savourait chaque seconde, envahi par une émotion profonde et nouvelle : la joie d'être encore en vie grâce à son chien qui somnolait à ses pieds.

Quelques jours plus tard, il se rendit au campement indien pour se procurer un autre canot. Mais, depuis que le vieux Chestapish était mort, plus personne ne construisait de canots d'écorce.

— Je veux bien te donner le mien, dit Namagoo, un jeune trappeur, mais je veux ton chien en échange.

— Ça, jamais! fit Jos. J'ai besoin d'un canot, certes, l'été n'est pas fini, mais jamais je ne vendrai Pax.

— Tu n'as pas d'attelage, alors pourquoi garder ce gros chien? Il me serait plus utile pour mener ma meute.

Jos n'avait pas raconté leur dernière aventure, c'était comme un secret entre Pax et lui.

— Même si je n'ai pas d'attelage, reprit-il, ce chien me rend de très grands services.

— Je t'en donnerai un des miens en échange, ils sont moins gros, tu auras moins à chasser pour le nourrir.

— Non, désolé, Namagoo, je garde mon chien.

— Eh bien, je garde mon canot.

Jos revint à sa cabane bien ennuyé. En été on ne peut se passer de canot pour pêcher, ni en automne pour chasser l'orignal. Il lui en fallait absolument un, et seuls les Indiens pouvaient le lui fournir, mais, si Namagoo refusait, tous refuseraient. Surtout que, loin des villages, l'argent les intéressait beaucoup moins que l'indispensable, comme un fusil ou un chien par exemple. Et Jos ne pouvait donner ni l'un ni l'autre.

Quelques jours passèrent, où le trappeur chercha vainement une autre solution, puis, un matin, deux vieux Indiens, Ashini et sa femme, se présentèrent à sa cabane.

— On a entendu parler de tes problèmes, dit Ashini, on a peut-être une solution...

— Ah oui? fit Jos, intrigué.

— On n'a pas de canot à t'offrir, mais on peut réparer le tien.

— Il est très abîmé...

— Tout se répare, dit Ashini. Je ne fais plus de canots depuis longtemps, mais si tu nous donnes un coup de main, avec ma femme on y arrivera.

— On ne risque rien à essayer et... vous voulez quoi en échange?

— Assez de tabac pour aller jusqu'à la prochaine vente de fourrures au printemps.

Jos eut un pincement au coeur: Ashini et sa femme fumaient la pipe à longueur de journée et, pour attendre le prochain passage du trafiquant de fourrures, il ne leur faudrait pas moins que sa réserve entière. Et lui devrait se priver totalement de fumer... pendant plus de deux saisons... dont l'hiver, avec ses jours courts et tristes...

Voyant que le trappeur hésitait, Ashini, se leva :

— C'était juste une proposition, on voulait pas t'ennuyer.

— Non, vous ne m'ennuyez pas, dit Jos. J'accepte.

Et il sortit d'une caisse son sac de tabac, ce savoureux mélange de virginie et de hollande, amoureusement conservé dans des feuilles de rhubarbe sauvage.

— Voilà, dit-il, c'est pour vous.

— Comprends-nous, dit Ashini avec un sourire malicieux, on ne rend plus grand service au campement, et les jeunes rechignent à nous acheter autant de tabac qu'on voudrait. Comme ça, on n'aura rien à leur demander.

— Oui, je comprends, dit Jos en voyant disparaître son sac.

Deux jours plus tard, ils partaient en emportant le bois, l'écorce et les outils nécessaires à la réparation du canot.

Jos put finir sa pêche d'été, chasser sur les lacs en automne, mais les soirées de cet hiver-là lui parurent interminables, sans rien à mettre dans sa pipe.

Il avait, pour se consoler, le bon regard de Pax compatissant.

Table des matières

Mot de l'auteur 7

Les deux amis 9

Le meilleur choix 27

Un repos bien mérité 45

Le numéro huit de Whitehorse 69

Le vieil homme et le loup 87

Jos et Pax 99

La collection Grande Nature – Histoires vécues

LIBRE!
Claude Arbour

Debout derrière ses chiens de traîneau sur une route de neige ou en canot sur un lac paisible au crépuscule, Claude Arbour parle de son quotidien dans la grande forêt laurentienne où il vit isolé depuis des années.

SUR LA PISTE!
Claude Arbour

Claude Arbour poursuit ici le remarquable récit de sa vie dans les bois, à l'écart de la civilisation moderne. Comme dans *Libre!*, il nous entraîne avec lui à la découverte de la vie qui bat tout près : castors, loups, huarts à collier, balbuzards...

BEN
Benjamin Simard

L'histoire vraie d'un coureur des bois d'aujourd'hui, un peu poète, parfois rebelle, qui vit au contact des orignaux, des ours et des loups dans le parc des Laurentides.

EXPÉDITION CARIBOU
Benjamin Simard

L'histoire vraie d'un coureur des bois d'aujourd'hui, d'un homme d'action qui vit avec les caribous dans l'impitoyable froid du Grand Nord.

Revoici l'auteur de *Ben*, poète à ses heures, qui raconte ses aventures : les tournées harassantes en avion, les dangereuses expéditions de capture, la magie de la toundra.

PIEN
Michel Noël

Fils d'une Blanche déracinée et d'un Métis tiraillé entre le progrès et les traditions de ses ancêtres, Pien observe, sent, vibre. Son monde, un coin du Nord ouvert au déboisement farouche des années 50, est hostile. Mais c'est un univers qui forge des coeurs passionnés.

PRIX LITTÉRAIRE DU GOUVERNEUR GÉNÉRAL DU CANADA

DOMPTER L'ENFANT SAUVAGE - tome 1
NIPISHISH
Michel Noël

Le missionnaire de la réserve a bien averti les Algonquins. « Mes chers amis, le gouvernement du Canada vous offre un grand cadeau: il va envoyer vos enfants à l'école! Enfin, ils apprendront à lire, à écrire et à bien se comporter en société. Ne vous inquiétez de rien, nous viendrons les chercher à la fin de l'été pour les mener au pensionnat. »

« Quoi? riposte Shipu, le père du jeune Nipishish. Les Blancs veulent nous arracher nos enfants? Jamais! »

DOMPTER L'ENFANT SAUVAGE - tome 2
LE PENSIONNAT
Michel Noël

Nipishish et ses camarades ont été transplantés contre leur gré dans un pensionnat indien. En effet, le ministère des Affaires indiennes, de concert avec le clergé catholique, a décidé de civiliser et d'instruire les «Sauvages». Mais, pour le privilège d'apprendre à lire et à compter, les jeunes autochtones paieront un prix terrible: vêtements confisqués, langue maternelle bannie, traditions ridiculisées, ils se verront dépouiller de leur identité.

ALERTE À L'OURS
André Vacher
Les habitants d'un petit village des Rocheuses canadiennes ne dorment plus. Ils sont terrorisés. Des ours attaquent, blessent et tuent les gens dans la forêt avoisinante. On organise des battues mais en vain. La tension monte dans la petite localité. Il faut faire cesser le carnage.

ENTRE CHIENS ET LOUPS
André Vacher
Cet ouvrage réunit huit histoires authentiques et pourtant à peine croyables tant les animaux du Grand Nord défient le sens commun par leur ruse et leur habileté. L'auteur les a recueillies en majorité au Yukon et dans les immenses Territoires du Nord-Ouest, souvent de la bouche même de ceux qui les ont vécues.